7/6/02

Also by Helen W. Cyr
A Filmography of the Third World (1976)
A Filmography of the Third World, 1976-1983 (1985)

British Library Cataloguing-in-Publication data available

Library of Congress Cataloging-in-Publication Data

Cyr, Helen W., 1926-
    The Third World in film and video, 1984-1990 / by Helen W. Cyr
        p.   cm.
    Continues: A filmography of the Third World, 1976-1983.
    Includes index.
    ISBN 0-8108-2380-2 (alk. paper)
    1. Developing countries—Film catalogs.   2. Minorities—United
States—Film Catalogs.   3. Developing countries—Videotape catalogs.
4. Minorities—United States—Videotape catalogs.   I. Cyr, Helen W.,
1926- Filmography of the Third World, 1976-1983. II. Title.
HC59.7.C975   1985 Suppl.
016.909'09724—dc20   90-25883

THE
THIRD WORLD
IN
FILM AND VIDEO,
1984-1990

by

HELEN W. CYR

The Scarecrow Press, Inc.

Metuchen, N.J., & London

1991

CONTENTS

iii

v

PREFACE

The latest continuation of the 1976 and 1895 publications of *A Filmography of the Third World* is being issued under a new title, *The Third World in Film and Video*, to reflect the fact that the new supplement now includes video cassettes as well as 16mm films. Otherwise, all is as before, i.e., the present volume provides titles and annotations about the so-called Third World, and the "third world in our midst," the major ethnic minorities in North America (Native Americans, Asian-Americans, Latinos, and Afro-Americans).

The purpose of this book is to help teachers, scholars, group leaders, and students locate 16mm films and video cassettes in distribution, for rental or sale, for use in broadening the public understanding of lesser-known geographic areas and peoples.

Films and videos listed cover a variety of matters, e.g., customs, history, economics, politics, religion, fine arts, technology, and travel. There are also a few fictional films, including theatrical feature-length productions.

Almost all the titles in this supplement were produced in the 1980s. A few earlier works were added because they either have been re-released recently or have been deemed to have special significance for the purpose of this book, regardless of date.

This film/video list is designed as an easy-to-use reference tool. Most indexes of audio-visual materials categorize them under broad subject treatment, by title only, so that the researcher must then locate desired information (annotation, date, distributor, and other data) elsewhere in the body of the volume. *The Third World in Film and Video*, on the other hand, presents information in one step under easy-to-find geographic categories organized by continent and area, or in the case of North America, by ethnic group. There are more recent titles exclusively on Third World topics here—over 1,100—than are to be found in other current publications, such as motion picture almanacs and major film/video indexes.

Care has been taken that none of the titles are repeats of items listed in earlier versions of this book. The author has searched for films and videos in distributors' catalogs, in festival programs, library catalogs, and from direct communication with independent filmmakers. The productions of small companies overlooked by the larger resource guides are included.

Every effort has been made to ensure up-to-date distributor information. And, wherever possible, Canadian distribution agents have been cited. Unfortunately, the audio-visual world is not so stable as the book publishing world. Films and videos frequently are transferred from one company to another, or go in and out of "availability" at an unpredictable rate. Also, companies, small and large, are merging or going out of business at a seemingly ever-increasing pace. With such a situation in flux, there is no way of guaranteeing the distribution of the titles covered.

Most of the videos selected for this book are educational, unrestricted programs that may be shown publicly to groups and classes without legal restraint, just like 16mm films. The reader should be warned that a few "home-use-only" tapes have been included because of their interest for Third World studies. Fortunately, under the "fair use" provisions of the copyright law, an individual teacher may show restricted material within the confines of the single classroom for an instructional purpose. It is forbidden, however, to circulate this type of videotape to others at the same institution.

The geographic framework of *The Third World in Film and Video* is strictly adhered to. This means that a country like Egypt, often classified for cultural-political factors as part of the "Middle East," is found here under "Africa" where it belongs geographically.

Preface

Similarly, Cuba is often treated as part of the Central American complex. In this book, Cuba is placed under "West Indies." North American blacks who emigrated from Caribbean countries have been classified as "Latinos" rather than "Afro-Americans." Filipinos in the U.S., despite the language spoken, have been categorized as Asian-Americans because, of course, their country of origin is in Asia.

As in earlier editions, there is generous coverage of Afro-Americans and Native Americans. It is unfortunate that there are comparatively fewer productions about Latinos and Asian-Americans. Filmmakers have given more attention than ever to certain crisis-ridden countries, Nicaragua and El Salvador being two cases in point. Colombia and Panama are still not adequately represented. Doubtless, some films and tapes are "in the works."

Each film/video description presents the following information: title; production company, producer, or filmmaker; release or copyright date; running time; color or black and white; format (16mm and/or video); distributor; a brief annotation. An alphabetical list of distributors with addresses and telephone numbers, and a title index are provided at the back of the book.

I wish to thank all who helped me with this work—especially the distributors who sent me copies of their catalogs, and Barry Stahl, Marc Sober, and Jackie Dear of the Audio-Visual Department at the Enoch Pratt Free Library, Baltimore.

H. W. Cyr
Baltimore, Maryland
January, 1990

THE THIRD WORLD IN FILM AND VIDEO, 1984-1990

THE THIRD WORLD

GENERAL

THE BUSINESS OF HUNGER. Robert Richter, 1984. 28 min. color. 16mm/Video. Maryknoll World.
Explores one of the major causes of hunger in Third World countries—the export of cash crops. Examines the situations of Latin America, Africa, Asia, and the U.S.

COMMODITIES: BLACK MARKET. Channel Four Television/UK, 1986. 26 min. color. Video. First Run/Icarus Films.
Documents the control of the seas and international trade by the British from 1650. Tells how opium exports from India to China helped finance operations and imports of the British East India Company.

COMMODITIES: GROW OR DIE. Channel Four Television/UK, 1986. 52 min. color. Video. First Run/Icarus Films.
Shows how most markets today are controlled by two or three companies that have bought out their competition. Tells how the focus is being shifted from the Atlantic to the Pacific Basin in the constant search for cheap raw materials.

COMMODITIES: LEAVING HOME FOR SUGAR. Channel Four Television/UK, 1986. 52 min. color. Video. First

3

Run/Icarus Films.
Studies in the sugarcane industry in the West Indies and in Zimbabwe, which was for 200 years an exceedingly profitable business.

COMMODITIES: TEA FORTUNES. Channel Four Television/UK, 1986. 52 min. color. Video. First Run/Icarus Films.
A history of the tea industry in China, India, Sri Lanka, and East Africa. Includes a profile of Sir Thomas Lipton. Compares British-controlled operations of the past with today's nationalized tea estates.

DIALOGUE ON INTERNATIONAL DEVELOPMENT. Aspire Films with Triune Productions, 1989. 20 min. color. 16mm/Video. Bullfrog Films.
A film designed to encourage discussion about international development programs. The participants represent Canadian governmental and non-governmental organizations. Questions raised are concerned with easing international tensions between the industrialized and developing nations.

ETHNIC DANCE AROUND THE WORLD. Wayne Mitchell, 1983. 24 min. color. 16mm/Video. BFA Educational Media.
Provides examples of dance all over the world—the Americas, Asia, Africa, Europe, and Australasia—to explain why people dance and why the dances differ from country to country.

THE FOOD MACHINE. Journal Films, 1988. 20 min. color. Video. Journal Films.
An account of the farm crisis in the U.S. and the trend to larger farms with fewer workers. Shows how this kind of farming is being transplanted to the Third World.

FOR EXPORT ONLY: PESTICIDES. Robert Richter, 1981. 56 min. color. 16mm/Video. First Run/Icarus Films.
Although banned in the U.S., harmful pesticides are exported to Third World countries where there are no restrictions. This is a report on the public health consequences of exposure to such chemicals.

FOR EXPORT ONLY: PILLS. Robert Richter, 1981. 56 min. color. 16mm/Video. First Run/Icarus Films.
Investigates the practice of exporting pharmaceuticals banned in the U.S. to Third World countries. Features interviews with officials and victims on four continents.

GLOBAL LINKS: CURSE OF THE TROPICS. WETA-TV, n.d. 30 min. color. Video. WETA-TV.
Takes a look at the dread disease "river blindness" on the people of the Volta River Valley in West Africa. Instructor's guides and teacher training tape available.

GLOBAL LINKS: EARTH—THE CHANGING ENVIRONMENT. WETA-TV, n.d. 30 min. color. Video. WETA-TV.
Impoverished nations have suffered from exploitation—for example, deforestation in the Amazon rain forest and erosion of the soil in Africa. Instructor's guides and teacher training tape available.

GLOBAL LINKS: EDUCATION—A CHANCE FOR A BETTER WORLD. WETA-TV, n.d. 30 min. color. Video. WETA-TV.
Shows how Third World nations are trying to educate citizens despite shortages of teachers and materials and conditions which make it necessary for children to labor at home. Instructor's guides and teacher training tape available.

GLOBAL LINKS: TRADITIONS AND THE 20TH CENTURY. WETA-TV, n.d. 30 min. color. Video WETA-TV.
The cultures of six Third World countries from West Africa to India are described. Probes the question of survival of traditions in an environment of modernization and development. Instructor's guides and teacher training tape available.

GLOBAL LINKS: THE URBAN DILEMMA. WETA-TV, n.d. 30 min. color. Video. WETA-TV.
Explains the enormous population growth of Third World cities, such as Shanghai and São Paulo, where the strain on public services is severe. Suggests possible solutions to the problem. Instructor's guides and teacher training tape available.

GLOBAL LINKS: WOMEN IN THE THIRD WORLD. WETA-
TV, n.d. 30 min. color. Video. WETA-TV.
Examines the status of women in Third World countries.
Demonstrates their abilities to affect change in their societies.
Instructor's guides and teacher training tape available.

THE GREAT AWAKENING. United Nations, n.d. 19 min. color.
16mm/Video. Lucerne Media.
Depicts the changes that have come about in Third World
countries in the transition from colonial rule to independence.
Gives interesting details, such as the fact that more than 50
independent nations have been admitted to the United Nations
in the last few decades.

GROWING UP IN THE WORLD NEXT DOOR. Asterisk
Productions, 1989. 59 min. color. 16mm/Video. Bullfrog Films.
A report on three teenagers in the Third World: one from Nepal,
one from Kenya, and one from St. Vincent in the Caribbean. They
were filmed at 12 years of age and then again at 18 years.
Describes their goals and dreams and how they were troubled in
some way by an international development project.

THE HUNGER BUSINESS. Journal Films, 1988. 20 min. color.
Video. Journal Films.
Studies the implications of food and programs for poorer nations.
Explains how grain exports can harm the very nations they are
intended to help.

INCREASE AND MULTIPLY? Robert Richter, 1989. 55 min.
color. Video. Filmakers Library.
Ellen Burstyn is the narrator for this video, which describes what
happens when family planning support is not funded. Shows how
people want to learn about limiting the size of their families
without recourse to illegal abortions and abandoned babies. Filmed
in Kenya, Zimbabwe, China, Guatemala, and Mexico.

LIFE IN THE DEVELOPING WORLD. UNICEF, NHK-TV
Japan, 1982. 4 parts. 30 min. each, color. Video. Great Plains
National.
A series which covers economic problems of women and children

in underdeveloped nations. 1. Bolivia: Indians of the Andes; 2. Haiti: Education for the Future; 3. Zaire: Health Care; 4. India: Migration to the City.

PEACEKEEPING: SITUATION REPORT—AN UPDATE. Lucerne Media, 1988. 30 min. color. 16mm/Video. Lucerne Media.
Describes the work of the United Nations peacekeeping troops made up of volunteers from many nations. Tells of their dedicated efforts to limit violence in troubled areas of the world.

THE PRICE OF PROGRESS. Nicolas Claxton, Central Independent Television, 1989. 53 min. color. Video. Bullfrog Films.
A hard-hitting film that explores three large resettlement projects in India, Indonesia, and Brazil sponsored by the World Bank. Analyzes the social, environmental, and economic problems involved in the bank's lending policies.

A QUESTION OF AID. Journal Films, 1988. 20 min. color. Video. Journal Films.
Explains how poor nations cope with hunger and malnutrition. Compares the situation in Kerala, India, with Bangladesh. One has high standards, the other is dependent on foreign aid.

SLUMS IN THE THIRD WORLD. Wayne Mitchell, 1983. 17 min. color. 16mm/Video. BFA Educational Media.
Uses the daily life of one family living in a slum of a Third World city to typify the worldwide problems of poor housing and a depressed lifestyle.

SUPER-COMPANIES. National Film Board of Canada, 1989. 57 min. color. 16mm/Video. Bullfrog Films.
Shows how super-companies think of the world as a single market. They do not work to improve conditions in their host countries. Instead they create social and environmental problems. Filmed on four continents.

TELLING THEIR OWN STORY. United Nations, 1988. 27 min. color. Video. First Run/Icarus Films.

Takes a look at a growing number of efforts to help areas without resources to have news broadcasts that are compatible with the needs of local audiences. Asiavision is shown coordinating the exchange of programs via satellite from countries like Sri Lanka, Malaysia, and the Philippines. In Papua New Guinea radio is used to reach the widely scattered population.

THE THIRD WORLD: AN INTRODUCTION. Wayne Mitchell, 1983. 21 min. color. 16mm/Video. BFA Educational Media.
Gives a detailed report on life in the Third World today. Explains the concept of the Third World and how most Third World countries were originally First World colonies.

TURNING THE TIDE: GROWING PAINS. Tyne Tees Television, 1988. 26 min. color. Video. Bullfrog Films.
This video is part of a series on environmental issues. It is concerned with hunger in a world that grows more than enough to feed everyone. Discusses the problems involved, such as growing crops in the wrong place and in the wrong way and selling them at the wrong price. Also tells how Third World countries raise rich crops for the rich world while their own people starve.

TURNING THE TIDE: THE GREAT GENE ROBBERY. Tyne Tees Television, 1988. 26 min. color. Video. Bullfrog Films.
This is part of a seven-part series on environmental issues. This particular program is concerned with the global problem of ever-increasing extinct species. With the loss of more and more species we lose the opportunity to find new food crops, medicines, and chemicals. Visits the Andes where certain relatives of the potato are threatened and tells how no amount of genetic engineering can protect food crops without genetic diversity.

WATER SUPPLY AND SANITATION IN DEVELOPMENT: PEOPLE AND PROBLEMS. National Film Board of Canada, 1985. 28 min. color. 16mm/Video. Indiana University.
This is the first part of a series on water management and sewage treatment in Third World regions. It introduces the worldwide problems of clean water and sanitary waste disposal, showing the relationship between these factors and enteric disease. Produced in collaboration with the World Bank and the United Nations

Center for Human Settlements.

WATER SUPPLY AND SANITATION IN DEVELOPMENT: PROBLEMS AND SOLUTIONS. National Film Board of Canada, 1985. 42 min. color. 16mm/Video. Indiana University. Provides fuller detail on some of the problems introduced in program 1. Through film animation, shows how enteric pathogens are transmitted in unsanitary conditions and follows construction of low-cost sytems designed to control human excreta at their source.

WATER SUPPLY AND SANITATION IN DEVELOPMENT: SOLUTIONS AND PEOPLE. National Film Board of Canada, 1985. 26 min. color. 16mm/Video. Indiana University. Shows how the people most affected by a project are the key to the success or failure of a scheme for adequate sanitation. Follows efforts to inform and gain the support of people for projects. Gives details of how a Malawi water supply system was developed.

AFRICA

GENERAL

AFRICA: 1. DIFFERENT BUT EQUAL; 2. MASTERING A
CONTINENT. RM Arts, 1987. 120 min. color. Video. Films
Inc.
Part 1 of this series tells how Africa was ravished for centuries
by the slave trade but how it produced some of the world's
greatest civilizations. Part 2 discusses how African peoples must
fight to survive in an often hostile environment.

AFRICA: 3. CARAVANS OF GOLD; 4. KINGS AND CITIES.
RM Arts, 1987. 120 min. color. Video. Films Inc.
Part 3 presents the history of the gold trade from Africa. Part 4
looks at some African kingdoms, such as Nigeria.

AFRICA: 5. THE BIBLE AND THE GUN; 6. THIS
MAGNIFICENT AFRICAN CAKE. RM Arts, 1987. 120 min.
color. Video. Films Inc.
Part 5 discusses the impact of Europeans who came to Africa:
explorers, missionaries, and others. Part 6 tells how all of Africa
came under colonial rule beginning in the 1880s.

AFRICA: 7. THE RISE OF NATIONALISM; 8. THE LEGACY.
RM Arts, 1987. 120 min. color. Video. Films Inc.
Part 7 discusses Africa's struggle for independence with particular

focus on Zimbabwe and South Africa. Part 8 presents interviews with African leaders who discuss the problems and successes of post-colonial Africa.

AFRICA: AN INTRODUCTION. Wayne Mitchell, 1981. 21 min. color. 16mm/Video. BFA Educational Media.
Describes the geography and climate of Africa along with the turmoil and struggle for stable governments.

AFRICA CALLS: ITS DRUMS AND MUSICAL INSTRUMENTS. WCAU-TV, n.d. 23 min. color. 16mm/Video. Carousel Film and Video.
Shows how Africans work, worship, and communicate via music. Features instruments used: drums, zazas, wooden flutes, bells, and gourds.

AFRICAN ODYSSEY. National Geographic, 1988. 59 min. color. 16mm/Video. National Geographic.
Two conservationists study lions and brown hyenas in the Central Kalahari Game Reserve in Botswana. Later they move to a wildlife park in Zambia.

AFRICAN RELIGIONS AND RITUAL DANCES. WCAU-TV, n.d. 19 min. color. 16mm/Video. Carousel Film and Video.
Traces the importance of dance in everyday life of Africans. The viewer sees the reenactment of a cult dance of the Yoruba—the "invocation to Igunnu."

AFRICAN SOUL: MUSIC, PAST AND PRESENT. WCAU-TV, n.d. 17 min. color. 16mm/Video. Carousel Film and Video.
Demonstrates how early African music provided the roots for American jazz and blues.

THE AFRICANS, A TRIPLE HERITAGE: 1. THE NATURE OF A CONTINENT. BBC-TV, WETA-TV, 1986. 60 min. Video. Films Inc.
Explores the role of geography in African history; for example, the program discusses how the Nile River was instrumental in the origin of civilization. Also discusses the introduction of Islam via the Arabs.

THE AFRICANS, A TRIPLE HERITAGE: 2. A LEGACY OF
LIFESTYLES. BBC-TV, WETA-TV, 1986. 60 min. color.
Video. Films Inc.
Compares simple African societies with the more complex. Traces
influences of Islam and the West.

THE AFRICANS, A TRIPLE HERITAGE: 3. NEW GODS.
BBC-TV, WETA-TV, 1986. 60 min. color. Video. Films Inc.
Tells about the impact of Islam and Christianity and how they
influence one another.

THE AFRICANS, A TRIPLE HERITAGE: 4. TOOLS OF
EXPLOITATION. BBC-TV, WETA-TV, 1986. 60 min. color.
Video. Films Inc.
How Africa's resources, both human and natural, have been
exploited over the years. Traces the counter-influences of the West
on Africa and Africa on the West.

THE AFRICANS, A TRIPLE HERITAGE: 5. NEW
CONFLICTS. BBC-TV, WETA-TV, 1986. 60 min. color.
Video. Films Inc.
Explains the conflicts brought about by the clash of traditional
African, Western, and Islamic influences and how these conflicts
have brought about the rise of nationalist movements.

THE AFRICANS, A TRIPLE HERITAGE: 6. IN SEARCH OF
STABILITY. BBC-TV, WETA-TV, 1986. 60 min. color. Video.
Films Inc.
Tells about the search by African countries for social order and
forms of government to bring about stability.

THE AFRICANS, A TRIPLE HERITAGE: 7. A GARDEN OF
EDEN IN DECAY? BBC-TV, WETA-TV, 1986. 60 min.
color. Video. Films Inc.
Explains how the fact that Africa doesn't consume what it
produces and consumes what it doesn't produce leads to serious
problems involving economic dependence and decay.

THE AFRICANS, A TRIPLE HERITAGE: 8. A CLASH OF
CULTURES. BBC-TV, WETA-TV, 1986. 60 min. color.

Video. Films Inc.
Ponders the future of Africa in light of the mixing of cultures and
the many problems caused by such cultural clashes.

THE AFRICANS, A TRIPLE HERITAGE: 9. GLOBAL
AFRICA. BBC-TV, WETA-TV, 1986. 60 min. color. Video.
Films Inc.
Tells about Africa's contributions to contemporary culture and the
influence of superpowers on Africa.

ARUSI YA MARIAMU (THE MARRIAGE OF MARIAMU).
TFC, 1985. 36 min. color. Video. African Family Films.
A discussion of traditional medicine and healing in Africa. Tells
about the art and science involved.

BETWEEN NORTH AND SOUTH: ISRAEL AND AFRICA.
Anti-Defamation League of B'nai Brith, 1986. 30 min. color.
Video. Anti-Defamation League of B'nai Brith.
Discusses the technical training programs conducted by Israel, in
which people from developing African countries are helped to
improve their quality of life.

BLOODLINES AND BRIDGES: THE AFRICAN
CONNECTION. PBS Video, n.d. 60 min. color. Video. PBS
Video.
Covers portraits of Africans: a collector of African art, a politician
who supports African rights, a traditional dance troupe, an orphan
in search of her roots, and a school that emphasizes African
values.

CHAIN OF TEARS. Toni Strasburg (UK), 1989. 52 min. color.
Video. California Newsreel.
Depicts the shocking life of the child victims of the apartheid
regime in Mozambique, Angola, and South Africa, where one child
dies every four minutes and children are subject to acts of
brutality and harassment.

CHILDREN OF THE FOREST. Kevin Duffy, 1985. 28 min. color.
16mm/Video. Pyramid Film and Video.
This is an edited classroom version of "Pygmies of the Rain

Forest." Describes the lives of the Mbuti Pygmies of equatorial Africa who have a lifestyle similar to that of their ancestors.

CHUCK DAVIS, DANCING THROUGH WEST AFRICA. Gorham Kindem, 1987. 28 min. color. 16mm/Video. Filmakers Library.
Depicts African village life and the importance of dance in the culture. Filmed in Senegal and Gambia. Features three ethnic groups: Wolof, Mandinka, and Diola.

CORRIDORS OF FREEDOM. Ingrid Sinclair (UK), 1987. 52 min. color. Video. California Newsreel.
Reviews the patterns of unequal trade back to the days of colonialism. Depicts the efforts of SADACC, the Southern African Development Coordination Conference, to improve economic conditions for Tanzania, Zambia, Malawi, Botswana, Lesotho, Swaziland, Angola, Mozambique, and Zimbabwe, all founders of SADACC.

DESTRUCTIVE ENGAGEMENT. Toni Strasburg (UK), 1987. 52 min. color. Video. California Newsreel.
An account of how apartheid permeates regions way beyond South Africa's borders in Front Line states: Zimbabwe, Mozambique, Botswana, Zambia, and Angola. Shows the destruction in Mozambique caused by the South African-backed resistance movement and how U.S.-supported rebels in Angola have planted mines in fields causing the crippling of an estimated 20,000 peasants.

FARMERS HELPING FARMERS. National Film Board of Canada, 1989. 28 min. color. 16mm/Video. Bullfrog Films.
This prize-winning film tells how a group of Canadian farmers are funding food-growing projects for farmers in Kenya and Tanzania. Funding helps Africans buy seeds, rent tractors, attend workshops, or build oxcarts.

LIVING AFRICA: A VILLAGE EXPERIENCE. Andre Lefebvre, 1984. 34 min. color. 16mm/Video. Indiana University.
Portrays a visit to a small village on the Senegal River in West Africa. Provides scenes showing the attempt to cope with the

changes brought about by contemporary life.

NORTH AFRICA: THE GREAT SAHARA. Coronet/MTI Film
and Video, 1988. 15 min. color. 16mm/Video. Coronet/MTI
Film and Video.
Shows how the Sahara is made up of deserts with sand dunes,
plains, plateaus, and mountains. Examines the influence of nomad
Touaregs, Romans, Arabs, European scientists, explorers, priests,
and now technology, on the Saharan nations.

RIVER JOURNEYS: THE CONGO. Churchill Films, 1986. 57
min. color. Video. Churchill Films.
Makes a 1,000-mile trip along the Congo River in central Africa
in a huge ferry.

RIVER JOURNEYS: THE NILE. Churchill Films, 1986. 57 min.
color. Video. Churchill Films.
A trip along the Nile covering 1,800 miles from southern Sudan
to the Mediterranean.

ROOTS OF HUNGER, ROOTS OF CHANGE. Asterisk
Productions, 1985. 28 min. color. 16mm. Church World
Service.
Studies the causes of hunger in part of the African Sahel.
Discusses efforts to correct the situation.

THE SOUTH-EAST NUBA. BBC-TV, 1983. 60 min. color.
16mm/Video. Films Inc.
About the Nuba people of Africa who live in a remote region
near the center of the Sudan. The Nuba are noted for their body
decoration and bracelet fighting.

A SPIRITUAL ORDERING: THE METAL ARTS OF AFRICA.
African-American Institute, 1983. 20 min. color. Video. Indiana
University.
Takes a look at metal objects from western and central Africa.
Examines the symbolism of the themes reflected in the work of
African artists. Includes footage describing the work of the Yoruba
people and of Congolese craftsmen.

THE TREE OF IRON. Peter Schmidt, 1988. 57 min. color.
     16mm/Video. Center for African Studies, University of Florida.
Explores present-day efforts to discover the techniques of ancient
African smelters who were able to turn out carbon steel of high
quality.

TREE OF SURVIVAL. Abdellatif Ben Ammar, 1984. 20 min.
     color. 16mm/Video. First Run/Icarus Films.
Shows how trees are being planted in the Sahel region of Africa
to stop the sands of the Sahara desert.

WITH THESE HANDS. Chris Sheppard, 1987. 33 min. color.
     16mm/Video. Filmakers Library.
Farming has been women's work in Africa. This is an account of
three African women farmers who are now beginning to assert
their power over the land.

ANGOLA

ANGOLA IS OUR COUNTRY. Jenny Morgan, 1988. 45 min.
     color. Video. Women Make Movies.
Traces the role of Angolan women in the affairs of their country
in the face of an expensive war.

CAMEROON

BAKA: PEOPLE OF THE FOREST. National Geographic, 1989.
     59 min. color. 16mm/Video. National Geographic.
A visit with the Baka people who live in a Cameroon rain forest.
Focuses on one family to depict daily life in the rain forest
environment.

CAPE VERDE ISLANDS

SONGS OF THE BADIUS. Constant Spring Productions, 1985.
    35 min. color. 16mm/Video. Constant Spring Productions.
Describes the role of songs and dances in the culture of the
people of the Cape Verde Islands near Africa.

EGYPT

ANCIENT LIVES. Peter Spry-Leverton, 1985. 25 min. color.
    Video. Films for the Humanities.
An Egyptologist visits a 3,000-year-old village in the Valley of the
Kings. He is able to describe daily life of the people from well-
preserved records.

EGYPT: PAST AND PRESENT. Lucerne Media, 1983. 13 min.
    color. 16mm/Video. Lucerne Media.
Shows Egypt to be a modern nation with a rich ancient past.
Focuses on the intermingling of old and new, skyscrapers, traffic
jams, in contrast with ancient methods of farming still in use.

EGYPT: QUEST FOR ETERNITY. National Geographic, 1982.
    59 min. color. Video. National Geographic.
Shows how archeologists study the monuments of ancient Egypt.

EGYPT: THE NILE RIVER KINGDOM. Stefan Quinth, 1988.
    20 min. color. 16mm\Video. Barr Films.
Depicts Egypt's ancient past and her modern society. Visits the
pyramids, the city of Luxor, the Valley of the Kings, and
Tutankhamen's tomb, along with present-day cities and towns.

HERITAGE OF THE PHARAOHS. International Adventure
    Video, 1983. 50 min. color. Video. International Adventure
    Video.
Reviews the history of the pharaohs of Egypt for a period of 17
centuries.

NATIONS OF THE WORLD: EGYPT. National Geographic,
    1988. 25 min. color. 16mm/Video. National Geographic.
A visit to modern Alexandria and Cairo, and a look at industry
and agriculture along the Nile. Also depicts the evolution from
monarchy to a parliamentary democracy.

PARADISE STEAMSHIP CO. VISITS: EGYPT AND ISRAEL.
    KCBS-TV, n.d. 21 min. color. Video. Carousel Film and
    Video.
A look at the historic treasures of Egypt and the history of the
Holy Land.

SADAT: THE PRESIDENCY AND THE LEGACY. UPI, 1984.
    26 min. color. Video. Journal Films.
Tells about the events that made Anwar el-Sadat an important
figure in 20th-century history.

ETHIOPIA

ETHIOPIA. Robin Lehman and Don Charles, 1986. 29 min. color.
    16mm/Video. BFA Educational Media.
Presented without narration, this film records the beauty and harsh
contrasts of the land that is Ethiopia. Shows scenes of nature and
the people who live there.

FACES IN A FAMINE. Robert Lieberman, Ithaca Filmworks,
    1985. 51 min. color. 16mm/Video. Filmakers Library.
Tells how the three-year drought in Ethiopia caused a devastating
famine of enormous proportions. Shows how relief workers from
Western countries are trying to help the starving Ethiopians.

FALASHA: AGONY OF THE BLACK JEWS. Matara Film
    Productions, 1983. 28 min. color. 16mm/Video. Filmakers
    Library.
Documents the persecution and rejection of the black Jews of
Ethiopia by Ethiopians and Israelis.

FALASHA—EXILE OF THE BLACK JEWS. S. Jacobovici, 1985.
    80 min. color. 16mm. New Yorker Films.
Gives the history of the black Jews of Ethiopia—the Falasha—who
practice pre-Talmudic Judaism despite centuries of persecution.

FALASHA: THE SAGA OF ETHIOPIAN JEWRY. Steve
    Benzell, n.d. 30 min. color. Video. Alden Films.
The history and culture of Ethiopian Jewry. Includes rare footage
shot in pre-revolutionary Ethiopia. The Falasha people are
thought to be the descendents of the Israelite tribe of Dan.

NO EASY WALK: ETHIOPIA. Bernard Odjidja, 1988. 60 min.
    color. Video. The Cinema Guild.
Uses newsreel footage, press releases, and interviews to reflect
both the European and the African perspective on African history.
This program traces Ethiopia's history from 1896, when Ethiopia
freed itself from colonial domination by Italy, to modern times.

NO PLACE TO BE ME. Reynolds Film Production Ltd., 1983.
    15 min. color. 16mm. Beacon Films.
Follows for one day the 12-year-old son of Ethiopian refugees who
now live in the Somalian desert. Documents the problems of food
and water scarcities faced by the refugees.

GHANA

NOT FAR FROM BOLGATANGA. Michael Rubbo, Barrie
    Howells, 1982. 28 min. color. 16mm/Video. National Film
    Board of Canada.
Shows how a developed country can bring technology to a Third
World country, in this case, the Canadian International
Development Agency helping the government of Ghana. Wells
were drilled and hand-operated pumps were installed to provide
a clean and convenient water supply.

IVORY COAST

SPITE. Catherine De Clippel, 1984. 54 min. color. Video.
    Filmakers Library.
Shows how people of the Ivory Coast look to their prophet-
healers for help with medical and psychological problems.

KENYA

THE AFRICAN RHINO. R. Thomsett, 1986. 28 min. color.
    16mm/Video. Modern Talking Pictures.
Emphasizes the government of Kenya's effort to protect the black
and white rhinos of East Africa. Shows the lifestyle of the animals
and gives a history of hunting in that region.

ELEPHANTS: THEIR LAST STAND. National Geographic, 1983.
    22 min. color. 16mm/Video. National Geographic.
A visit to Kenya to study hungry elephants that must compete
with farmers for available resources.

FACING TOMORROW. Lucerne Media, n.d. 56 min. color.
    16mm/Video. Lucerne Media.
A look at the largest conference ever involving women, part of
the United Nations' Decade for Women, which took place in
Nairobi, Kenya. The official goals for the decade were peace,
equality, and development.

NO EASY WALK: KENYA. Bernard Odjidja, 1988. 60 min.
    color. Video. The Cinema Guild.
Depicts Kenya's history from the arrival of the first white people
who settled there in the 19th century to the Mau-Mau rebellion
in 1952, a struggle for land rights. Shows the frustration of the
Kenyans—in particular the Kokoyu and their leader Jomo
Kenyatta.

SPEAKING OF NAIROBI. Signe Johansson, Barbara Janes,
    Barbara Doran, 1986. 56 min. color. 16mm/Video. Indiana

University.
In July 1985 a United Nations women's conference was held in
Nairobi, Kenya. Women from all over the world discussed issues
such as peace, development, and equality.

THE WEDDING CAMELS. David and Judith MacDougall, 1980.
  108 min. color. Video. University of California Extension
  Media Center.
Shows the wedding negotiations between two Turkana families,
nomads of northeastern Kenya. In Turkana with English subtitles.

MALI

YEELEN. Souleymane Cisee, 1987. 105 min. color. 16mm.
  Cinecom International.
Yeleen means "brightness," suggested by the fact that the film was
shot in early morning when the sun was rising. The structure of
the story is based on Mande oral literature and presents in mythic
style the tale of a young man who tries to escape the wrath of his
father. Winner of a special jury prize in Cannes.

MOROCCO

MOROCCO, BODY AND SOUL: ALTA. First Run/Icarus Films,
  1987. 26 min. color. 16mm/Video. First Run/Icarus Films.
Presents a famous Moroccan female balladeer who travels with
dancers and musicians to perform at various occasions all over
Morocco.

MOROCCO, BODY AND SOUL: HYMNS OF PRAISE. First
  Run/Icarus Films, 1987. 26 min. color. 16mm/Video. First
  Run/Icarus Films.
Part of a series of three films about the diversity and beauty of
Moroccan culture. This film focuses on an annual religious
pilgrimage. Shows the ceremonies, the constant stream of people

from all over Morocco, and people dancing themselves into a trance.

MOROCCO, BODY AND SOUL: LUTES AND DELIGHTS.
    First Run/Icarus Films, 1988. 26 min. color. 16mm/Video. First
    Run/Icarus Films.
An outstanding Moroccan orchestra performs Arab-Andalusian music brought to North Africa by Jews and Muslims driven out of Spain. Combines Arab and Moroccan poetry with music utilizing lutes, violins, cellos, and percussion instruments to express a wide range of human emotions.

ROUTES OF EXILE: A MOROCCAN JEWISH ODYSSEY.
    Eugene Rosen, n.d. 90 min. color. 16mm. The Diaspora Film
    Project.
This documentary includes rare archival footage and interviews with a wide variety of people to tell the history of the Moroccan Jews from ancient times to the turbulent present. Shows how Jews and Arabs lived in peace side by side in North Africa for thousands of years. Follows the Moroccan exodus to other countries.

TIMGHRIWIN: MASS MARRIAGE OF BERBERS IN THE
    ATLAS MOUNTAINS; MARRIAGE DESTINED FOR
    DIVORCE. Austrian Federal Institute for Scientific Film,
    1988. 45 min. color. 16mm/Video. BFA Educational Media.
The Berbers of the High Atlas region in South Morocco celebrate TIMGhRIWIN, a five-day ceremony for the first marriage of their children. Many children are rushed into marriage and are divorced right after the ceremony. This film shows how the ceremony functions more as an initiation ritual than a marriage celebration. Also available in a 101 min. version showing ceremonies all over the High Atlas region.

MOZAMBIQUE

CHOPI MUSIC OF MOZAMBIQUE. Ron and Ophera Hallis,

1988. 28 min. color. 16mm/Video. Flower Films.
Shows how the culture of the Chopi people of the Inhambane Province of Mozambique is gradually being destroyed by the civil war. Explains how the Chopi have continued to play their xylophones from the early 16th century to the present.

KILLING A DREAM. Anders Nilsson and Gunilla Aakesson, 1986. 32 min. color. Video. First Run/Icarus Films.
An inside look at the war waged inside Mozambique by South African-sponsored guerrillas. Traces the systematic destruction brought by terrorists.

MOZAMBIQUE: RIDING OUT THE STORM. Alter Cine, 1989. 29 min. color. 16mm/Video. California Newsreel.
Depicts the struggle of the Mozambique people to survive a brutal war. A young student teacher takes the viewer to scenes of destruction during his perilous journey to find his family. Tells how he has survived five RENAMO guerrilla attacks. Visits a women's agricultural co-op and a refugee camp.

MOZAMBIQUE: THE STRUGGLE FOR SURVIVAL. Bob and Amy Coen, 1988. 57 min. color. Video. The Cinema Guild.
A prize-winning film about Africa's poorest nation, where the people must deal with famine and the Mozambique National Resistance, a terrorist army supported by South Africa. Documents the founding of the group, the terrorist atrocities committed, and the significance of the conflict.

SAMORA MACHEL, SON OF AFRICA. Ron Hallis, 1989. 28 min. color. Video. First Run/Icarus Films.
This is a portrait of Mozambican President Samora Machel, which includes an exclusive interview given to the filmmaker shortly before Machel's death in a plane crash. Uses archival footage to describe his political beliefs and actions.

NAMIBIA

NAMIBIA: AFRICA'S LAST COLONY. Paul Hamann and Peter
    Salmon, BBC-TV, 1984. 52 min. color. Video. California
    Newsreel.
Namibians take the viewer through their terrorized land in which
South Africa tries to maintain control. Also traces Namibia's
beleagured past when the Germans, then the British, enriched
themselves off the vast mineral resources. Some scenes will make
the viewer turn away in horror.

NAMIBIA: INDEPENDENCE NOW! Pearl Bowser, 1985. 50 min.
    color. 16mm/Video. Third World Newsreel.
Documents the struggle of the people of Namibia, which is under
South African rule illegally. Shows that a settlement like Cuanza
Sul in Angola, a refuge for fleeing Namibians, is a productive
community preparing for eventual return to Namibia. Available
in a variety of sound tracks, including Spanish, French, and
German.

SOUTHWEST AFRICA: THE FORGOTTEN DESERT.
    Coronet/MTI Film and Video, 1988. 15 min. color.
    16mm/Video. Coronet/MTI Film and Video.
An account of the geography, the people, and European influences
in Southwest Africa's two deserts: the Namib and the Kalahari.
Tells how the Bantu and Bushman people originally lived as
hunters and herdsmen in the deserts, but after World War I, when
South Africa took control of Namibia, they worked as laborers in
white-owned farms and mines.

NIGER REPUBLIC

AN AFRICAN RECOVERY. Sandra Nichols, United Nations,
    1988. 28 min. color. Video. First Run/Icarus Films.
Investigates ways of coping with devastating droughts, such as
those experienced in Africa in the early and mid-1980s. Shows
various projects in Niger tailored to local needs.

DEEP HEARTS. Harvard University Study Center, 1980. 53 min. color. 16mm/Video. Phoenix Films and Video.
A film about the nomadic Bororo Fulani of the Niger Republic. Shows them at a gathering at which ritual dances are performed to celebrate their pride as an independent and beautiful people.

NIGERIA

SONS OF THE MOON. Dierdre LaPin, Francis Speed, 1984. 25 min. color. 16mm/Video. University of California Extension Media Center.
A bard of the Ngas people of Nigeria tells how the moon influences the growth of crops and schedules all important human events.

VILLAGE OF THE RAIN FOREST. Journal Films, 1983. 23 min. color. 16mm/Video. Journal Films.
A look at village life in Nigeria as viewed through the eyes of children. Shows how villages still represent traditions, but when city-educated children return to their rural homes they introduce new methods.

SENEGAL

REASSEMBLAGE. Jean-Paul Bourdier and Trinh T. Mioh-ha, 1982. 40 min. color. 16mm. Third World Newsreel.
Using experimental film techniques, this film explores the cultural images of the diverse peoples of Senegal. Scenes include women at work, indigenous music, and interaction and communication of people.

SOUTH AFRICA

ADAPT OR DIE. Christopher Isham, 1983. 48 min. color. Video.
  ABC Video Enterprises.
A report on the black trade union movement in South Africa and
its struggle for power.

THE ANVIL AND THE HAMMER. International Defence and
  Aid Fund for Southern Africa, England, 1985. 40 min. color.
  Video. Third World Newsreel.
Depicts the growing unity of a wide variety of South Africans
(former political prisoners, workers, clergy, students, freedom
fighters, and others) in the fight to end apartheid. Shows the
brutality of the South African police and army to unarmed
Africans. Nelson Mandela's daughter is shown reading his rejection
of conditional release to a gathering in Soweto.

BIKO: BREAKING THE SILENCE. Mark Kaplan, Richard
  Wickstead, 1987. 52 min. color. Video. Filmakers Library,
  California Newsreel.
This program commemorates the tenth anniversary of the death
in South Africa of Steve Biko, the activist who inspired African
blacks. Shot in Zimbabwe and South Africa, it includes some
scenes from Richard Attenborough's *Cry Freedom*.

CHANGING THIS COUNTRY. Peter Entell, 1988. 58 min. color.
  Video. California Newsreel.
The first film to depict the strength of South Africa's labor
movement. Shows how the struggle is moving from the factory to
the freedom movement outside. Filmed in Port Elizabeth; includes
scenes of demonstrations and brutality.

CHILDREN OF APARTHEID. CBS News, 1987. 49 min. color.
  Video. California Newsreel.
From the "CBS Reports" TV show, with Walter Cronkite as host
in a discussion on young people in South Africa. Features Zindzi
Mandela and Roxanne Botha, daughters of Nelson Mandela and
President P. W. Botha respectively, who live drastically different
lifestyles.

CLASSIFIED PEOPLE. Yolande Zauberman, Obsession Films, 1986. 55 min. color. Video. Filmakers Library.
Examines the complications and absurdities of family life that can arise in a country that classifies people by color. Uses an elderly South African couple as an example. The husband, who had a white mother and black father, is classified "colored." His children from his first marriage with a white woman are classified "white." Later the children were embarrassed when their father chose a black woman for his second wife.

CRY FREEDOM. Richard Attenborough, 1987. 157 min. color. 16mm/Video. Swank Films (16mm)/MCA Home Vision (Video).
A theatrical feature-length film that tells the story of Steven Biko, black South African activist, and the white editor who tries to bring Biko's story to public attention. Based on a book by Donald Woods. With Kevin Kline, Denzel Washington, and Penelope Wilton.

THE CRY OF REASON: BEYERS NAUDE, AN AFRIKANER SPEAKS OUT. Southern Africa Media Center, 1986. 20 min. color. Video. California Newsreel.
Describes the work of the former general secretary of the South Africa Council of Churches to end apartheid. Narrated by Mark Mathabane. An Academy Award nominee.

DAVID GOLDBLATT IN BLACK AND WHITE. Bernard Joffa Productions, 1988. 52 min. color. Video. Wombat Film and Video.
David Goldblatt, photographer, reveals the diversity and controversy in South Africa through his black-and-white photographs.

FOR FREEDOM IN SOUTH AFRICA. Judea Crisfield, 1986. 57 min. color. Video. Crisfield Films and Video.
Tells about the anti-apartheid movement of the U.S. and the U.S. foreign policy regarding South Africa.

FREE MANDELA. International Defence and Aid Fund for Southern Africa, 1988. 40 min. color. Video. California

Newsreel.
In July 1988 South African activist Nelson Mandela's 75th birthday was celebrated in a concert in London. Features many famous people: Stevie Wonder, Miriam Makeba, Whoopi Goldberg, Natalie Cole, and others. Presents historical background about Mandela. His colleagues talk about harassment and torture. Also includes scenes of the Mandela celebrations around the world.

GIRLS APART. New Internationalist, 1987. 39 min. color. Video.
    California Newsreel.
Describes the life and attitudes of two 16-year-old girls in South Africa. One is a black girl who lives in Soweto; the other is white and lives in Johannesburg.

ISITWALANDE. International Defence and Aid Fund for
    Southern Africa, England, 1980. 55 min. color. 16mm/Video.
    Third World Newsreel.
Isitwalande is the decoration of heroism given to three men (one African, one Asian, and one white) who helped organize the Congress of the People which created the Freedom Charter, a document of liberation for South Africa. Tells how over 100 leaders of the African National Congress, which sponsored the Congress, were arrested for high treason. Includes interviews with organizers.

MAIDS AND MADAMS. Channel Four Television, London, 1986.
    52 min. color. Video. Filmakers Library.
Gives an inside view of life for South Africa's black domestic workers who must live apart from their own families in conditions of poverty. Winner of many prizes.

MANDELA. P. Davis, 1983. 58 min. color. 16mm/Video.
    California Newsreel.
This film was shot clandestinely to tell the story of Nelson and Winnie Mandela, leaders in the struggle for black rights in South Africa.

MAPANTSULA. Max Montocchio, 1988. 104 min. color.
    16mm/Video. California Newsreel.

The first anti-apartheid feature film that concentrates on black South Africans. *Mapantsula* is Zulu for "petty criminal," in this case, a fellow named Panic who is a *totsi*, a rebellious underworld figure popular in black South African fiction. Not just Panic, but those around him, join in the anti-apartheid movement in various ways—a rent strike, a student demonstration, a fight for back pay. This film was banned in South Africa. Contains strong language. In English, Zulu, Sotho, and Afrikaans with English subtitles.

NELSON MANDELA: THE STRUGGLE IS MY LIFE. Lionel Ngakane, England, 1985. 30 min. color. Video. Third World Newsreel.
Uses the words of Nelson Mandela, archival film footage, and interviews with African National Congress leaders to give a view of Mandela and the struggle for freedom he represents. Shows Mandela's statement to South Africans in answer to Prime Minister Botha's offer to release him.

NO EASY ROAD. BBC-TV, 1988. 50 min. color. Video. Films Inc.
BBC-TV reporter Michael Buerk, who covered South Africa, was expelled for four years. Now he talks about life and work in this racially troubled country.

THE RIBBON. Harriet Gavshon, 1987. 50 min. color. 16mm/Video. First Run/Icarus Films.
A film by a South African woman to describe the recent establishment of women's organizations in South Africa. The women, wanting to make a public statement, took up the idea of making a Peace Ribbon on which they have sewn, drawn, or painted their visions of peace. The ribbon eventually reached a length of 500 meters.

ROBBEN ISLAND: OUR UNIVERSITY. Lindy Wilson, 1988. 53 min. color. 16mm/Video. Lindy Wilson Productions.
Three former black political prisoners discuss what conditions are like on Robben Island, a South African maximum security prison. They also discuss the liberation struggle.

SALESTALK. Hugo Cassirer, 1984. 29 min. color. 16mm. Felix
    Films.
A tale about an old black maid and the white woman she works
for, who are shown as they grow old together. Set in South Africa.

SONG OF THE SPEAR. International Defence and Aid Fund for
    Southern Africa, England, 1986. 57 min. color. 16mm/Video.
    Third World Newsreel.
Follows the Amandla Group, a troupe of performers in South
Africa, who represent the closely tied cultural and political
expressions of the anti-apartheid movement. Explains how music,
dance, and performance can be used in the struggle.

SOUTH AFRICA. John Tiffin for CBS News, n.d. 19 min. color.
    Video. Carousel Film and Video.
Raises the question whether South Africa is a racist state or a
country in transition. A "60 Minutes" program hosted by Morley
Safer.

SOUTH AFRICA: THE SOLUTION. Facet Films, n.d. 38 min.
    color. Video. Beacon Films, Journal Films.
Based on a book of the same name by Frances Kendall and Leon
Louw. Analyzes South Africa's past and present with a vision of
the way South Africa could be. Proposes a solution that would
accommodate the needs of all the South African people.

SOUTH AFRICA TODAY: A QUESTION OF POWER. Journal
    Films, 1987. 55 min. color. Video. Journal Films.
Presents opposing views on the problems of South Africa. Two
South African newspaper editors, one an Afrikaner and the other
a black nationalist, discuss their viewpoints. The film optimistically
suggests the possibility of a shared future.

SOUTH AFRICA UNEDITED. David Goodman, 1986. 30 min.
    color. Video. American Friends Service Committee.
Discusses repression and resistance in South Africa and the attack
on media coverage. Uses uncensored footage.

SOUTH AFRICAN CHRONICLES. The Varan Workshop of
    Johannesburg, 1987. 105 min. color. Video. First Run/Icarus

Films.
Depicts daily life in South Africa as filmed by members of the
Varan Workshop, a multiracial group of young men and women.
Includes scenes of an election campaign in a small town, a
meeting of an extreme right-wing Afrikaner group, old people in
Soweto collecting their pensions, a health care center, and the
like—all testimony to the realities of apartheid.

SPEAR OF THE NATION: HISTORY OF THE ANC. Thames
     Television, BELBO Filmproductions, NOVIB, 1986. 50 min.
     color. Video. California Newsreel.
Documents the 75-year history of the African National Congress
(ANC) to show that the first 50 years of this group were non-
violent, contrary to the statements of critics. Filmed secretly in
South Africa. Includes interviews with President Oliver Tambo,
Albertina Sidulu, Thabo Mbaki, and military chief Joe Slovo.

THE SUN WILL RISE. International Defence and Aid Fund for
     Southern Africa, 1983. 35 min. color. 16mm/Video. First
     Run/Icarus Films.
A secretly made film about the armed struggle inside South Africa
as exemplified by the story of young members of the African
National Congress who fled the country as they were sentenced
for actions to end apartheid.

TALK ABOUT ME, I AM AFRICA. Chris Austin, 1980. 54 min.
     color. Video. First Run/Icarus Films.
A clandestinely filmed report on apartheid in South Africa.
Theatrical and musical groups demonstrate cultural resistance to
apartheid.

THE TWO RIVERS. Mark Newman and Edwin Wes, 1985. 60
     min. color. 16mm/Video. First Run/Icarus Films.
The narrator and co-writer of this film is Rashaka Ratshitanga,
a writer and poet who lives in Venda, a rural area of South
Africa. When South Africa recently declared Venda an
"independent state," he opposed this policy and was detained
incommunicado for long periods of time.

VOICES OF *SERAFINA!* Nigel Nobel, 1988. 85 min. color. 16mm. New Yorker Films.
A feature-length documentary about the life experiences and performances of the teenagers who dance, sing, and speak in the South African musical, *Serafina!*—a powerful statement against the horrors of apartheid. Includes a moving scene in which the viewer observes the visit of Miriam Makeba who meets with the young people backstage.

WINNIE. Alexandra Gleysteen, 1987. 15 min. color. Video. Carousel Film and Video.
About Winnie Mandela, wife of the famous former political prisoner, Nelson Mandela. Shows political strife in South Africa.

WITNESS TO APARTHEID. Sharon Sopher, 1985. 58 min. color. 16mm/Video. California Newsreel.
Victims of apartheid, young and old, testify as to the torture and repression they have experienced in South Africa.

A WORLD APART. Chris Menges, 1988. 112 min. color. Video. Paramount Home Video.
This is a theatrical feature-length film about the suffering of children whose parents are active in the struggle against apartheid in South Africa. The setting is 1963 and the story is told from the point of view of a 13-year-old girl. With Barbara Hershey, Jeroen Krabbe, Jodhi May.

WOZA ALBERT! BBC-TV, 198? 55 min. color. Video. California Newsreel, Films Inc.
Includes excerpts from an internationally acclaimed play, produced for the BBC-TV series, "Everyman," which explores what it would be like if Christ went to South Africa today. Discusses black oppression in South Africa.

SUDAN

THE AVOIDABLE FAMINE. Journal Films, 1988. 20 min. color.

Video. Journal Films.
The Sudan area used to produce plenty of food. Now, because of a change in farming methods, there is famine and desertification of the land. Examines the reasons for these changes and what is happening to Sudan's economy.

TANZANIA

KOPJES: ISLANDS IN A SEA OF GRASS. Alan Root, 1988. 55
    min. color. 16mm/Video. Benchmark Films.
Shows how the granite rock formations, known as *kopjes*, located on the plains in Tanzania, serve as the habitat for a wide variety of animal life.

SERENGETI DIARY. National Geographic, 1989. 59 min. color.
    16mm/Video. National Geographic.
Two men, one a photographer, the other a Masai tribesman, tell why they've lived in the Serengeti for decades. An inside look at Serengeti culture.

THE YEAR OF THE WILDEBEEST (REVISED). Alan Root,
    1984. 30 min. color. 16mm. Benchmark Films.
Looks at the 2,000-mile migration of a million wildebeest in Tanzania.

TOGO

WATER FOR TONOUMASSE. Garry Beitel, 1987. 28 min. color.
    Video. Filmakers Library.
A study of women in a village of southern Togo, who must walk many miles each day for their water supply. Explains how they are trying to improve the conditions of their daily life.

UPPER VOLTA (BURKINA FASO)

YAABA. Idrissa Ouédraogo, 1989. 90 min. color. 16mm. New
    Yorker Films.
Burkina Faso (Upper Volta) is the setting for this feature-length
film by an African filmmaker about a young boy and girl who
befriend an old woman, *yaaba* (grandmother), who has been
rejected by the villagers. Combines real and mythological elements.
Winner of the International Critics Prize at the Cannes Film
Festival.

ZAMBIA

THE DEBT CRISIS: AN AFRICAN DILEMMA. Steve
    Whitehouse, United Nations, 1988. 20 min. color. Video. First
    Run/Icarus Films.
Traces the debt crisis of Africa with particular reference to
Zambia, one of the most hard hit in economic decline. Describes
the collapse of the copper market and the lack of ability even to
maintain its public transportation system.

MWE BANA BANDI—CHILDREN'S SONGS FROM ZAMBIA.
    Kristina Tuura, 1988. 29 min. color. Video. Villon Films.
Covers daily life in Wapamesa, a Zambian village. Also presents
songs sung by the children.

ZIMBABWE

AFTER THE HUNGER AND DROUGHT. Olley Marumba,
    1988. 54 min. color. Video. California Newsreel.
An insightful account of the role of the writer in society.
Zimbabwe's leading literary figures, such as Dumbudzo Marechera
and Stanlake Samkange, debate this issue as well as matters of
tradition, race, class, and gender in literature. Recommended for

courses on African literature and African studies in general.

NKULELERO MEANS FREEDOM. Ron and Ophera Hallis,
   1982. 28 min. color. 16mm/Video. First Run/Icarus Films.
A report on Zimbabwe's educational system that developed in
refugee camps during the recent war. The system is based on
education with production.

NO EASY WALK: ZIMBABWE. Bernard Odjidja, 1988. 60 min.
   color. Video. The Cinema Guild.
Documents the uprising in March 1896 of the Ndebele people in
Rhodesia (now Zimbabwe) against the European settlers who had
taken over their land for gold and mineral mining. Although the
struggle ended in defeat, 84 years later a guerrilla war brought
independence. Includes interviews with black and white
Zimbabweans.

THE STRUGGLING PEOPLE. BBC-TV, 1987. 28 min. color.
   Video. Films Inc.
Shows how Zimbabwe and other African nations are trying to curb
population growth through the education of women.

ZIMBABWE: THE NEW STRUGGLE. Ron Hallis, 1985. 58 min.
   color. Video. First Run/Icarus Films.
A documentary about Zimbabwe today. Reports on social and
economic development, and the debate over the country's future
as a Marxist one-party state. Covers the history of Zimbabwe.
Interviews officials and people at the grass-roots level.

ASIA

GENERAL

ASIA: AN INTRODUCTION (REVISED). Wayne Mitchell, 1981.
21 min. color. Video. BFA Educational Media.
Examines the characteristics of each major region in Asia.
Explains how values and political systems are in constant change.

ASIAN THEATRE: TECHNIQUES AND APPLICATION.
Michigan State University, 1983. 15 programs/28—91 min.
each, color. Video. Michigan State University.
A series of 15 programs on Asian acting techniques. 1. Kabuki
Acting Technique I: The Body (60 min.); 2. Kabuki Acting
Technique II: The Voice (29 min.); 3. Acting Techniques of the
Noh Theatre of Japan (29 min.); 4. Acting Techniques of Topeng,
Masked Theatre of Bali (39 min.); 5. Kalarippayatt, Martial Art
of India (35 min.); 6. Acting Techniques of Kutivattam, Sanskrit
Theater of India (55 min.); 7. Asian Concepts of Stage Discipline
and Western Actor Training (33 min.); 8. Conversation with R.
C. Scott (28 min.); 9. Kabuki for Western Actors and Directors
(40 min.); 10. Actor Training and Kalarippayatt, Martial Art of
India (45 min.); 11. Adapting Topeng, the Masked Theatre of Bali
(46 min.); 12. Seraikella Chhau: The Masked Dance of India (38
min.); 13. Noh, the Classical Theatre of Japan (29 min.); 14. From
India to East Lansing—Surpanak ha—Producing a Sanskrit Drama
(31 min.); 15. Seraikella (The Amorous Demoness) (91 min.).

CENTRAL ASIA: THE DESERT OF TAMERLANE. Coronet/MTI Film and Video, 1988. 15 min. color. 16mm/Video. Coronet/MTI Film and Video.
An account of the physical features, social and economic evolution, and the long succession of occupants in the Turkestan deserts which run from Mongolia to the Caspian Sea.

SOUTHWEST ASIA (MIDDLE EAST)

General

THE ARAB WORLD. Lucerne Media, 1986. 22 min. color. 16mm/Video. Lucerne Media.
Gives a look at the world of the Arabs in the Middle East. Provides information about the geography, history, religion, and economics of the vast area they inhabit. Also discusses the role of women, the life of the nomadic Bedouins, and relations with Israel.

THE DEAD SEA IN BIBLICAL TIMES. Doko Video Ltd., 1984. 26 min. color. Video. Doko Communications.
Examines the history of the Dead Sea in ancient times.

THE DERVISHES OF KURDISTAN. Brian Moser, 1986. 52 min. color. Video. Filmmakers Library.
The Dervish tribesmen live in an area between Iran and Iraq. Shows them performing amazing rituals without pain due to their deep faith in Islam.

THE HOLY KORAN. F. Cockburn, 1982. 60 min. color. Video. Mastervision.
Explains the importance of Islam in today's world. Describes Islam's contributions to culture.

LEAGUE OF ARAB STATES. Marilyn Perry, 1980. 28 min. color. Video. Marilyn Perry TV Productions.
An observer of the League of Arab States, Ambassador to the

United Nations, Clovis Maksoud, talks about the role of the league.

LEBANON, ISRAEL AND THE PLO. UPI, 1984. 28 min. color.
     Video. Journal Films.
Provides the background of the confrontation involving Lebanon, Israel, and the PLO.

MIDDLE EAST: ANCIENT AND MODERN—THE FALL AND
     RISE OF THE MIDDLE EAST. TV Ontario, 1984. 25 min.
     color. 16mm/Video. Encyclopaedia Britannica Educational
     Corporation.
Studies the conditions that have held back progress in the Middle East from the time of the European Renaissance to the present. Reports on the impact of the oil trade, technology, and independence.

MIDDLE EAST: CAPTAINS AND KINGS—AUTHORITY IN
     THE MIDDLE EAST. TV Ontario, 1984. 25 min. color.
     16mm/Video. Encyclopaedia Britannica Educational
     Corporation.
Compares the Middle East with the West in the preference for authoritarian rule under a monarch or military leader. Mentions the countries that are exceptions to this political orientation.

MIDDLE EAST: CHANGE—TURKEY AND SAUDI ARABIA.
     TV Ontario, 1984. 25 min. color. 16mm/Video. Encyclopaedia
     Britannica Educational Corporation.
Explains how change of a non-violent nature has affected the Middle East. Compares Turkey and Saudi Arabia in their response to change, showing how one emphasized modernization over heritage and the other maintained its Arab, Islamic traditions.

MIDDLE EAST: FAMILY MATTERS—THE ROLE OF THE
     FAMILY IN THE MIDDLE EAST. TV Ontario, 1984. 25
     min. color. 16mm/Video. Encyclopaedia Britannica Educational
     Corporation.
Discusses the importance of family life for the people of the Middle East and the conflicts that have come about with the recent fragmentation of the extended family.

MIDDLE EAST: HOLY LAND—JUDAISM, CHRISTIANITY, AND ISLAM IN THE MIDDLE EAST. TV Ontario, 1984. 25 min. color. 16mm/Video. Encyclopaedia Britannica Educational Corporation.
Presents the Middle East as the birthplace of three of the world's religions. Points out the role of religion in the region's culture and development.

MIDDLE EAST: HOMELAND—ISRAEL AND PALESTINE. TV Ontario, 1984. 25 min. color. 16mm/Video. Encyclopaedia Britannica Educational Corporation.
Discusses the struggle for the same territory by the Israelis and Palestinians.

MIDDLE EAST: INDEPENDENCE—EGYPT AND ALGERIA. TV Ontario, 1984. 25 min. color. 16mm/Video. Encyclopaedia Britannica Educational Corporation.
Explores the various ways in which Middle Eastern countries achieve independence. Focuses on Egypt and Algeria, which, although located in Africa, are considered part of the Middle Eastern bloc.

MIDDLE EAST: JOURNEY INTO THE FUTURE (REVISED). Lucerne Media, 1987. 15 min. color. 16mm/Video. Lucerne Media.
Shows a young man who is a farmer and lives in a village in a traditional atmosphere. He also is shown on his other job in a more modern world: working as a diver for an oil company in order to earn enough money to support his family.

MIDDLE EAST: NEW FRONTIERS—THE MIDDLE EAST FOLLOWING WORLD WAR I. TV Ontario, 1984. 25 min. color. 16mm/Video. Encyclopaedia Britannica Educational Corporation.
Explains how 26 nation-states came into being after World War I. Describes the impact of Western nationalism on the social order of the Middle East.

MIDDLE EAST: REVOLUTION—IRAQ AND IRAN. TV Ontario, 1984. 25 min. color. 16mm/Video. Encyclopaedia

Britannica Educational Corporation.
Covers the post-World War II period in the Middle East. Looks at Iran and Iraq in particular.

MIDDLE EAST: SECTS AND VIOLENCE—FRAGMENTATION WITHIN RELIGIONS. TV Ontario, 1984. 25 min. color. 16mm/Video. Encyclopaedia Britannica Educational Corporation.
Shows that disputes over territory among sects cause as much tension in the Middle East as the major differences among the faiths.

MIDDLE EAST: THE DESERT OF GOD. Coronet/MTI Film and Video, 1988. 15 min. color. 16mm/Video. Coronet/MTI Film and Video.
Explains how four great religions, all dedicated to the worship of one God, were born in Middle Eastern deserts. Moses, Jesus, Mohammed, and King Amenhotep IV were equally inspired by visions in the desert. Poses the question of why deserts have such profound effects on spiritual longings. Gives viewers a look at the various deserts of the Middle East.

MIDDLE EAST: THE MIDDLEMEN—THE PIVOTAL ROLE OF THE MIDDLE EAST. TV Ontario, 1984. 25 min. color. 16mm/Video. Encyclopaedia Britannica Educational Corporation.
Explains why the Middle East is in constant turmoil and how it has been a crossroads for trade, religion, and ethnic influences throughout many centuries.

MIDDLE EAST: THE STORY OF OIL, CHIEF ECONOMIC RESOURCE OF THE MIDDLE EAST. TV Ontario, 1984. 25 min. color. 16mm/Video. Encyclopaedia Britannica Educational Corporation.
An account of how the growth of the oil industry in the Middle East affects its society and also changed Western lifestyles.

MIDDLE EAST: THE TORCHBEARERS—BRIDGING THE DARK AGES. TV Ontario, 1984. 25 min. color. 16mm/Video. Encyclopaedia Britannica Educational Corporation.

Introduces Islamic learning and explains how Islam's preservation of knowledge played a role between the fall of Rome and the onset of the European Renaissance.

PEOPLE OF THE ARABIAN GULF. Beacon, 1987. 18 min.
   color. 16mm/Video. Beacon Films.
The values of the people of the Arabian Gulf have not changed much, even though they have been transformed from a nomadic tribal culture to a more affluent lifestyle. Focuses on the countries of the Organization of Petroleum Exporting Countries (OPEC): Kuwait, Bahrain, Qatar, Saudi Arabia, and the United Arab Emirates.

SHOOT AND CRY. National Film Board of Canada, 1988. 58
   min. color. 16mm/Video. First Run/Icarus Films.
Two young men, one a Palestinian and the other an Israeli, discuss frankly what life is like for each. The phrase, "shoot and cry," was used in the 1982 war in Lebanon to describe Israeli soldiers who supposedly would shoot first, then cry later.

SUEZ CANAL: POLITICS OF CONTROL. UPI, 1984. 18 min.
   color. Video. Journal Films.
A report on the nationalization of the Suez Canal. Discusses the reaction worldwide.

TALKING TO THE ENEMY: VOICES OF SORROW AND
   RAGE. Mira Hamermesh, 1988. 54 min. color. Video.
   Filmakers Library.
When a Palestinian journalist and an Israeli editor try to open a dialogue on peace with the people of a kibbutz, they open old wounds. Shows how each felt compassion for the other.

Iran

THE AYATOLLAH'S REVOLUTION. UPI Television, 1980. 26
   min. color. Video. Journal Films.
Documents the return of Ayatollah Khomeini to Iran in 1979 and its effects on religion. Also tells how his return was instrumental in the deposing of the shah.

BANI SADR FLEES. UPI, 1984. 15 min. color. Video. Journal
Films.
About the rise and fall of Bani Sadr, the first president after the
revolution in Iran.

ESCAPE FROM IRAN: THE CANADIAN CAPER. Les Harris,
1987. 96 min. color. Video. Chip Taylor Communications.
A docudrama that describes how Canadian diplomats gave shelter
to, and helped smuggle out, six Americans held in the Iran
hostage crisis.

ESCAPE FROM IRAN: THE INSIDE STORY. Les Harris, 1987.
58 min. color. Video. Chip Taylor Communications.
Depicts the escape of six Americans in the Iran hostage crisis.
With interviews of survivors.

IRAN. BBC-TV, Jenny Cropper, 1984. 60 min. color. Video.
Films Inc.
Traces the beginnings of the Iranian revolution through footage
smuggled out of Iran.

IRAN—A REVOLUTION BETRAYED. BBC-TV, 1984. 60 min.
color. Video. Films Inc.
Gives the background of the Iranian revolution and its impact on
politics and religion.

IRAN: ADRIFT IN A SEA OF BLOOD. Ron Hallis, 1986. 27
min. color. Video. First Run/Icarus Films.
Examines the feelings of Iranians of all walks of life about the
war with Iraq, which began in 1980. Tells how the Iranians firmly
adhere to Islam and its leaders.

IRAN: BEHIND THE VEIL. Louise Vance, 1985. 97 min. color.
Video. Turner Program Services.
Tells how Khomeini came to power and of the many changes that
have taken place since the 1979 revolution.

JOURNAL FROM TEHRAN. Pershing Sadegh-Vaziri, 1986. 20
min. color. Video. Pershing Sadegh-Vaziri.
After an absence of seven years, an Iranian filmmaker returns to

her native Iran and observes the many changes that have occurred since the revolution.

KHOMEINI PROFILE. UPI, 1984. 17 min. color. Video. Journal Films.
Gives the background for the rise to prominence of Ayatollah Khomeini.

THE LAND OF THE PEACOCK THRONE. WGBH-TV, 1983. 15 min. color. Video. King Features Entertainment.
Uses archival footage to depict the forty years of upheaval in Iran. Also includes discussion of the hostage crisis.

THE SHAHSAVAN NOMADS OF IRAN. Dallalfar, Safizadeh, 1984. 28 min. color. 16mm. Safi Productions.
Follows the seasonal migration of the Shahsavan nomads in northwest Iran. Shows daily activities in both winter and summer camps.

SMITHSONIAN WORLD: ISLAM. Adrian Malone, 1987. 58 min. color. Video. WETA-TV.
A study of the origins and current condition of Islam. Discusses Muslim beliefs and their impact on society.

Israel

ABRAHAM'S PEOPLE. Anti-Defamation League of B'nai Brith, 1983. 53 min. color. Video. Anti-Defamation League of B'nai Brith.
Presents the complete history of the Jews in the Middle East.

BEN-GURION: ONE PLACE, ONE PEOPLE. Nielson-Ferns International, 1980. 24 min. b/w. Video. Coronet/MTI Film and Video.
A portrait of the Israeli prime minister who wanted to establish an independent Jewish state in Palestine.

THE HOLY LAND: A PILGRIMAGE. Episcopal Radio-TV Foundation, 1986. 28 min. color. Video. Episcopal Radio-TV

Foundation.
A tour of Jerusalem featuring Christian, Judaic, and Islamic aspects.

HOLY LAND: 5,000 YEARS—AN INCREDIBLE JOURNEY. Doko Video Ltd., 1984. 58 min. color. Video. Doko Communications.
Gives a historical tour of Israel with focus on Biblical landmarks.

THE HUNDRED YEARS WAR: PERSONAL NOTES. Ilan Ziv, 1983. 120 min. color. (60 min. each part). Video. First Run/Icarus Films.
A panoramic view of history on the West Bank and political struggle within the Israeli community. In two parts. Part I covers the invasion of Lebanon and Israeli policies in the West Bank. Part II studies the way in which Israeli society is influenced by its West Bank policies.

IMPRESSIONS. Alden Films, n.d. 28 min. color. 16mm/Video. Alden Films.
A travelogue about the land of Israel. Shows the diversity, topographical contrasts, traces of the ancient past, modern life, and cultural features.

ISRAEL AND THE ARAB STATES. BBC-TV, 1981. 20 min. color. Video. Films Inc.
The history of the founding of the state of Israel and Arabian disputes over territory.

ISRAEL AND THE PALESTINIANS: THE CONTINUING CONFLICT. Amran Nowak Associates, 1983. 37 min. color. 16mm/Video. BFA Educational Media.
This history of the conflict in the Middle East begins with the first settlements in what was to become Israel and continues on through the Israeli invasion of Lebanon in 1982. Presents interviews with statesmen and historians and uses archival footage and other materials.

ISRAEL—THE GOLAN AND SINAI QUESTION. UPI, 1984. 19 min. color. Video. Journal Films.

Describes the history of Golan and Sinai and their role in the Middle East Peace Plan.

ISRAEL—THE OTHER REALITY. Wombat, 1989. 58 min. color. Video. Wombat Film and Video.
Shows that, despite the conflict between Israel and the Arabs, there are unexpected examples of cooperation and love between Arabs and Jews. Shows them joined in business, in celebration, in day-to-day living, and in marriage.

ISRAEL: THE PROMISE OF THE JEWISH PEOPLE, FEATURING BOB GRANT. Yisrael Lifschutz, n.d. 58 min. color. Video. Alden Films.
Bob Grant of radio-talk-show fame in New York narrates this exploration of the 4,000-year history of the Jewish people in Israel.

JERUSALEM: GATES OF TIME. Israel Film Service, n.d. 26 min. color. Video. Alden Films.
Describes efforts of recent decades to restore the old city of Jerusalem. Depicts how architects, city planners, and archeologists are involved in preservation projects and development for the future.

JERUSALEM: THE HOLY CITY. Around the World in Sight and Sound, 1984. 16 min. color. Video. Around the World in Sight and Sound.
A travel film about Jerusalem featuring King David's tomb, the Garden of Gethsemane, and the tomb of Herod.

JOIN HANDS AND SING. Israel Information Media Services, n.d. 10 min. color. Video. Alden Films.
Explains how the memory of Dr. Martin Luther King, Jr., and his teachings are celebrated in Israel today by schoolchildren and by pilgrimages to a forest named for him. His daughter Yolanda King reviews his beliefs in freedom and justice.

MIRACLE OF SURVIVAL (AGAINST ALL ODDS). Lucerne Media, n.d. 49 min. color. 16mm/Video. Lucerne Media.
Covers 70 years of history of Palestine and Israel through the Six Day War. Traces the ups and downs of development leading to

the Israel of today.

MODERN ISRAEL. Around the World in Sight and Sound, 1984.
      17 min. color. Video. Around the World in Sight and Sound.
Takes a look at Israel's sights including Haifa, Tel Aviv, the Sea
of Galilee, and Jerusalem.

NATIONS OF THE WORLD: ISRAEL. National Geographic,
      1988. 25 min. color. 16mm/Video. National Geographic.
Covers Israel's ancient and modern history and depicts the struggle
to be a productive state despite unfriendly neighbors and a lack
of natural resources. Also discusses Israel's geographic beauty,
religious groups, and life on a kibbutz.

NATURE CONSERVATION IN ISRAEL. Alden Films, n.d. 23
      min. color. Video. Alden Films.
Documents how Israelis are bringing back the wildlife that used
to be native to the region: fallow deer, wild sheep, ibex, and
vultures.

NAZARETH IN AUGUST. Norman Cowie, Ahmed Damian, Dan
      Walworth, 1986. 58 min. color. Video. Third World Newsreel.
Nazareth is the largest Arab city in Israel, with 55,000 Arabs.
Documents how their continued existence there is a struggle. They
are fighting for equal rights and adequate funding for their city.
Presents interviews with Arab and Jewish officials, activists, and
workers.

A PEOPLE IS BORN. WNET-TV, 1984. ("Heritage: Civilization
      and the Jews" series.) 60 min. color. 16mm/Video. Films Inc.
About the origin of the Jewish people and their development from
the 6th century B.C. to 3500 B.C.

PEOPLE OF ISRAEL. Beacon Films, 1987. 18 min. color.
      16mm/Video. Beacon Films.
Tells how Israel is a new nation with a predominantly Jewish
population. Through the eyes of a native-born Israeli woman, the
viewer observes the lifestyle, the factors of education, compulsory
military service for men and women, and socializing. Makes visits
to the Memory Museum, which commemorates the victims of the

Holocaust, and to the Jewish Orthodox section of Jerusalem.

A PERSPECTIVE ON ISRAEL WITH BARBARA TUCHMAN.
Anti-Defamation League of B'nai Brith, 1986. 29 min. color.
Video. Anti-Defamation League of B'nai Brith.
Historian Barbara Tuchman talks about Israel's status as the only
democratic state in the Middle East and Israel's efforts for
survival.

SHALOM IN ACTION. Journal Films, 1987. 55 min. color.
Video. Journal Films.
Observes the Shalom dance company performing at various places
in Israel: Eliat on the Red Sea, Northern Galilee, and Jerusalem.
Gives background history of Israel. Also geography and culture.

SHATTERED DREAMS: PICKING UP THE PIECES. Victor
Schonfeld, 1987. 173 min. color. 16mm. New Yorker Films.
A British film about Israel as a country in crisis. Compares the
Zionist dreams of the 1940s with the problems of today: war,
dissension, discrimination, and economic difficulties. Explores the
unofficial grass-roots efforts to reconcile interests of Arabs and
Jews. In English, and Hebrew and Arabic with English subtitles.

THIS IS ISRAEL. Doko Video Ltd., 1983. 53 min. color. Video.
Doko Communications.
A visit to the Holy Land, showing important landmarks.

TREASURES OF THE HOLY LAND: ANCIENT ART FROM
THE ISRAELI MUSEUM. Metropolitan Museum of Art,
1986. 30 min. color. Video. Home Vision.
Gives the viewer a chance to examine the artistic treasures of
ancient Israel.

Jordan

DESERT REGIONS: NOMADS AND TRADERS. Wolfgang
Bayer, 1980. 15 min. color. Video. BFA Educational Media.
Compares the Bedouins of Jordan with the Navajo Indians of
Monument Valley.

JORDAN AND THE MEDITERRANEAN CANAL. Marilyn
    Perry TV Productions, 1983. 28 min. color. Video. Marilyn
    Perry TV Productions.
Crown Prince Hussein of Jordan discusses the canal being built
from the Mediterranean to the Dead Sea.

JORDAN, LAND AND PEOPLE. Jordan Ministry of Information,
    1981. 28 min. color. Video. Marilyn Perry TV Productions.
A report on how Jordan has grown in the last 29 years under the
rule of King Hussein.

PETER USTINOV'S PEOPLE: KING HUSSEIN OF JORDAN.
    Sheamus Smith, 1989. 48 min. color. Video. Chip Taylor
    Communications.
Covers Peter Ustinov's visit with King Hussein, in which the
monarch discusses his continuing work to bring peace and stability
to the Middle East.

WELCOME TO JORDAN. Around the World in Sight and
    sound, 1984. 19 min. color. Video. Around the World in Sight
    and Sound.
A travel film that covers the highlights of Jordan. Takes a look
at the Citadel, the Red Sea, and the Dead Sea.

Lebanon

BARRICADES: LEBANON'S CIVIL WAR. The Media Guild,
    1986. 52 min. color. Video. The Media Guild.
Shows how three women manage to lead ordinary lives in civil-
war-torn Lebanon.

BEIRUT! NOT ENOUGH DEATH TO GO AROUND. Jacques
    Vallée, 1984. 57 min. color. 16mm/Video. National Film
    Board of Canada.
An account of the day-to-day struggle of the Beirut populace to
survive. Shows the rubble and devastation brought by the war.

BEIRUT: ON A CLEAR DAY YOU CAN SEE PEACE. Alia
    Arasoughly, 1985. 30 min. color. Video. Women for Women

in Lebanon.
A study of living conditions in Beirut, Lebanon. Focuses on homeless women and children.

MIDDLE EAST: IDENTITY—LEBANON. TV Ontario, 1984. 25 min. color. Video. Encyclopaedia Britannica Educational Corporation.
Gives an account of the present unrest in Lebanon and the dissension that stems from the withdrawal of the French in 1940.

RETREAT FROM BEIRUT. Sherry Jones, Nancy Sloss, 1985. 52 min. color. Video. Washington Media Associates.
Covers U.S. involvement in Lebanon. Explains what led to the deaths of 241 U.S. servicemen there.

WAR GENERATION: BEIRUT. BBC-TV, 1988. 50 min. color. Video. The Cinema Guild.
Discusses the atmosphere of violence in Beirut as seen through the eyes of children. A 23-year-old man and some teenagers talk about their feelings regarding the conflict and their involvement in what is going on.

WOMEN OF SOUTH LEBANON. MTC, Lebanon, 1986. 71 min. color. 16mm/Video. Third World Newsreel.
Lebanese women tell of the 1982 Israeli invasion of south Lebanon. The filmmakers were barred from filming at the time, but by 1985 they were able to proceed with their report on the popular resistance in south Lebanon and on the life and traditions of the inhabitants. In Arabic with English subtitles.

Palestine

ARE YOU LISTENING: PALESTINIANS. Martha Stuart Communications, n.d. 29 min. color. Video. Martha Stuart Communications.
An extended family of Palestinians without a country came from many places (from St. Paul, Minnesota, to Saudi Arabia) to Paris for a marriage celebration. Explores their feelings about not being able to return to their homeland, the negative connotations of

being Palestinian, and their grief over family separations.

CONFLICT IN THE WEST BANK—SPRING 1983. Esti Galili
    Marpet, 1983. 30 min. color. Video. Maxi Cohen Film and
    Video Productions.
Shows what the occupation of the West Bank is doing to the
Palestinian people.

COURAGE ALONG THE DIVIDE. Victor Schonfeld, 1987. 75
    min. color. Video. Filmakers Library.
A documentary that explains how a growing number of Israelis
are opposing the occupation of the West Bank and the Gaza
Strip just as some Arabs are opposing the use of violence as a
way to deal with the Israelis. Shows the poor living conditions
and the brutality experienced by the Palestinians.

DOES THE CACTUS HAVE A SOUL? Gilles Dinnematin,
    1987. 56 min. color. Video. The Cinema Guild.
Describes the destruction of hundreds of Palestinian villages from
the pre-1948 period to the present. Includes interviews with
elderly Arabs who used to be village residents before they had to
flee to Lebanon and other countries, or to camps in the Gaza
Strip. Arab farmers discuss the Israeli policy of land confiscation.
Israeli settlers discuss their attitudes on this issue. In French and
Arabic with English subtitles.

GAZA GHETTO. P. Holmquist, J. Mandell, P. Bjorklund, 1984.
    82 min. color. 16mm/Video. First Run/Icarus Films.
Tells about a Palestinian family that fled from their home in
Dimra in 1948, as Israeli troops approached, to settle in a refugee
camp in Gaza. Then in 1967 Gaza also was occupied by Israeli
troops. Includes interviews with General Ben Eliezer, director of
Israeli settlement in Gaza.

NATIVE SONS: PALESTINIANS IN EXILE. Tom Hayes, 1985.
    57 min. color. 16mm/Video. Foglight Films.
Tells about the life of three Palestinian families who now live in
Lebanon. Narrated by Martin Sheen.

PALESTINIAN PORTRAITS. The United Nations, 1988. 22 min.

color. 16mm/Video. First Run/Icarus Films.
Various Palestinian professionals discuss their love for their
homeland and how they live in exile.

PALESTINIANS OF '83. United Nations, 1983. 26 min. color.
    Video. University of California Extension Media Center.
Tells how living conditions of Palestinians have changed since the
invasion of Lebanon by Israelis.

VOICES FROM GAZA. Antonia Caccia and Maysoon Pachachi,
    1989. 51 min. color. 16mm/Video. First Run/Icarus Films.
The people of the Gaza Strip, 70% of whom are refugees, discuss
their experiences and daily life in refugee camps.

Saudi Arabia

PILGRIMAGE TO MECCA. Marilyn Perry, 1980. 28 min. color.
    Video. Marilyn Perry TV Productions.
The Minister of Information of Saudi Arabia tells how the
government helps with the annual pilgrimage of Muslims to
Mecca.

SAUDI ARABIA: 1. THE KINGDOM. Pacific Productions, 1986.
    59 min. color. Video. Films Inc.
This series studies historical information in contrast with present-
day Arabian life. The first program explores how the Saudi family
gets and maintains its power.

SAUDI ARABIA: 2. RACE WITH TIME. Pacific Productions,
    1986. 59 min. color. Video. Films Inc.
Takes a look at the problem with traditional values caused by the
invasion of Western technology and culture.

SAUDI ARABIA: 3. OIL, MONEY AND POLITICS. Pacific
    Productions, 1986. 59 min. color. Video. Films Inc.
Explores the worldwide power of oil and oil's importance in Saudi
Arabia's domestic affairs.

SAUDI ARABIA TODAY. Exxon Corporation, 1984. 28 min.

color. Video. Modern Talking Picture Service.
An introduction to Saudi Arabia—its land, politics, and customs.

THE SAUDIS. CBS News, 1980. 49 min. color. Video. BFA
   Educational Media.
Covers the political and business scene in Saudi Arabia.

Turkey

BACK TO ARARAT. PeÅ Holmquist, 1988. 60- or 100-min.
   version, color. 16mm/Video. First Run/Icarus Films.
Depicts the dream of most Armenians—to return to the holy land
of Mount Ararat in what is now Turkey. Reflects on the first
genocide of the 20th century—the destruction of Armenia—when
1.5 million Armenians were killed or driven from their homeland.

SOUTH ASIA

General

IN SEARCH OF A HOLY MAN. Hartley Film Foundation,
   1986. 30 min. color. 16mm/Video. Hartley Film Foundation.
Covers a trip to Tibet, to Dharamsala, India, where the Dalai
Lama lives in exile, and to Lumbini, Nepal, the birthplace of the
Buddha. Studies the influence of Buddhism in the Asiatic world.

Afghanistan

AFGHANISTAN: THE FIGHT FOR A WAY OF LIFE. Stephen
   Olsson, 1986. 58 min. color. Video. Telesis Productions
   International.
A prize-winning film about the history and culture of Afghanistan.
Gives the background of the war there.

JHAD—AFGHANISTAN'S HOLY WAR. Jeff B. Harmon,
   Alexander Linday, 1986. 52 min. color. 16mm. International
   Media Associates.

Haji Abduly Latif tells about the war in Afghanistan.

Himalayan States
(For Nepal, see separate section, page 58.)

CAVE OF DREAMS. Frank Heimans, 1983. 50 min. color.
  16mm. Australian Film Commission.
Explains why thousands of people make an annual pilgrimage to
a cave in the Himalayas of Kashmir that has been drawing visitors
for 3,000 years.

SHERPA. Robert Godfrey, 1984. 28 min. color. 16mm. Centre
  Productions.
Studies the famous mountain-climbing guides, the Sherpas. Looks
at the way of life of one Sherpa family.

India

ADITI: THE LIVING ARTS OF INDIA. Phyllis Ward, 1986. 41
  min. color. Video. Smithsonian Institution.
Presents the work of India's artisans and performers who were
represented in the Smithsonian Institution's living exhibit, "Aditi:
A Celebration of Life."

AHIMSA NON-VIOLENCE. Marion Hunt, 1987. 58 min. color.
  Video. Direct Cinema.
An account of the origins of the Jain religion in India many
centuries ago. Modern Jains live in many countries and adhere to
ahimsa, or non-violence in all matters.

AHMEDABAD: LIFE OF A CITY IN INDIA. Howard Spodek,
  1984. 30 min. color. 16mm. University of Wisconsin.
Shows how Ahmedabad became an industrial center when it was
under British rule. Gives the history of the city, including its
passage from Hindu to Muslim influences.

BEING MUSLIM IN INDIA. J. Elder, 1984. 40 min. color.
  16mm. University of Wisconsin.
Examines the life of a Muslim family in Lucknow, India. The

head of the family has three wives, two of whom discuss what it is like to live in an extended family.

BENARES: STEPS TO HEAVEN. New Zealand National Film
    Unit, 1985. 30 min. color. 16mm/Video. Wombat Film and
    Video.
A tour of the sacred city with its many temples, ashrams, palaces, rituals and proximity to the holy river, the Ganges.

BOMBAY: OUR CITY. Anand Patwardhan, 1985. 57 min. color.
    16mm/Video. First Run/Icarus Films.
Describes the life of the four million slum dwellers of Bombay. Shows the lack of city utilities that these people must endure. An 82-minute version is also available.

BOY OF INDIA: RAMA AND HIS ELEPHANT. Coronet/MTI
    Film and Video, 1985. 12 min. color. 16mm/Video.
    Coronet/MTI Film and Video.
A visit with Rama and his father, an elephant handler. Revised from the earlier 1956 production.

BRIDES ARE NOT FOR BURNING. UPI, 1977. 24 min. color.
    Video. Journal Video.
A report on the custom of dowry, which exists in India even though banned.

CIRCLES-CYCLES KATHAK DANCE. Robert Gottlieb, 1988.
    28 min. color. Video. University of California Extension
    Media Center.
Mythology and daily events of village life make up the subject matter of *kathak*, the classic 1,000-year-old dance form of North India. Shows how the dance is influenced by Hindu and Muslim cultures.

DIVISION OF HEARTS. Satti Khanna and Peter Chappell, 1987.
    57 min. color. Video. First Run/Icarus Films.
A report on the 1947 partition of India into independent India and Pakistan. Hindus, Sikhs, and Muslims became victims of mutual suspicion. Witnesses recall their experiences of the period

of turmoil when over 500,000 people lost their lives.

GIVEN TO DANCE: INDIA'S ODISSI TRADITION. Ron Hess,
   1985. 57 min. color. 16mm. University of Wisconsin.
Odissi is an Indian classical dance form. Explains what the now
defunct dance ritual meant in the Hindu faith. Includes a
performance by the last female dancers.

INDIA AND THE INFINITE: THE SOUL OF A PEOPLE.
   Hartley Productions, 1980. 30 min. color. 16mm/Video.
   Hartley Film Foundation.
A detailed account of the extreme contrasts in India, including
religion, music, and art.

INDIA: HISTORY AND HERITAGE. Wayne Mitchell, 1987. 31
   min. color. 16mm/Video. BFA Educational Media.
A detailed study of the history and culture of India. Describes the
spirituality, diversity, and complexity of India, a country in which
more than 1,500 languages and dialects are spoken.

INDIA: LAND OF SPIRIT AND MYSTIQUE. Bill Youmans and
   Chip Duncan, 1988. 55 min. color. Video. International Video
   Network.
A video that describes the history and culture of northern India.

INDIA SPEAKS. Paula Lee Hallow, 1986. 21 min. color.
   16mm/Video. Walt Disney Educational Media Company.
Covers the cultural and economic diversity of India, the largest
democracy in the world.

INDIA—THE BRIGHTEST JEWEL. BBC-TV, 1981. 20 min.
   color. Video. Films Inc.
Documents India's struggle for independence in the 1930s and
1940s.

INDIA TODAY. World Vision Educational Resources/New
   Zealand, 1981. 17 min. color. Video. International Film
   Bureau.
A study of government, religion, education, and transportation in

India.

KALAKSHETRA: DEVOTION TO DANCE. Anthony Meyer,
    1985. 50 min. color. Video. Centre Productions.
Tells how people come annually to the Kalakshetra Festival of
the Arts. Features traditional and modern dances of India.

KATHPUTLI: THE ART OF RAJASTHANI PUPPETEERS.
    Smithsonian Folklife Programs, 1988. 30 min. color.
    16mm/Video. Smithsonian Institution Folklife Programs.
Itinerant families in Rajasthan, India, perform an ancient art
form—the *kathputli* puppet theater. Participants tell how they
create and operate the wooden puppets.

LOVING KRISHNA. Film Study Center, Harvard University,
    1986. 40 min. color. 16mm/Video. Centre Productions.
Examines the sacred cult of Krishna in the continuing link among
worship, arts and crafts, and everyday life. Shows two major
festivals for Krishna. Filmed in Vishnupur, West Bengal, a town
of temples, crafts, and markets.

NO LONGER SILENT. International Film Bureau, 1986. 57 min.
    color. 16mm/Video. International Film Bureau.
Depicts recent efforts by women of India to overcome social,
political, and cultural alienation and to raise the consciousness of
poor women. Discusses such things as dowry burnings of brides
and advertising techniques applied to consumerism of a small
percentage of Indian women without concern for the 70% who
are poorer.

PARADISE STEAMSHIP CO. VISITS: INDIA. KCBS-TV, n.d.
    21 min. color. Video. Carousel Film and Video.
A tour of India, including Vernassi, the sacred city, and the
Ganges. Examines the cultural and religious aspects of daily life.

PEOPLE OF INDIA. Beacon Films, 1987. 18 min. color.
    16mm/Video. Beacon Films.
Follows three sets of people in different strata in Indian society
to show disparate and shared features of their lives. All of the

people studied are devoted to the Hindu faith.

PETER USTINOV'S PEOPLE: THE GANDHIS OF INDIA.
Sheamus Smith, 1989. 48 min. color. Video. Chip Taylor
Communications.
Gives an account of Peter Ustinov's planned interview with Indira
Gandhi that could not take place because of her assassination,
which Ustinov witnessed. This profile was completed with the
help of Mrs. Gandhi's son, Rajiv.

SERPENT MOTHER. Film Study Center, Harvard University,
1986. 27 min. color. 16mm/Video. Centre Productions.
Filmed in Vishnupur, West Bengal, a town where daily life and
religious worship are intertwined. This is the story of the myth of
the Hindu goddess Manasha. Shows rituals that are part of the
annual festival of snakes. An award-winning film.

SHIVA'S DISCIPLES. Griffin Productions, 1985. 50 min. color.
16mm/Video. Centre Productions.
The god of dance, Shiva, is the focus of a cult in Kerala, a
southern state in India. Shows the rituals and festivals involved
with Shiva. Richard Attenborough is narrator.

SONS OF SHIVA. Film Study Center, Harvard University, 1986.
27 min. color. 16mm/Video. Centre Productions.
Observes the annual festival of Shiva, the Hindu god of
destruction, as filmed in Vishnupur, West Bengal. The
worshippers renounce everyday life to be "Sons of Shiva."
Includes the unique singing of Bauls, an order of wandering
monks.

THE SPICES OF INDIA. Jill Roach, 1985. 26 min. color. Video.
Beacon Films.
Describes the use of spices in the kitchens of the poor and the
well-to-do in India. Shows how the art of mixing spices is an
integral part of Indian culture.

WORK OF LOVE. William Livingston, 1983. 28 min. color.
16mm. Ikonographics, Inc.
A portrait of Mother Teresa of Calcutta at work. Includes scenes

of Calcutta and the countryside of India.

Nepal

LORD OF THE DANCE, DESTROYER OF ILLUSION.
   Richard Kohn, 1985. 108 min. color. 16mm/Video. First
   Run/Icarus Films.
A film made in Nepal to show activities at two Buddhist
monasteries where Sherpas and Tibetans preserve an unusual way
of life. Shows details of the ancient Mani-Rimdu festival of
"awakening."

NEPAL: THE PEOPLE AND THE CULTURE. UPI, 1984. 28
   min. color. Video. Journal Films.
A documentary that looks at the lifestyle of the people, the
culture, and the history of Nepal.

OSSIAN: AMERICAN BOY/TIBETAN MONK. Thomas
   Anderson, 1983. 28 min. color. Video. Thomas Anderson.
Filmed in the Kathmandhu Valley in the Kingdom of Nepal. This
is the study of the American boy who was recognized as a
reincarnation of a High Lama. He lives as a monk in a Tibetan
Buddhist monastery.

PARADISE STEAMSHIP CO. VISITS: NEPAL, KCBS-TV, n.d.
   21 min. color. Video. Carousel Film and Video.
A visit to a country of 15 million people where the life
expectancy is 46 years. Includes coverage of local crafts and the
daily struggle to survive.

Pakistan

PEOPLE OF PAKISTAN. Oxford Ethnographic Films, 1987. 18
   min. color. 16mm/Video. Beacon Films.
Shows how the Islamic religion and the laws of the state are
intertwined. People adhere to Muslim-prescribed dress, food,
hygiene, and family obligations, and are accordingly ill at ease
when they have to leave the country.

WHO WILL CAST THE FIRST STONE? Channel Four Television/UK, 52 min. color. Video. The Cinema Guild.
A clandestinely filmed report on the impact of Islamization on women in Pakistan. Focuses on the stories of three women. Tells how the law discriminates against women and is used to intimidate women. Not an anti-Islamic film but a critique of Pakistan's Hudood Ordinances that punish people on religious grounds.

Sri Lanka

IRAMUDUN. Barrie Machin, 1983. 45 min. color. Video. Australian Film Commission.
The first complete view of the exorcism in Sri Lanka of a sickness-causing demon from a patient who could not be helped by Western medicine.

TWO THOUSAND YEARS IN ONE GENERATION. National Video Communications, 1985. 20 min. color. 16mm/Video. Coronet/MTI Film and Video.
Gives details about the impact of new technology on the people of Sri Lanka.

EAST ASIA

China

ADVENTURES IN THE CHINA TRADE. U.S. Government, 1981. 28 min. color. Video. New York State Education Department.
Discusses the commercial life of China and prospects for future American trade with China.

ARE YOU LISTENING: ENERGETIC CHINESE VILLAGERS. Martha Stuart Communications, 1981. 29 min. color. Video. Martha Stuart Communications.
Rural villagers of the Xinbu Brigade in China tell how they

developed energy self-sufficiency and how they benefit from it. Also probes Chinese village life. Available in Cantonese or English-language voice-over.

BEIJING. University of California Extension Media Center, 1981. 45 min. color. 16mm/Video. University of California Extension Media Center.
Studies the people of Beijing, China, and captures the special character of the Chinese capital.

BRUSH DANCE. Centre Productions, 1986. 21 min. color. 16mm/Video. Centre Productions.
Portrays the calligraphic work of a 20-year-old Chinese girl who shares the distinction of being a master calligrapher with about two dozen Chinese men in their seventies and eighties. Shows that at present she is teaching at a college in California.

BUDDHISM IN CHINA. China Institute in America, 1983. 30 min. color. Video. Indiana University.
The history of Buddhism and its influence on China's political and cultural life.

THE CHILDREN OF SOONG CHING LING. Soong Ching Ling Foundation, 1985. 30 min. color. 16mm/Video. Pyramid Film and Video.
Portrays the medical care and education available for China's children today. Explains that policies for medical care and education were developed by the widow of Sun Yat-sen.

CHINA: A HISTORY. Centre Productions, 1988. 23 min. color. 16mm/Video. Barr Films.
A recounting of China's rich history and many contributions: great public works, the martial arts, acupuncture, fine pottery and porcelain, and great philosophers. Shows how this rich heritage has influenced modern China.

CHINA: A HOLE IN THE BAMBOO CURTAIN. WWWL-TV, New Orleans, n.d. 28 min. color. 16mm/Video. Carousel Film and Video.
An award-winning film about the People's Republic of China.

Shows scenes of people in daily life: children at schools, handicrafts, industry, and the practice of acupuncture. Also includes antiquities such as the Great Wall and the Imperial Palace.

CHINA: A HUMAN GEOGRAPHY. Centre Productions, 1988. 22 min. color. 16mm/Video. Barr Films.
A beautifully photographed view of China. Contains an account of geographical features, particularly in four regions of China—Inner Mongolia, the Himalayas, China proper, and Tibet.

CHINA AFTER MAO. Michigan Media, 1980. 29 min. each, color. 10 programs. Video. Michigan Media.
Top American experts on China talk about the many changes that have occurred in the post-Mao period. In ten programs: 1. Lifestyle; 2. Education; 3. The Arts; 4. Trade and Economics; 5. Law and Justice; 6. Political Leadership and Stability; 7. U.S./China Relations; 8. Relations with the World; 9. Science and Technology; 10. The Road Ahead.

CHINA DISCOVERY. Barry Stoner, 1984. 28 min. color. Video. KCTS-TV.
Discusses and observes the exhibition held in Seattle in 1984—"China: 7,000 Years of Discovery."

CHINA: LAND OF MY FATHER. Disney Educational Productions, 1985. 28 min. color. 16mm/Video. Coronet/MTI Film and Video.
A Chinese-American journalist visits China in search of her heritage. Includes observations of the polite people and culture she encounters. She interviews a female journalist, who, like herself, is a working mother, and who gives a rare view of a professional woman's role in Chinese society. This film has won at least three major awards.

CHINA LOOKS WEST. UPI, 1984. 25 min. color. Video. Journal Films.
An account of China's new attitude toward international economics.

CHINA MISSION: THE CHESTER RONNING STORY. National Film Board of Canada, 1980. 58 min. color. Video. National Film Board of Canada.
A portrait of Chester Ronning, using interviews and archival footage. Ronning, the son of missionaries, spent much of his life in China.

CHINA: SICHUAN PROVINCE. National Geographic, 1988. 25 min. color. 16mm/Video. National Geographic.
Depicts modern Beijing and China's most populous province, Sichuan. Studies the region's geography, agriculture, industry, major cities, schools, and religious heritage.

CHINA SINCE MAO. BBC-TV, 1987. 20 min. color. Video. Films Inc.
Reviews Chairman Mao's achievements and what happened to Chinese society, politics, and economic growth after his death in 1970.

CHINA: THE AWAKENING GIANT OF ASIA. Around the World in Sight and Sound, 1984. 21 min. color. Video. Around the World in Sight and Sound.
A tour of Beijing, Shanghai, and Canton, featuring important sites, such as the Great Wall and the Forbidden City.

CHINA: THE LONG MARCH. Independent Productions, 1986. 48 min. color. Video. Coronet/MTI Film and Video.
Traces the route of the Long March across China that occurred fifty years ago as part of the revolution. Uses archival footage, historical paintings, and modern scenes of landscapes never seen before.

CHINA: THE MIDDLE KINGDOM, PART 1. Highlight International Films, 1985. 25 min. color. Video. Journal Films.
Tells how the Chinese have managed to preserve their cultural heritage and assimilate it into modern life.

CHINA: THE MIDDLE KINGDOM, PART 2. Highlight International Films, 1985. 25 min. color. Video. Journal Films.
Takes a look at the Chinese commune, in which farming is the

main industry. Explains how communes provide education and cultural training for their members.

CHINA—THE YEAR OF THE COUNTING. United Nations, 1983. 54 min. color. 16mm/Video. Barr Films.
Gives details of China's 1982 census, its first in modern times. Discusses implications for the future.

CHINA TODAY. WGBH Boston, 1983. 22 min. color. Video. King Features Entertainment.
Studies the roles of Dr. Sun Yat-sen and Mao Tse-tung in China's development.

CHINA: WORKING AND LIVING IN THE SOUTH. Around the World in Sight and Sound, 1984. 21 min. color. Video. Around the World in Sight and Sound.
A visit to the sites of southern China's cities.

CHINA: ZHAO XUAN AT SCHOOL. Centre Productions, 1988. 15 min. color. 16mm/Video. Barr Films.
Follows a junior-high-level student through the day. Describes the buildings, the market, and the school system in the People's Republic of China through his eyes.

CHINESE GODS. Four Seas Films, 1980. 90 min. color. Video. Video Gems.
Using colorful animation this program deals with Chinese mythology around 1000 B.C., the period of the Shang Dynasty. The tale involves war and bitter rivalries.

THE CHINESE WAY OF LIFE. Sandler Films, 1986. 24 min. color. 16mm/Video. AIMS Media.
A documentary about the beauty of China, the ancient culture which blends with the modern society of the People's Republic of China. Shows industrial development, unusual specialized farming, Beijing (the capital city), the Great Wall, and the Forbidden City (now a large museum).

A DAY ON THE GRAND CANAL WITH THE EMPEROR OF CHINA. Philip Haas, 1988. 46 min. color. 16mm. New Yorker Films.

Contemporary artist David Hockney takes the viewer on a witty examination of a Chinese scroll depicting an inspection tour taken by the Emperor of China in 1689. Shows the details of life in 17th-century China and the differences of Eastern and Western perception.

DEPENDING ON HEAVEN. Peter Entell, 1987. 28 min. color.
    16mm/Video. First Run/Icarus Films.
A lyrical film treatment which tells about a Mongolian family moving its herds across northern China. Uses interviews, song, and legends to describe the life of the Mongols.

ENERGETIC CHINESE VILLAGERS. United Nations, 1984. 20
    min. color. Video. Martha Stuart Communications.
Some villagers in the People's Republic of China explain how they maintain their energy system. Also includes a look at village life. In Chinese with English narration.

FACES OF CHINA. Raphael and Jocelyn Green, 1988. 23 min.
    color. 16mm/Video. International Film Bureau.
A look at urban and rural China. Shows people at work and enjoying sports and entertainment.

FEEDING AND CLOTHING CHINA'S MILLIONS. National
    Film Board of Canada, 1988. 14 min. color. 16mm/Video.
    Barr Films.
Shows how China struggles to feed and clothe its people with three main crops—wheat, rice, and cotton—which are cultivated by hand, not by machines as in the Western world. Demonstrates how almost everyone in the rural villages is involved.

FIRST MOON: CELEBRATION OF THE CHINESE NEW
    YEAR. R. Gordon, C. Hinton, K. Kline, 1987. 37 min. color.
    16mm/Video. New Day Films.
Describes the ritual of the Chinese New Year as celebrated by the people of Long Bow, a village in China. Shows how certain Western influences have crept in.

THE HUMAN FACE OF CHINA. Film Australia, 1980. 28 min.
    each, color. Video. Coronet/MTI Film and Video.

A five-part series on China. Each program covers the lifestyle of ordinary people in a single province. 1. It's Always So in the World; 2. Mind, Body and Spirit; 3. One Hundred Entertainments; 4. Something for Everyone; 5. Son of the Ocean.

A LOOK AT SOUTHERN CHINA. Around the World in Sight and Sound, 1987. 19 min. color. Video. Around the World in Sight and Sound.
A travel film featuring a visit to the cities of Kunming and Guilin, located in southern China.

LOOKING FOR MAO. PBS, 1980. 58 min. color. Video. PBS Video.
A portrait of modern China and how it was faring six years after Mao's death.

LOTUS. Arthur Dong, Rebecca Soladay, 1988. 27 min. color. 16mm/Video. Direct Cinema.
The story of this film is set in rural China of 1914. Explains, through the life of Lotus, a traditional Chinese woman with bound feet, how women lived duty bound to the father, or, if married, to the husband, or, if widowed, to the son. Although foot-binding was banned in 1911, many women continued the practice as a key to a favorable marriage. In this story Lotus must decide whether or not to bind the feet of her seven-year-old daughter in this period of transformation.

MING GARDEN. Gene Searchinger, 1983. 29 min. color. 16mm. Metropolitan Museum of Art.
A report on the cultural exchange project between the People's Republic of China and the U.S. that brought about the installation of a Ming-style Chinese garden courtyard.

ON THE MOVE: THE CENTRAL BALLET OF CHINA. Catherine Tatge, 1986. 58 min. color. 16mm. Simarka Productions, Inc.
Covers the first U.S. tour of the famous Central Ballet of China.

ONE MAN'S REVOLUTION: MAO TSE-TUNG. BBC-TV, 1981. 20 min. color. Video. Films Inc.

Covers the career of Chinese leader Mao Tse-tung.

PARADISE STEAMSHIP CO. VISITS: CHINA. KCBS-TV, n.d.
   21 min. color. Video. Carousel Film and Video.
A visit to China with views of the Children's Palace, the Peking
Opera, and the zoo. Tells about China before and after the
cultural revolution.

PEOPLE'S REPUBLIC OF CHINA: THE CALL OF THE
   GREAT WALL. Centre Productions, 1988. 29 min. color.
   Video. Centre Productions.
Discusses China's efforts toward disarmament and demilitarization.

PETER USTINOV IN CHINA: BEIJING TO TIBET, PART I.
   John McGreevy, 1989. 30 min. color. Video. Chip Taylor
   Communications.
Observes Peter Ustinov as he visits Beijing, where he mingles
with the crowds and tours the quiet parts of the city: the Ming
Tombs, the Forbidden City, and Mao's burial place.

PETER USTINOV IN CHINA: BEIJING TO TIBET, PART II.
   John McGreevy, 1989. 30 min. color. Video. Chip Taylor
   Communications.
Peter Ustinov visits the Beijing Opera and the Olympic School.
He then follows the ancient route of Marco Polo to Lanchow.
During his journey he meets Muslims, farmers, and Tibetan
monks.

PETER USTINOV IN CHINA: TIBET TO HONG KONG,
   PART I. John McGreevy, 1989. 30 min. color. Video. Chip
   Taylor Communications.
Follows Peter Ustinov in his visit to a remote village of Tibet. He
is seen touring the region of caves where people live and work.

PETER USTINOV IN CHINA: TIBET TO HONG KONG,
   PART II. John McGreevy, 1989. 30 min. color. Video. Chip
   Taylor Communications.
Follows Peter Ustinov as he visits the great archeological
discovery, the Buried Armies of the first emperor of China, who
is also responsible for the Great Wall. Then Ustinov moves on

to bustling Hong Kong.

SILENT ARMY. WTTW-TV, 1980. 29 min. color. Video. PBS
   Video.
A study of the culture of the Bronze Age in China from 1700
B.C. to A.D. 200.

SMALL HAPPINESS: WOMEN OF A CHINESE VILLAGE.
   Kathy Line, Dan Sipe, 1985. 58 min. color. 16mm/Video. New
   Day Films.
Features rare views of the Chinese countryside with particular
focus on the people of Long Bow village. Interviews with Chinese
women reveal their experiences with love, marriage, childbearing,
birth control, foot-binding, and work.

A TASTE OF CHINA: FOOD FOR BODY AND SPIRIT. Sue
   Yung Li, 1984. 29 min. color. 16mm/Video. University of
   California Extension Media Center.
Traces the influence of religion on Chinese cuisine. A Taoist
priestess demonstrates how the opposing forces of *yin* and *yang*
are harmonized in cooking. Also visits an herb shop, an herbal
medicine restaurant, and two Buddhist monasteries to show how
Buddhism brought about the development of vegetarian cuisine.

A TASTE OF CHINA: MASTERS OF THE WOK. Sue Yung
   Li, 1984. 29 min. color. 16mm/Video. University of California
   Extension Media Center.
Describes the evolution of Chinese cuisine from simple peasant
food to lavish imperial cooking. Observes two master chefs
preparing a 28-course feast. Shows how Chinese cuisine is related
to Chinese culture.

A TASTE OF CHINA: THE FAMILY TABLE. Sue Yung Li,
   1984. 29 min. color. 16mm/Video. University of California
   Extension Media Center.
Compares the lives of two families, a rural family and a family in
an urban setting. The rural family is shown cooking and eating
together. The husband of the urban family is shown preparing a
fast meal for the family while his wife works in a nearby factory.

A TASTE OF CHINA: WATER FARMERS. Sue Yung Li, 1984. 29 min. color. 16mm/Video. University of California Extension Media Center.
Observes the farmers' way of life in the water country of the Yangzi River delta, a land filled with hundreds of canals. Shows the activity along the canals with wedding boats, traveling vendors, and rowboats.

THEY LOOK A LOT LIKE US: A CHINESE ODYSSEY. Terry Woolf, 1987. 29 min. color. Video. Kudluk Productions.
A group of Inuit children from Coppermine, Canada, travel through China to Mongolia, where anthropologists believe their ancestors lived.

TO TASTE A HUNDRED HERBS: GODS, ANCESTORS AND MEDICINE IN A CHINESE VILLAGE. Kathy Kline, Richard Gordon, Carma Hinton, Dan Sipe, 1986. 60 min. color. 16mm/Video. New Day Films.
A study of a Chinese doctor who combines traditional Chinese medical practice with his Catholic faith.

A WEEK IN THE LIFE OF A CHINESE STUDENT. Sandler Films, 1986. 20 min. color. 16mm/Video. AIMS Media.
A much-awarded documentary about students in a junior middle school in Beijing gives a view of life in the People's Republic of China. Shows daily routines at school and at home.

THE XINBU ENERGY STORY (Series). Martha Stuart Communications, n.d. 8 tapes/20 min. each. Video. Martha Stuart Communications.
Describes the Xinbu system of energy conversion. Includes details about the operation of a communal bio-gas digester. In Cantonese with English subtitles.

Hong Kong

ASIAN INSIGHT: HONG KONG/SINGAPORE. Film Australia, 1987. 48 min. color. Video. Films Inc.
This program recounts the events that brought Western powers

to Asia and compares the social structures of Hong Kong and
Singapore.

BEHIND THE PAINTED SCREEN: TWO FACES OF HONG
KONG. Polonius Productions, 1984. 24 min. color.
16mm/Video. International Film Bureau.
A tour of Hong Kong featuring all the important sights.

HONG KONG: LIVING ON BORROWED TIME. UPI, 1984.
28 min. color. Video. Journal Films.
An account of Hong Kong, its people, and its trade, as it is today
before it reverts to Chinese rule.

HONG KONG: RICH AND POOR. Around the World in Sight
and Sound, 1984. 16 min. color. Video. Around the World in
Sight and Sound.
A travel film about Hong Kong. Shows landmarks and scenic
views.

HONG KONG TODAY. World Vision Educational
Resources/New Zealand, 1981. 16 min. color. Video.
International Film Bureau.
Discusses the immigrant people of Hong Kong who are 98%
Chinese. Also shows views of present-day Hong Kong.

THE HUMAN FACE OF HONG KONG: BETTER RICH
THAN RED. Film Australia, 1987. 48 min. color. Video.
Films Inc.
Describes the powerful men who run the Jockey Club in Hong
Kong, and how their lives alternate between running horse racing,
big business, and government.

THE HUMAN FACE OF HONG KONG: RUNNING FROM
THE GHOST. Film Australia, 1987. 48 min. color. Video.
Films Inc.
Tells how ordinary people have no access to the government
bureaucracy, which seems to exist merely to maintain the laissez-
faire, low-tax "economic miracle" that is Hong Kong.

Japan

AMERICAN GAMES, JAPANESE RULES. David Fanning, 1988
    (Frontline Series). 60 min. color. Video. PBS Video.
Americans who live in Japan talk about the special features of
Japanese society, from baseball to business.

AQUACULTURE IN JAPAN. Iwanami Productions, 1984. 20
    min. color. 16mm. Filmfair Communications.
Aquaculture, the breeding of marine life, helps Japan with the
problem of food shortage. Aquaculture is providing a larger
supply of animal protein.

ASIAN INSIGHT: JAPAN. Film Australia, 1987. 48 min. color.
    Video. Films Inc.
Reveals the history of Japan, a complex and paradoxical country.

CHACONNE   FOR   TRADITIONAL   JAPANESE
    INSTRUMENTS. NHK-TV, 1987. 19 min. color. Video. Japan
    Society.
A Japanese musical ensemble plays music on traditional Japanese
instruments.

CHILDREN   OF   JAPAN: LEARNING   THE   NEW,
    REMEMBERING THE OLD. Paula Haller, 1987. 21 min.
    color. 16mm/Video. Coronet/MTI Film and Video.
The letters of an 11-year-old Japanese boy to an American pen
pal evoke a view of life in Japan. Includes a visit to the boy's
school and a tour of the scenic archipelago.

CHILDREN OF THE TRIBE. National Film Board of Canada,
    1986. 28 min. color. 16mm/Video. Centre Productions.
Discusses the basic approach to child rearing in Japan, which calls
for dependence, not independence. Shows patterns of parenting,
education, and how close ties to family and commitment to
academic achievement provide strong influences on children.

COMMUNITY DIVIDED. NHK-TV, 1987. 45 min. color. Video.
    Japan Society.

Shows the stress on traditional life in a Japanese village when the government plans to industrialize the area.

A COUPLE OF CHANGES. Michael Goldberg, 1983. 55 min. color. Video. Video Out.
How the culture of Vancouver, Canada, compares with Japanese culture, as seen through the eyes of a Japanese couple.

DO YOUR UTMOST. Journal Films, 1988. 30 min. color. Video. Journal Films.
A study of competition in Japan. Observes two young people striving for success in a culture that encourages people to "do their utmost."

DOLL'S FESTIVAL OBSERVED IN LOCAL JAPAN. NHK-TV, 1987. 8 min. color. Video. Japan Society.
A film without narration that shows how the Hina-Matsuri, or Doll's Festival, is celebrated by young girls in Japan.

THE ELECTRONIC TRIBE. WTTW-TV, 1988. 55 min. color. Video. Coronet Film/MTI Film and Video.
Provides a contrast between a rural population, steeped in traditions, and city dwellers, aligned to Western ideals. Gives the background for the Japanese proclivity for forming cohesive organizations and thinking collectively, both of which have contributed to Japan's productive manufacturing.

FIGHTING FESTIVAL. Keiko Ikeda, 1985. 30 min. color. Video. University of California Extension Media Center.
Observes the annual Fighting Festival. This 500-year-old event features ritually structured brawls involving descendents of Japanese fishermen and farmers.

FISHING IN JAPAN. NHK-TV, 1987. 33 min. color. Video. Japan Society.
Ancient and modern fishing techniques of the Japanese are described.

FUTURE WAVE: JAPAN DESIGN. David Rabinovitch, 1988. 27 min. color. Video. University of California Extension Media

Center.
Documents how Japanese design has helped create a consumer
lifestyle eventually exported around the world. Shows how the
Sony Walkman was developed. Observes a fashion show and
explains the role of design in product development, packaging,
marketing, advertising, and sales.

THE GENIUS OF JAPAN. WGBH-TV, 1983. 14 min. color.
    Video, King Features Entertainment.
Covers the history of Japan from the end of World War II to the
present.

THE GODS WHO STAY AT HOME. NHK-TV, 198? 16 min.
    color. Video. Japan Society.
About the pattern of life in a village in northeast Japan in which
the men fish most of the year and the women remain at home
growing crops and gathering seaweed. The women are shown
performing a "Good Fortune" dance.

HELLFIRE: A JOURNEY FROM HIROSHIMA. John Dower,
    1986. 58 min. color. 16mm/Video. First Run/Icarus Films.
Reviews the work of two Japanese artists, painters who won fame
for murals of Hiroshima.

HIRAIZUMI—CAPITAL OF THE NORTH. NHK-TV, 198? 30
    min. color. Video. Japan Society.
Includes highlights of Japan's past glories—the ruins of Moetzuji
Temple, of Chusonji Temple, the Golden Hall, and Buddhist
artifacts.

HONEY ROAD. NHK-TV, 198? 40 min. color. Video. Japan
    Society.
Migrant bee workers travel, along with their bees, from Kyushu
to Hokkaido in Japan.

THE HUMAN FACE OF JAPAN. Learning Corporation of
    America, 1982. 6 tapes/28 min. each, color. Video.
    Coronet/MTI Film and Video.
The lifestyles of the Japanese are explored in this six-part series:
1. The Career Escalator; 2. Lifetime Employment; 3. A Working

Class Couple; 4. Raw Fish and Pickle; 5. The Rice Ladle; 6. Tomorrow and Yesterday.

IN THE EMPEROR'S NAME. Centre Productions, 1988. 58 min. color. Video. Centre Productions.
An account of the World War II Japanese naval warriors who embodied the samurai tradition in modern times. Tells how they believed there was no higher goal than death in the service of the Emperor. Depicts the suicide raid on a naval base in Sydney harbor.

INTRODUCTION TO FLOWER ARRANGEMENT. NHK-TV, n.d. 30 min. color. Video. Japan Society.
A master teacher demonstrates the Sogetsu school of flower arrangement.

JAPAN: AN INTRODUCTION (REVISED). Wayne Mitchell, 1981. 22 min. color. Video. BFA Educational Media.
Describes the industrialization of Japan and the ancient cultural traditions that are practiced.

JAPAN AT WORK. Journal Films, 1988. 30 min. color. Video. Journal Films.
A program about the combining of culture, organization, and the nature of work to create the unique Japanese workplace. Shows the interaction of worker and employer in three case studies.

JAPAN, INC. National Film Board of Canada, 1986. 28 min. color. 16mm/Video. Centre Productions.
An award-winning film about Japan's success in the industrial world. Shows the factors that lead to success.

JAPAN REACHES FOR THE 21ST CENTURY. WETA-TV, n.d. 60 min. color. Video. WETA-TV.
A look at present-day Japanese who seem to be preparing to become world leaders in the next century. Reviews details of, and reasons for, Japan's success in the years since World War II. Describes efforts to fulfill Japan's vision for the future. Host is Daniel Schorr.

JAPAN: RHEUMATISM CURE. UPI, 1984. 12 min. color.
  Video. Journal Films.
How the Japanese treat rheumatism, including the use of extreme
cold and physical activity.

JAPAN, THE CROWDED ISLANDS: 1. CITY: TOKYO. BBC-
  TV, 1982. 20 min. color. Video. Films Inc.
Program 1 of this series about modern life in Japan observes a
day in Tokyo, with urban activity and traditional family life.

JAPAN, THE CROWDED ISLANDS: 2. COUNTRYSIDE:
  OBITSU. BBC-TV, 1982. 20 min. color. Video. Films Inc.
Shows how some city workers commute from rural areas where
farmland is at a premium.

JAPAN, THE CROWDED ISLANDS: 3. FACTORY:
  HIROSHIMA. BBC-TV, 1982. 20 min. color. Video. Films
  Inc.
An account of how Hiroshima has been completely rebuilt since
nuclear devastation.

JAPAN, THE CROWDED ISLANDS: 4. BACK OF BEYOND:
  IWATE. BBC-TV, 1982. 20 min. color. Video. Films Inc.
Tells how mountain farmers of Japan increase their income with
forestry and fishing.

JAPAN, THE CROWDED ISLANDS: 5. TOO FAR, TOO
  FAST? BBC-TV, 1982. 20 min. color. Video. Films Inc.
Explains how interior towns are making an effort to attract
industry away from the overcrowded coastal towns.

JAPAN: THE NATION FAMILY. CBC Productions, 1980. 51
  min. color. 16mm/Video. Wombat Productions.
Part of the "Nova" series, a program about the growth of
technology in Japan.

JAPAN: THE SUPERACHIEVERS. Canadian Broadcasting
  System, 1987. 51 min. color. 16mm/Video. Barr Films.
This prize-winning documentary focuses on Japan's industrial and
electrical genius. Her prowess with technology is traced with

examples, such as the fact that ancient steel making, originally developed in China, was improved by Japan and used for samurai sword making.

THE JAPAN THEY DON'T TALK ABOUT. NBC News, 1986. 50 min. color. Video. Films Inc.
An acclaimed NBC News White Paper studies the harsh realities of Japan's "economic miracle": long working hours, cramped and expensive housing, and other problems.

JAPANESE WOMAN. John Taylor, Don Hopkins, 1986. 52 min. color. Video. Centre Productions.
Explores the status of women in Japan. Describes lifestyles, social values, labor practices, and the women's movement.

JAPANESE YOUNG WOMEN. Hoso-Bunko Foundation, 1984. 29 min. color. Video. Martha Stuart Communications.
Some Japanese women in their twenties and thirties frankly discuss life in contemporary Japan.

JAPAN'S GRAND KABUKI IN AMERICA. Centre Productions, 1986. 28 min. color. Video. Centre Productions.
Dick Cavett is the host for this program that follows the 91-member Grand Kabuki Company backstage for interviews with leading actors during a tour in the U.S. in 1985. Discusses their unique approach to theater.

JIZO CHILDREN'S FESTIVAL. NHK-TV, n.d. 30 min. color. Video. Japan Society.
A study of Kyoto's Nishijin weaving district as it gets ready for a festival dedicated to the Buddhist deity of children.

KENDO: THE PATH OF THE SWORD. Camera 3 Productions, 1980. 29 min. color. Video. Camera 3 Productions.
The history and role of the martial arts in Japan.

THE KOTO. Ohio University Telecommunications Center, 1979. 30 min. color. Video. Ohio University Telecommunications Center.

Includes performances and the history of the *koto*, a traditional stringed instrument.

THE LEGACY OF THE SHOGUNS. WTTW-TV, 1988. 56 min.
    color. Video. Coronet/MTI Film and Video.
Traces the 17th-century traditions of discipline and rigid hierarchy that kept Japan in isolation for centuries. Also shows how these same traditions led to the build-up of military power in World War II and the move to leadership in modern world economics.

LIFETIME EMPLOYMENT. Film Australia, 1982. 28 min. color.
    Video. Coronet/MTI Film and Video.
Observes the lifestyle and working conditions of industrial employees, with focus on an assembly-line worker in an automobile plant in Japan.

LOST   GENERATION.   Hiroshima-Nagasaki   Publishing
    Committee, 1983. 20 min. color. 16mm/Video. Films Inc.
Reports on what happened when the U.S. dropped atom bombs on Hiroshima and Nagasaki in 1945. Survivors discuss the effects of the bombings.

MADE   IN   JAPAN: CULTURAL   INFLUENCES   ON
    INDUSTRY, PART I. WABC-TV, 1982. 16 min. color.
    16mm/Video. Coronet/MTI Film and Video.
Analyzes Japan's economic miracle and compares it with the recent plight of the American system.

MADE IN JAPAN: BUSINESS PRACTICES AND CHANGING
    LIFESTYLES, PART II. WABC-TV, 1982. 22 min. color.
    16mm/Video. Coronet/MTI Film and Video.
An account of business practices that have led to Japan's booming economy, particularly in steel production and electronic consumer goods.

MANUFACTURING   MIRACLES: A   JAPANESE   FIRM
    REINVENTS ITSELF. California Newsreel, 1987. 32 min.
    color. 16mm/Video. California Newsreel.
Traces post-war organizational development in Japan with focus

on the Mazda firm. Studies the social cost of industrial success.

MUDDY RIVER. Kohei Oguri, 1984. 105 min. b/w. 16mm. New
    Yorker Films.
Depicts the experiences of a young boy as he grows up in the
environs of Osaka in 1956. In Japanese with English subtitles.

NARUKAMI OPERA (FATHER THUNDER). NHK-TV, n.d. 58
    min. color. Video. Japan Society.
Presents the Kabuki play "Narukami" in a performance by
bunraku puppets controlled by handlers who use traditional
methods.

NATIONS OF THE WORLD: JAPAN. National Geographic,
    1988. 25 min. color. 16mm/Video. National Geographic.
Visits villages and cities of Japan. Also describes how Japan has
become prominent in manufacturing and trade.

NO MORE HIBAKUSHA. National Film Board of Canada, 1983.
    55 min. color. 16mm/video. First Run/Icarus Films.
Studies the *hibakusha*, the survivors of the Hiroshima and
Nagasaki bombings in 1945. Includes interviews that recall painful
memories. Shows the anti-war demonstration in New York in
1982.

NO MORE HIROSHIMA. Jacques Vallée, 1984. 26 min. color.
    16mm/Video. First Run/Icarus Films.
Follows two survivors of the Hiroshima and Nagasaki atomic
bombings on their mission as representatives of the Japanese
Peace Movement at the United Nations Special Session on
Disarmament in New York in June 1982.

NOH MASKS. NHK-TV, n.d. 30 min. color. Video. Japan
    Society.
There is no narrative in this program about Noh masks. Shows
Japanese mask makers at work.

OUR ANCESTORS—THE WORLD OF JOMON. NHK-TV, n.d.
    22 min. color. Video. Japan Society.

Examines structures and artifacts to learn about the prehistoric period in Japan.

PARADISE STEAMSHIP CO. VISITS: TOKYO. KCBS-TV, n.d. 21 min. color. Video. Carousel Film and Video.
A look at the old and the new in Japan: a subway station, a fish market, an elementary school, and shops of Japanese designers.

PEOPLE AND PRODUCTIVITY: WE LEARN FROM THE JAPANESE. Pacific Basin Institute, 1982. 28 min. color. Video. Encyclopaedia Britannica Educational Corporation.
Explains what has made Japanese businesses so competetive in the modern market. Discusses their business philosophies.

PEOPLE OF JAPAN. Beacon, 1987. 18 min. color. 16mm/Video. Beacon Films.
Even though outwardly the Japanese people appear to have changed with the times, the age-old philosophy of life remains untouched. To demonstrate this fact, the film focuses on the employees of a small business office. Shows their family life, social behavior, business practices, and the role of Shintoism and Buddhism.

A PROMISE. Yoshishigue Yoshida, 1986. 123 min. color. 16mm. New Yorker Films.
Yoshishigue Yoshida, a New Wave Japanese film director, presents a study of the relationship between young people and the old. The mercy killing of an elderly woman is the taking off point for this probe of modern Japanese life. In Japanese with English subtitles.

A PROPER PLACE IN THE WORLD. WTTW-TV, 1988. 59 min. color. Video. Coronet/MTI Film and Video.
Discusses the factors that led to World War II and General MacArthur's post-war reform policies for Japan that eventually produced great economic prosperity. Shows Japan's efforts to deal with some of the problems connected with success: overindustrialization, overcrowding, and a fast-paced competetive lifestyle.

RAN. Akira Kurosawa, 1985. 161 min. color. Video. CBS Fox Video.
An award-winning feudal epic set in 16th-century Japan based on the story of Shakespeare's play, *King Lear*. With Tatsuya Nakadai, Akira Terao and Mieko Harada. In Japanese with English subtitles.

RAW FISH AND PICKLE. Learning Corporation of America, 1982. 28 min. color. Video. Coronet/MTI Film and Video.
A profile of a fishing family in rural Japan.

RESTORATION OF THE GOLDEN SHRINE. NHK-TV, n.d. 50 min. color. Video. Japan Society.
Describes features of the restoration work done on the Golden Hall of the Chusonji Temple in Hiraizumi, Japan.

SATORI IN THE RIGHT CORTEX. John Taylor, Don Hopkins, 1986. 29 min. color. 16mm/Video. Centre Productions.
The spiritual goal of Zen Buddhism is *satori*, a flash of intuitive enlightenment. This film is an impressionistic treatment, presenting images of the Japanese "way of breathing." Shows scenes of monks in a monastery, Shintoist and Buddhist street festivals, masked rituals, and many other religious events.

SHODO: THE PATH OF WRITING. Camera 3 Productions, 1980. 29 min. color. Video. Camera 3 Productions.
About the art of calligraphy in ancient and modern Japan.

SURVIVORS: 40 YEARS AFTER HIROSHIMA (REVISED). Frances Politeo and Steven Okazaki, 1988. 35 min. color. Video. Mouchette Films.
This is a revised version of the culturally acclaimed documentary about Hiroshima and Nagasaki survivors who talk freely about their fears, trauma, and other experiences. Some have migrated to the U.S.

THE SWORD AND THE CHRYSANTHEMUM. WTTW-TV, 1988. 55 min. color. Video. Coronet/MTI Film and Video.
Draws a contrast between the samurai and ninja warriors and the

tea ceremony and sensitive garden design. These cultural contrasts are reflected in Japanese business behavior and social structure.

TOMORROW AND YESTERDAY. Learning Corporation of America, 1982. 28 min. color. Video. Coronet/MTI Film and Video.
How the Japanese observe the traditions of ancient times despite their participation in the new technology.

TRADITIONAL JAPANESE MASKS. NHK-TV, n.d. 15 min. color. Video. Japan Society.
How the Japanese use masks and what they look like.

VIDEO LETTERS FROM JAPAN. The Asia Society, 1985. 60 min. 6 programs. Video. The Asia Society.
Japanese culture as described in six programs: 1. My Day and Tokyo Sunday; 2. Summer Vacation and Tohuku Diary; 3. My Family and Making Things; 4. My Town and Nobles and Samurai; 5. Living Arts; 6. Our School and Sessions and Activities.

THE WORLD OF YUKAR—THE LIFE OF THE AINU 100 YEARS AGO. NHK-TV, n.d. 30 min. color. Video. Japan Society.
The lifestyle of the Ainu people a century ago is described in the Ainu epic, *Yukar*. Consists of three program: 1. (Winter) Bear Killing Ritual; 2. (Summer) Domestic Customs; 3. Hunting/Fishing Rituals.

ZEN. NHK-TV, n.d. 36 min. color. Video. Japan Society. Shows how young monks are trained and looks at the practice of Zen. Without narration.

Korea

KOREA: LAND OF THE MORNING CALM. P. Newman and Carol Kucera, 1985. 23 min. color. Video. Centre Productions.
A history of Korean culture and a look at present-day Korean society.

KOREA: THE FAMILY. Centron Films, 1980. 18 min. color. Video. Centron Films.
Tells how traditional Korean life is being changed by urbanization and industrialization.

KOREAN SPRING. Caltex, 1980. 20 min. color. Video. New York State Education Department.
An overview of Korea's history, culture, and economic outlook.

THE KOREAN WAR: AGGRESSION. Lou Reda Productions, 1988. 15 min. color. 16mm/video. Coronet/MTI Film and Video.
This is the first episode of a three-part series. The film starts with the North Korean invasion of South Korea. Uses archival footage to show the Inchon invasion and the capture of Seoul. Depicts the reactions of South Korea, the U.S., and the United Nations.

THE KOREAN WAR: ESCALATION. Lou Reda Productions, 1988. 15 min. color. 16mm/Video. Coronet/MTI Film and Video.
In the second part of this series the viewer sees the United Nations forces, consisting mostly of U.S. troops, move north to the Yalu River despite warnings from the Chinese. Shows the fall of Pyong Yang, the break up of the 8th Army and the X Corps. The Chinese enter the war; U.S. forces retreat.

THE KOREAN WAR: NEGOTIATION. Lou Reda Productions, 1988. 15 min. color. 16mm/Video. Coronet/MTI Film and Video.
In this last part of the series viewers learn about the Yalu defeat and the realization that victory might be impossible. Shows General Ridgeway's arrival and the removal of General MacArthur from command. A truce is finally signed at Panmunjom after over three years of war. Considers the U.S. role in the political struggles of the Far East.

THE KOREAN WAR: THE UNTOLD STORY. Carol Fleisher, USAA, 1988. 34 min. color. 16mm/Video. Pyramid Film and Video.

Some of the survivors of the Korean War discuss their experiences in America's first "undeclared" war. Narrated by Loretta Swit.

MR. OH: A KOREAN CALLIGRAPHER. Toshi Washizu and
    Richard Mellott, 1985. 20 min. color. Video. Asian Art
    Museum of San Francisco.
Introduces the training and philosophy of calligraphy in Korea as expressed by a master calligrapher.

ONE CHILD AT A TIME. Centre Productions, 1988. 29 min.
    color. Video. Centre Productions.
A study of the work of an organization called Heal the Children that helps children all over the world to come to the U.S. for badly needed medical treatment—in this case, how three South Korean children came to the U.S. for treatment. Tells about the culture of these children.

Taiwan

FROM COURTYARD HOUSE TO BLOCK APARTMENT.
    Wynette Yao, 1987. 23 min. color. Video. First Run/Icarus
    Films.
A documentary on the range of housing from traditional to modern in Taiwan as seen by a Chinese-American. Analyzes why the courtyard way of life is nearing extinction.

TAIWAN, THE BEAUTIFUL ISLAND. Shih Chien-Chen, 1986.
    28 min. color. 16mm. Taipei Chinese Information and Culture
    Center.
Gives the viewer a tour of Taiwan's special attractions.

SOUTHEAST ASIA

General

ANIMALS OF ASIA. Centron Films, 1980. 16 min. color. Video.

Centron Films.
Describes the variety of animal life in Southeast Asia.

THE BAJAO: SEAGOING NOMADS. Wayne Mitchell, 1983. 18
   min. color. 16mm/Video. BFA Educational Media.
Describes the life of the Bajao nomads of Southeast Asia who
live entirely on outrigger canoes. Shows how they gather the
things they need from coral reefs and uninhabited islands.

INDOCHINA REFUGEES. Martha Stuart Communications, 1981.
   60 min. color. Video. Martha Stuart Communications.
Explores the reasons for becoming refugees as told by
Cambodians, Laotians, and Vietnamese who have settled in the
U.S.

INDOCHINA REVISITED: A PORTRAIT BY JEAN
   DESPUJOLS. Judy Williams, 1984. 28 min. color. 16mm.
   Meadows Museum of Art.
The French artist portrayed the land and culture of the 1930s in
French Indochina, which included Vietnam, Cambodia, and Laos.
This is a culture that no longer exists. Shows the paintings and
provides dances by Royal Thai dancers.

RIVER JOURNEYS: MEKONG. Cornell University, 1985. 55
   min. color. Video. Cornell University
A visit to Vietnam, Cambodia, and Laos via the Mekong River.

Indonesia

ASIAN INSIGHT: INDONESIA. Film Australia, 1987. 48 min.
   color. Video. Films Inc.
Reports on Indonesia's independence gained in 1945 and traces
Dutch influence on Indonesian society. Shows the cultural
diversity of the region.

THE HUMAN FACE OF INDONESIA: BUT I'LL ALWAYS
   CONTINUE TO WRITE. Film Australia, 1987. 26 min. color.
   Video. Films Inc.
This is part of a series designed to inform viewers about

Indonesia's life and culture. This program is a profile of a Djakarta newspaper reporter who works hard to bring the story of Djakarta's impoverished groups to the attention of her readers.

THE HUMAN FACE OF INDONESIA: HELPING THE PEOPLE TO HELP THEMSELVES. Film Australia, 1987. 26 min. color. Video. Films Inc.
Two doctors are shown serving poor people in a remote community, the province of Nusa Tenggara Timur in Indonesia.

THE HUMAN FACE OF INDONESIA: JOURNEY TO A NEW LIFE. Film Australia, 1987. 26 min. color. Video. Films Inc.
Tells how, in order to alleviate overcrowding, the Indonesian government has started to relocate people to less-populated provinces, such as East Kalimantan.

THE HUMAN FACE OF INDONESIA: MASTER OF THE SHADOWS. Film Australia, 1987. 26 min. color. Video. Films Inc.
Explores the question of whether Bali, one of the most famous places in Indonesia, can survive the impact of tourism that threatens the traditional culture.

THE HUMAN FACE OF INDONESIA: WE ARE NOTHING WITHOUT THE PEOPLE. Film Australia, 1987. 26 min. color. Video. Films Inc.
A doctor, who is also governor of Nusa Tenggara Timur, and his wife discuss their medical work for their poor province and talk about the role of the military in Indonesia.

INDONESIA, A GENERATION OF CHANGE: LEGACY OF A JAVANESE PRINCESS. Barbara Barde, 1987. 28 min. color. Video. Chip Taylor Communications.
Studies several Indonesian women to learn how the next generation of women will balance their traditional role with the new opportunities to enter the world of employment.

INDONESIA, A GENERATION OF CHANGE: A PLACE IN THE SUN. Barbara Barde, 1987. 28 min. color. Video. Chip Taylor Communications.

Four different cultural groups explore Indonesia's search for unity among the 300 different ethnic groups who live there.

INDONESIA, A GENERATION OF CHANGE: OUT OF THE SHADOWS. Barbara Barde, 1987. 28 min. color. Video. Chip Taylor Communications.
Traces Indonesia's history and discusses its plan for the future. Explores the problems connected with rapid industrialization.

INDONESIA, A GENERATION OF CHANGE: TANAH AIR—OUR LAND, OUR WATER. Barbara Barde, 1987. 28 min. color. Video. Chip Taylor Communications.
Depicts the many environmental problems faced by Indonesia, such as overpopulation, resource depletion, and the destruction of rain forests.

INDONESIA, A GENERATION OF CHANGE: TO DREAM THE IMPOSSIBLE DREAM. Barbara Barde, 1987. 28 min. color. Video. Chip Taylor Communications.
Shows how Indonesia struggles to strike a balance between ever-evolving new technology and the creation of new jobs in a country where two million enter the labor force every year.

INDONESIA, A GENERATION OF CHANGE: TRADING PLACES—INDONESIA MEETS THE WEST. Barbara Barde, 1987. 28 min. color. Video. Chip Taylor Communications.
Discusses foreign aid, investments, and trade in Indonesia as a relatively new nation.

INDONESIA—PRESSURE OF POPULATION. Journal Films, 1988. 20 min. color. Video. Journal Films.
Discusses the problems that must be faced in Indonesia due to the great diversity there. Focuses on the city of Djakarta to show solutions sought by the government.

Kampuchea

BEYOND THE KILLING FIELDS—REFUGEES ON THE THAI-CAMBODIAN BORDER. Jeff Harmon, 1987. 45 min.

color. 16mm. Loyola Marymount University.
Tells about the refugees' lives on the Thai-Cambodian border.

CAMBODIAN DANCE. Cornell University, 1979. 50 min. color.
Video. Cornell University.
Demonstrates Cambodian classical and folk dances.

KAMPUCHEA: THE PAST AND THE FUTURE. UPI, 1984. 24
min. color. Video. Journal Films.
A review of Kampuchea's history and present-day problems.

WORLD IN ACTION: NO MAN'S LAND. David Darlow, 1983.
26 min. color. Video. Filmakers Library.
Shows how Kampuchean refugees are trapped along a strip
between Thailand and Kampuchea because they are forbidden to
enter either country.

Malaysia

ASIAN INSIGHT: MALAYSIA. Film Australia, 1987. 48 min.
color. Video. Films Inc.
Explains that Malaysia is a Muslim state in a Chinese-dominated
environment. Tells about Chinese economic strength in a country
where the Chinese are a minority.

BORNEO PLAYBACK: A SABAH STORY. C. Kreeger
Davidson, 1984. 57 min. color. Video. C. Kreeger Davidson.
Describes the return visit of a Peace Corps woman to Sabah,
Malaysia, where she discovers the many changes that have taken
place in the transformation from British colony to the Federation
of Malaysia.

LATAH: A CULTURE SPECIFIC ELABORATION OF THE
STARTLE REFLEX. Ronald C. Simons, 1983. 39 min. color.
16mm/Video. Indiana University.
People who startle readily are called *latahs* and have a specific
role in Malay society. This film was made in a small village on
the Straits of Malacca and presents a *latah* who tells how she
started becoming startled during a depression in her life and how,

when this was noticed by others, she was startled repeatedly until she became a *latah*. Discusses the *latah* role and shows *latahs* in and out of *latah* states.

LIFE ALONG A MALAYSIAN RIVER. Hugh Baddeley Productions, n.d. 17 min. color. 16mm/Video. International Film Bureau.
Depicts life in the tropical rain forests of Sarawak, Malaysia, through the daily routines of two young men. One lives in a Dyak longhouse and the other on the outskirts of Kapit. Shows them using the Rajang River as their highway and covers geography, people, transportation, education, exports, and natural resources. Observes family life, use of space, cooking, weaving, and games.

MAGICAL MALAYSIA. Polonius Productions, 1984. 11 min. color. Video. International Film Bureau.
A tour of Malaysia covering the important sites and the life of the people.

Philippines

ASIAN INSIGHT: PHILIPPINES. Film Australia, 1987. 48 min. color. Video. Films Inc.
Discusses the Spanish and American colonization in the Philippines and explains how colonial influences can be traced in Filipino culture today.

THE BATAK: A FORGOTTEN PEOPLE. John Ferretti, 1984. 43 min. color. 16mm. John Ferretti.
Observes the daily life of a fast-disappearing tribe of 250 people, the Batak, who live on the island of Palawan in the Philippines.

CELSO AND CORA. Gary Kildea, 1983. 109 min. color. 16mm/Video. First Run/Icarus Films.
A prize-winning feature-length film about a family of street vendors living in a squatter area of Manila. Reveals the poverty faced daily with courage and humor.

COLLISION COURSE. BBC-TV, 1980. 45 min. color. Video.

Cornell University.
Explores human rights violators in the Philippines.

FIRST IN THE PHILIPPINES. Robert Koglin, 1984. 62 min.
color. 16mm/Video. Salmon Studios.
Covers the Spanish-American and the Philippine-American wars
with particular focus on a regiment from Oregon.

LAND OF THE SUN RETURNING. Caltex, 1981. 28 min. color.
Video. New York State Education Department.
Covers the changing culture and customs of the modern
Philippines.

MESSAGE FROM THE STONE AGE: THE STORY OF THE
TASADAY. John Nance, 1984. 16 min. color. 16mm. New
Dimension Films.
The obscure Tasaday people of the Philippines were discovered
in 1971. This is a report on their environment and Stone Age
culture.

PERFUMED NIGHTMARE. Kidlat Tahimik, 1982. 91 min. color.
16mm. Flower Films.
A partly autobiographical story about a young man of the
Philippines and his reactions to American colonialism. He is
particularly impressed with the new technology, but reacts against
some aspects of American colonization.

PHILIPPINES: BLACKBOARD NEWSPAPER. UPI, 1984. 15
min. color. Video. Journal Films.
A documentary about the Filipino people. Covers their culture
and lifestyles.

THE PHILIPPINES: LIFE, DEATH, AND REVOLUTION.
DCTV, 1986. 57 min. color. Video. Downtown Community
TV Center.
A portrait of life in the Philippines before and after the rule of
Marcos as told by Filipino people.

THE PHILIPPINES: RICARDO THE JEEPNEY DRIVER.
Handel Film Corporation, 1984. 22 min. color. 16mm/Video.

Handel Film Corporation.
An award-winning film about the history of the Philippines and
its ethnic, social, and economic aspects, as seen through the eyes
of a driver of a "jeepney," an unusual vehicle made of old jeeps
left over from World War II.

PHILIPPINES: THE PRICE OF POWER. Jeffrey Chester and
    Charles Drucker, 1986. 28 min. color. 16mm/Video. First
    Run/Icarus Films.
Studies the roots of the "People's Power" revolution of 1986 in
the Philippines. Focuses on the Igorots, tribal Filipinos who are
traditional farmers in the mountains.

TO SING OUR OWN SONG. BBC-TV, 1983. 49 min. color.
    16mm/Video. Films Inc.
A visit with a resister to the dictatorship of Ferdinand Marcos in
the Philippines. Expresses the concern for the poor in contrast
with a selfish elite.

THE VANISHING EARTH. Interim Media Productions, 1985. 30
    min. color. Video. Cornell University.
About the problems of the T'boli people who live in the hills of
the Philippines.

Singapore

ASIAN INSIGHT: HONG KONG/SINGAPORE. Film Australia,
    1987. 48 min. color. Video. Films Inc.
This program recounts the events that brought Western powers
to Asia and compares the social structures of Hong Kong and
Singapore.

KNOWZONE: WILDLIFE FOR SALE. Coronet/MTI Film and
    Video, 1987. 30 min. color. 16mm/Video. Coronet/MTI Film
    and Video.
The "Knowzone" programs are adaptations from the "Nova"
series. This one describes the flourishing illegal trade in
endangered wildlife. Visits Singapore to give a view of this
successful business in operation.

SINGAPORE. BFA Educational Media, 1987. 14 min. color. 16mm/Video. BFA Educational Media.
Compares old and new Singapore. Talks about the people—a blend of Malaysian, Chinese and Indian—and the country's importance as a harbor and international trade center.

SINGAPORE: CROSSROAD OF THE ORIENT. Handel Film Corporation, 1987. 22 min. color. 16mm/Video. Handel Film Corporation.
Despite its small size, Singapore has a great impact on Asia and is important as a port. This film discusses Singapore's financial operations and industrial development. Describes various ethnic groups that live in Singapore and how the country achieved independence. All of this is seen through the eyes of four generations of one family.

Thailand

ASIAN INSIGHT: THAILAND. Film Australia, 1987. 48 min. color. Video. Films Inc.
Tells how Thailand has never known colonial rule. Explains that most of the people are Buddhists and covers the history of Buddhism and the monarchy in Thailand.

LEE'S PARASOL. Coronet/MTI Film and Video, 1980. 25 min. color. 16mm/Video. Coronet/MTI Film and Video.
A young girl in Thailand is shown designing a parasol for a Buddhist festival.

THAILAND BICENTENNIAL. UPI, 1984. 27 min. color. Video. Journal Films.
An account of the history of Thailand with discussion of social, political, and economic problems there today.

THAILAND: LAND OF FREEDOM. Polonius Productions, 1984. 28 min. color. 16mm/Video. International Film Bureau.
A tour film showing the unusual features of Thailand.

THAILAND: LIFE ALONG THE KHLONGS. Handel Film

Corporation, 1984. 22 min. color. 16mm/Video. Handel Film Corporation.
Describes family life along the Khlongs of Bangkok, Thailand. Follows a typical Khlong family during their morning swim, shopping in a floating market, and riding the water school bus to a festival.

THAILAND TODAY. World Vision Educational Resources/New Zealand, 1981. 16 min. color. 16mm/Video. International Film Bureau.
An overview of Thailand, highlighting rural areas, Bangkok, temples, classical dance, and production for export.

Vietnam

BOAT PEOPLE. Ann Hui, 1983. 106 min. color. 16mm. New Yorker Films.
A docudrama that serves as an exposé of the failures of the Communist regime in post-war Vietnam. Focuses on a Japanese photojournalist who returns to South Vietnam three years after the war. In Mandarin with English subtitles.

CA DAO, THE FOLK POETRY OF VIETNAM. David Grubin, 1984. 9 min. color. Video. Penn State University.
A musicologist talks about *ca dao*, the short lyric poems that are part of the oral musical tradition of Vietnam. The professor and his daughter sing *ca dao* and perform traditional instrumental music.

KIM PHUC. VARA-TV, 1984. 25 min. color. 16mm/Video. First Run/Icarus Films.
In 1972 a little Vietnamese girl was hit by napalm. This is a report on her a decade later.

SURNAME: VIET; GIVEN NAME: NAM. Trinh T. Minh-ha, 1989. 108 min. color. 16mm. Women Make Movies.
Uses experimental and documentary styles to describe the life of Vietnamese women. With interviews, archival footage, home movies, and poetry.

VIETNAM, A TELEVISION HISTORY. WGBH-TV, 1983. 13
  parts, 60 min. each, color. Video. Films Inc.
A report on Vietnam from the start of the revolution in 1945 to
the evacuation of Saigon in 1975. In 13 programs: 1. Roots of
War; 2. First Vietnam War, 1946-1954; 3. America's Mandarin,
1954-1963; 4. LBJ goes to War, 1964-1965; 5. America Takes
Charge, 1965-1976; 6. With America's Enemy, 1954-1967; 7. TET,
1968; 8. Vietnamizing the War, 1969-1973; 9. No Neutral Ground:
Cambodia and Laos; 10. Peace at Hand; 11. Homefront U.S.A.;
12. The End of the Tunnel, 1973-1975; 13. Legacies.

VIETNAM: FIVE YEARS AFTER THE WAR. UPI, 1980. 11
  min. color. Video. Journal Video.
An account of the many problems that followed the end of the
Vietnam war.

VIETNAM—TALKING TO THE PEOPLE. Jon Alpert, 1985. 52
  min. color. Video. Downtown Community TV Center.
A close look at daily life in Vietnam ten years after the war.
Covers the countryside and inside homes and factories.

WHEN NIGHT COMES. Bob Kane, 1988. 23 min. color. Video.
  CGI.
A visit to Vietnam to look at the impact of more than thirty
years of war on family life and culture.

WHY VIETNAM? Joe Domanick, 1986. 101 min. color. Video.
  Churchill Films.
Complete coverage of the issues of the Vietnam war. Discusses
impact on the Vietnamese.

THE PACIFIC

[Includes Hawaii, Oceania (Islands of Central and South Pacific); Australasia (Australia, New Zealand, New Guinea and neighboring islands); Melanesia (Northeast of Australia); Micronesia (Mariana, Caroline, and Marshall Islands); and Polynesia (area between Hawaii and New Zealand)]

ANGELS OF WAR. Andrew Pike, Hank Nelson, Gavan Daws, 1982. 54 min. color. 16mm/Video. Filmakers Library.
The people of Papua New Guinea recall the incidents of World War II that touched them personally, when Americans, Australians, and Japanese passed through their island. Uses archival footage and old propaganda feature films to portray what happened.

AS FROZEN MUSIC. Juniper Films, 1986. 55 min. color. Video. Wombat Film and Video.
Reports on the creative life of the new Sydney Opera House, which at first was a subject of controversy but is now a source of pride for Australians. Features opera stars, such as Joan Sutherland and Janet Baker, ballet's Robert Helpmann, jazz singer Cleo Laine, and the Sydney Youth Orchestra.

THE AUSTRALIAN WAY OF LIFE. AIMS Media, 1988. 21 min. color. 16mm/Video. AIMS Media.
An overview of Australia's early settlers, the Europeans, the wildlife, agriculture, mining, and manufacturing. Discusses the

heritage and contributions of the aborigines who have lived on the island for 40,000 years and provides views of city life and life "outback" in the dry, flat inland area.

AUSTRALIA'S UNUSUAL ANIMALS. National Geographic, 1983. 23 min. color. 16mm/Video. National Geographic.
Describes Australia's unusual mammals (marsupials, monotremes, and others) and strange reptiles and amphibians.

CANE TOADS. Tristram Miall, 1988. 46 min. color. 16mm/Video. Australian Film Commission.
The cane toad was introduced into Australia in 1935 and has multiplied to become a pest of major proportions. Presented in an entertaining account.

CANNIBAL KILLERS. Cine-Pic Hawaii, n.d. 11 min. color. 16mm/Video. Cine-Pic Hawaii.
The Polynesians who settled the Hawaiian Islands were not cannibals. However, cannibals from the South Pacific may have reached Hawaii, since some legends tell about the practice of cannibalism. This particular legend tells about a chief and a mountain boy who collaborate to get rid of a cannibal on their island.

"CANNIBAL TOURS." Dennis O'Rourke, 1986. 70 min. color. 16mm/ Video. Direct Cinema.
Explores the differences and similiarities of the indigenous people of Papua New Guinea and the white tourists. Lush jungle vegetation and the roar of cicadas, frogs, and other creatures must compete with Mozart and the sound of a shortwave radio.

CHRIS AND MASAKO WATASE. Phyllis Kido, n.d. 10 min. color. 16mm/Video. Cine-Pic Hawaii.
Studies three generations of the Japanese Watase family in Hawaii from 1890 to 1984. The filmmaker Phyllis Kido, who is a granddaughter of the Watase family, takes the viewer to various places on Kauai where the family settled and lived.

COULDN'T BE FAIRER. Dennis O'Rourke, 1984. 50 min. color. 16mm/Video. Direct Cinema.

A hard-hitting documentary about a side of aboriginal society in Australia that is seldom seen by white people. Discusses the problems of alcoholism, racial violence, and political oppression. Also presents an account of the work of Mick Miller, an aboriginal activist.

DEATH OF THE GODS. Cine-Pic Hawaii, n.d. 11 min. color. 16mm/Video. Cine-Pic Hawaii.
Recounts the story of two young priests (*kahuna*) and how they were affected by the decree (issued in 1819 by King Kamehameha II and high priest Hewahewa) to destroy all images of the gods. The film includes a restored temple, actual wooden images, and reenactment of rituals.

DREAMINGS: THE ART OF ABORIGINAL AUSTRALIA. Janet Bell and Michael Riley, 1988. 30 min. color. Video. First Run/Icarus Films.
Explores the Australian aboriginal artwork, which reflects the 40,000-year-old belief system of the aborigines. Shows modern aboriginal artists at work on paintings with mystical significance.

EASTER ISLAND: PUZZLE OF THE PACIFIC. ABC Eagle, 1982. 28 min. color. Video. Films Inc.
A study of the achievements of the mysterious ancient inhabitants of Easter Island.

FAMILIAR PLACES. David MacDougall, 1981. 53 min. color. 16mm/Video. University of California Extension Media Center.
Observes a group of Australian aborigines and an anthropologist in the process of mapping the traditional territorial lands of an aboriginal family.

FIJI. Marilyn Perry TV Productions, 1980. 28 min. color. Video. Marilyn Perry TV Productions.
Ambassador Berenado Vunibobo talks about life in Fiji.

THE FIRESTICK. Cine-Pic Hawaii, n.d. 11 min. color. 16mm/Video. Cine-Pic Hawaii.
A Hawaiian legend about Wiki, brother of Pele, who places the

fire of the volcano into the hibiscus plant as a gift for the villagers who formerly had made long journeys to a volcano to obtain fire.

GALAPAGOS: MY FRAGILE WORLD. WETA-TV, n.d. 60 min. color. Video. WETA-TV.
Discusses the rare species of plants and animals found in the Galapagos Islands. A resident conservationist and photographer talk about the fight to preserve threatened species. Narrated by Cliff Robertson.

GALAPAGOS—MY SPECIAL LAND. Joseph O'Brien, 1983. 13 min. color. 16mm/Video. United Nations.
An old-timer talks of the past and present of the Galapagos Islands and the efforts of the Ecuadoran government to protect the ecosystem of the islands.

GHOST ISLAND. Cine-Pic Hawaii, n.d. 11 min. color. 16mm/Video. Cine-Pic Hawaii.
A Hawaiian legend about a fellow named Paki who is rescued from his overturned canoe by two spirits from a floating island. Paki outwits the two spirits and after winning their friendship sails home with their gifts—melia blossoms.

GIFT-GIVING RITUAL OF OLD HAWAII. Cine-Pic Hawaii, n.d. 10 min. color. 16mm/Video. Cine-Pic Hawaii.
Observes a pageant at the *heiau* (temple) of Pu'ukohola that recreates the gift-giving ritual to King Kamehameha.

HALF LIFE: A PARABLE FOR THE NUCLEAR AGE. Dennis O'Rourke, 1985. 86 min. color. 16mm/Video. Direct Cinema.
The terrifying story of the U.S. testing of the hydrogen bomb in the Marshall Islands, which contaminated the area for centuries to come. The native residents were not warned or evacuated during the detonation in March 1954. Officials said the neglect of the people was a mistake, but the evidence in this documentary indicates the incident may have been intentional.

HAWAII: CONTINUING TRADITIONS. Gail Evenari, Lawrence

Lansburgh, 1985. 28 min. color. Video. Chevron U.S.A.
Describes the historical and cultural traditions of ancient Polynesia
in Hawaii. Shows how these traditions are handed down to young
Hawaiians.

HAWAII: PARADISE LOST? Wolfgang Bayer, 1984. 18 min.
    color. 16mm/Video. BFA Educational Media.
Provides a background history of Hawaii before statehood in 1959.
Then describes how Hawaii began to experience the growth and
problems found on the mainland. Also covers geography, climate,
and culture.

HAWAIIAN HULA. Cine-Pic Hawaii, n.d. 30 min. color.
    16mm/Video. Cine-Pic Hawaii.
A noted hula master, Eleanor Leilehua Hiram, demonstrates the
hula, "Ula No Weo." She explains the meanings of the hand, leg,
and body motions. This study of the hula is fostered by the
University of Hawaii Committee for the Study and Preservation
of the Hawaiian Language, Art, and Culture.

HERE'S NEW ZEALAND. Journal Films, 1982. 18 min. color.
    Video. Journal Films.
Portrays New Zealand as a place of peace and beauty. Shows
snow-covered mountains, lakes, beaches, and a modern economy.

THE HOUSE-OPENING. Judith MacDougall, 1980. 45 min. color.
    16mm/Video. University of California Extension Media Center.
Observes a new aboriginal ceremony designed to expel the spirit
of a deceased man so that his widow can move back into their
house.

THE HUMAN FACE OF THE PACIFIC: ATOLL LIFE ON
    KIRIBATI. Film Australia, 1987. 28 min. color. Video. Films
    Inc.
This is part of a series which attempts to reveal the romantic
islands of the South Seas as a heterogeneous group of countries
and colonies trying to deal with the challenges of the modern
world while preserving their cultural identities. This particular
program studies Kiribati, which became independent in 1979.
Depicts its isolation and preservation of ancient culture.

THE HUMAN FACE OF THE PACIFIC: MARSHALL
    ISLANDS—LIVING WITH THE BOMB. Film Australia,
    1987. 28 min. color. Video. Films Inc.
Tells how the people of the Marshall Islands, a United States
Trust Territory, had to be relocated and their culture destroyed
due to nuclear bomb testing in the area.

THE   HUMAN   FACE   OF   THE   PACIFIC: NEW
    CALEDONIA—A LAND IN SEARCH OF ITSELF. Film
    Australia, 1987. 28 min. color. Video. Films Inc.
Examines the differences between the Kanala, who want to retain
their tribal society in Caledonia, and the Caledonian French, who
are more interested in economic progress.

THE HUMAN FACE OF THE PACIFIC: PLACE OF POWER
    IN FRENCH POLYNESIA. Film Australia, 1987. 28 min.
    color. Video. Films Inc.
Describes the reemergence of traditional arts and rituals after
years of French rule had nearly extinguished the Polynesian
culture of Tahiti.

THE HUMAN SIDE OF THE PACIFIC: FIJI—LEGACIES OF
    EMPIRE. Film Australia, 1987. 28 min. color. Video. Films
    Inc.
Studies the differences between the Indian people who were
brought to Fiji during colonial times and the native Fijians who
want to repossess the land taken from them by British rule. Shows
how sugarcane is the center of the division between the two
groups.

THE HUMAN SIDE OF THE PACIFIC: WESTERN SAMOA—I
    CAN GET ANOTHER WIFE BUT I CAN'T GET
    PARENTS. Film Australia, 1987. 28 min. color. Video. Films
    Inc.
Discusses the mass emigration of Western Samoans to New
Zealand. Focuses on a young couple who must leave their close-
knit families.

KAHUNA. Cine-Pic Hawaii, n.d. 5 min. color. 16mm/Video. Cine-
    Pic Hawaii.

Even today belief in the power of the *kahuna anaanaa*, the priest who practices sorcery and can will a person to death, persists in Hawaii. This film recounts a 1960 incident of death by sorcery.

KALU FROM THE SEA. Cine-Pic Hawaii, n.d. 11 min. color. 16mm/Video. Cine-Pic Hawaii.
An ancient Hawaiian storyteller tells about Paki, who, while swimming in the sea, is attacked and assumes that Kalu, a sea creature in human form, is responsible. Paki slays Kalu only to discover afterward that a shark-man was the guilty party. The storyteller warns the viewer about making hasty conclusions—"Remember Kalu."

KENJI. George Tahara, 1985. 29 min. color. 16mm/Video. Cine-Pic Hawaii.
Depicts boyhood remembrances of plantation life in Hawaii around 1900. Kenji is the 13-year-old Hawaii-born son of the Nakamura family from Japan who came to Hawaii in 1886. This film was produced as part of the centennial celebration of the arrival of the first Japanese immigrants to Hawaii.

KIONI'S POI POUNDER. Cine-Pic Hawaii, n.d. 11 min. color. 16mm/Video. Cine-Pic Hawaii.
A Hawaiian legend about Kioni, a boy who attacks a shark with a poi pounder and finds that the shark has become a boy. He enslaves the shark-boy and plays pranks on the boy. Eventually Kioni decides to make amends for the way he has treated the shark-boy by giving the boy his poi pounder. To this day the poi pounder can be seen in Kaneohe Bay, Oahu, and no one has been harmed by sharks around this island.

KOLEA THE MOON CHILD. Cine-Pic Hawaii, n.d. 5 min. color. 16mm/Video. Cine-Pic Hawaii.
A Hawaiian legend about Kolea, a moon child who loses his human form while visiting Kauai Island and is transformed into a golden plover by Hind, the goddess of the moon, so that he can fly home. As a result, Kolea visits Hawaii each winter and flies home in the spring. Filmed on the island of Kauai.

LANI AND THE SHARKMAN. Cine-Pic Hawaii, n.d. 9 min.
    color. 16mm/Video. Cine-Pic Hawaii.
This is a story taken from an ancient Hawaiian song that tells
about a hula dancer who plays with the affection of a stranger,
only to discover that he is the feared sharkman, who seeks his
victim when the flowers of the wiliwili tree bloom.

LEGEND OF THE ILIMA BLOSSOMS. Cine-Pic Hawaii, n.d.
    11 min. color. 16mm/Video. Cine-Pic Hawaii.
Tells the story of the ilima blossoms in Hawaii and why they
could be worn only by those of royal blood.

LIFE IN SAMOA. Cine-Pic Hawaii, n.d. 11 min. color.
    16mm/Video. Cine-Pic Hawaii.
Depicts village life in Samoa. Includes a marriage ceremony filmed
on Ta'u Island.

LOUSY LITTLE SIXPENCE. Alec Morgan, Gerald Bostock,
    1983. 54 min. color. 16mm/Video. Coronet/MTI Film and
    Video.
Using old film footage, photographs, and memories of elders, this
production traces the history of the New South Wales Protection
Board's treatment of the aborigines from 1909 to the present.

MAGIC GIFT OF RONGO. Cine-Pic Hawaii, n.d. 11 min. color.
    16mm/Video. Cine-Pic Hawaii.
A Hawaiian legend about how the secret of net making is given
to a young fisherman who befriends a visitor from Kahiki.

MAORI LEGENDS OF NEW ZEALAND: KAHUKURA'S NET.
    New Zealand National Film Unit, 1987. 5 min. color.
    16mm/Video. Wombat Film and Video.
A legend told in film animation about Kahukura, who, in a
dream, is led to an unusual discovery by the spirits of his
ancestors.

MAORI LEGENDS OF NEW ZEALAND: MAUI CATCHES
    THE SUN. New Zealand National Film Unit, 1987. 5 min.
    color. 16mm/Video. Wombat Film and Video.
A legend about Maui, who is asked to use magical means to catch

the sun to make him go more slowly and thereby ensure a longer day. An animated film.

MAORI LEGENDS OF NEW ZEALAND: PANIA OF THE REEF. 5 min. color. 16mm/Video. Wombat Film and Video. A legend about a young chief who loves a sea maid, Pania. He loses her and their child to the sea forever. An animated film.

MAORI LEGENDS OF NEW ZEALAND: RATA AND THE CANOE. New Zealand National Film Unit, 1987. 5 min. color. Wombat Film and Video. An animated film of a story based on the spirit world of the Maori people of New Zealand. When Rata is sent to find a giant tree in the forest to build a large canoe, he forgets to ask permission of Tana, the god of the forest, and magic things begin to happen.

MAORI LEGENDS OF NEW ZEALAND: RAU TAPU (MAGIC FEATHER). New Zealand National Film Unit, 1987. 5 min. color. 16mm/Video. Wombat Film and Video. About a fellow named Po who travels to Hawaiiki, a faraway land where he has many adventures. By the time he returns home he has picked up the power to fly. An animated film.

MAORI LEGENDS OF NEW ZEALAND: TE HOUTAEWA'S RUN. New Zealand National Film Unit, 1987. 5 min. color. 16mm/Video. Wombat Film and Video. This legend tells the story of the giant warrior, Te Houtaewa, who steals food from his enemies and is able to elude them with his speed and cunning. An animated film.

MAORI LEGENDS OF NEW ZEALAND: TINIRAU'S PET WHALE. New Zealand National Film Unit, 1987. 5 min. color. 16mm/Video. Wombat Film and Video. A tale about Kae, a clever old priest who abuses his friend Chief Tinirau. The women of his tribe cast a spell to help Tinirau get revenge. An animated film.

MARGARET MEAD AND SAMOA. Cinetel, 1988. 51 min. color. Video. Wombat Film and Video.

About Derek Freeman, a young anthropologist who in 1940 traveled to Samoa to see for himself the Polynesian culture so glowingly described by Margaret Mead. Instead, he found Mead's Samoa to be a fabrication. After 40 years of study Freeman published his refutation and shocked the world of anthropology.

MILLYA RUMARRA (BRAND NEW DAY). I. F. Productions, 1984. 49 min. color. 16mm/Video. Coronet/MTI Film and Video.
A study of aboriginal culture in Australia. Follows a nine-day exchange between some aborigines and a group of white Australian children. Examines cultural similarities and differences. Also reveals the aboriginal struggle during the 200 years since the Europeans settled in Australia.

MOANI AND THE SACRED PRINCE. Cine-Pic Hawaii, n.d. 11 min. color. 16mm/Video. Cine-Pic Hawaii.
A Hawaiian legend about Moani, a village boy who takes care of a lame prince. One day on an outing with the prince he is captured by a guard and thrown into a shark-infested sea. The prince rescues the boy and his joy is so great that his lameness is miraculously healed.

MOTU THE SENTINEL. Cine-Pic Hawaii, n.d. 11 min. color. 16mm/Video. Cine-Pic Hawaii.
A storyteller recounts the story of a sentinel on duty guarding a post at a boundary line who captures a rival chief, only to have the tables turned on him. Eventually the rival chief and the sentinel develop a respect for each other.

NAI'A AND THE FISH GOD. Cine-Pic Hawaii, n.d. 9 min. color. 16mm/Video. Cine-Pic Hawaii.
A Hawaiian legend about Nai'a, the son of a high priest, who fails in his duty to look after the fish god. The god becomes angry and brings starvation to the villagers by removing the fish from the sea. Nai'a, in order to become a sacrifice to appease the god, is turned into a porpoise. To this day Nai'a leads fishermen to where fish are plentiful.

NATIONS OF THE WORLD: AUSTRALIA. National

Geographic, 1988. 26 min. color. 16mm/Video. National
Geographic.
Tells about the aboriginals who were the first people to inhabit
the continent of Australia. Reenacts the arrival of Europeans from
England. Describes the miners and farmers who work "outback"
to create the country's wealth.

THE NEW PACIFIC: 1. THE PACIFIC AGE. BBC/NVC, 1987.
50 min. color. Video. Films Inc.
This is a series devoted to exploration of cultural, historical,
economic, and political aspects of the important Pacific Basin
that supports one third of the world's population. This first
program discusses how world trade has been transformed by
dynamic economic growth of Pacific countries.

THE NEW PACIFIC: 2. ECHOES OF WAR. BBC/NVC, 1987.
50 min. color. Video. Films Inc.
Shows how the Pacific's strategic significance for world powers
increases as the Pacific's prosperity increases.

THE NEW PACIFIC: 3. RETURN TO PARADISE. BBC/NVC,
1987. 50 min. color. Video. Films Inc.
Studies the impact of technological change on traditional values
among the Pacific island peoples.

THE NEW PACIFIC: 4. OVER RICH, OVER SEXED AND
OVER HERE. BBC/NVC, 1987. 50 min. color. Video. Films
Inc.
Explains how the traditional culture of the Pacific people is being
strengthened by tourism.

THE NEW PACIFIC: 5. FIFTY WAYS TO GET
ENLIGHTENED. BBC/NVC, 1987. 50 min. color. Video.
Films Inc.
Describes the major religions found in the Pacific—Islam,
Buddhism, Hinduism, and Christianity.

THE NEW PACIFIC: 6. FOR RICHER, FOR POORER.
BBC/NVC, 1987. 50 min. color. Video. Films Inc.
Compares wedding practices in Pacific nations to reveal a variety

of attitudes.

THE NEW PACIFIC: 7. JUGS TO BE FILLED OR CANDLES
     TO BE LIT. BBC/NVC, 1987. 50 min. color. Video. Films Inc.
A report on the differences of schools and universities in Japan,
Korea, California, Samoa, and Papua New Guinea.

THE NEW PACIFIC: 8. SHADOW OF THE RISING SUN.
     BBC/NVC, 1987. 50 min. color. Video. Films Inc.
Discusses how the prosperity of the Pacific Rim countries creates
a challenge to American economic dominance.

NEW ZEALAND: THE FILM. Gary Hannam and Ian John, 1985.
     29 min. color. Video. Wombat Film and Video.
Explores New Zealand in a fast-paced, action-packed style.
Features yachting, windsurfing, river rafting, wilderness tramping,
gold panning, skiing, golfing, fishing, and visits cities such as
Auckland and Christchurch. Also includes a look at Maori culture.
With a distinctive music track.

PACIFIC PARADISE? Journal Films, 1988. 30 min. color. Video.
     Journal Films.
Discusses how South Pacific islands have been dominated by the
U.S. and Europe. The result is the destruction of traditional ways
of life. Examines the past and future for three Pacific nations.

THE PACIFIC: PARADISE IN PAIN. Otto Schuurman, 1985. 60
     min. color. Video. The Cinema Guild.
Explains how residents of New Caledonia, Palau, Hawaii, and the
Marshall Islands are confronting colonial domination by France,
military domination by the U.S., and economic influence by Japan
and Southeast Asia.

PEOPLE IN CHANGE: PART I. NEW GUINEA PATROL AND
     EXCERPTS FROM YUMI YET. Film Australia, 1988. 42
     min. color. Video. Films Inc.
Presents two films: one, made in 1958 about an Australian patrol
officer in Papua New Guinea during the colonial administration,
and the other a documentary of Papua New Guinea's
independence celebrations. Part of a series concerned with the

influence of other cultures on the traditions of Papua New Guinea.

PEOPLE IN CHANGE: PART II. TOWARDS BARUYA MANHOOD. Film Australia, 1988. 3 programs/53 min., 42 min., 48 min. color. Video. Films Inc.
Studies life of the Baruya people in the eastern highlands of Papua New Guinea. In three programs shows how the Baruya culture has been relatively free from European contact.

POHINAHINA, BOY FROM THE SUN. Cine-Pic Hawaii, n.d. 11 min. color. 16mm/Video. Cine-Pic Hawaii.
According to a Hawaiian legend, the silver sword plant of Haleakala Crater bears the name Pohinahina in honor of a boy from the sun who decided to settle at the crater, even though it meant losing his mortal form.

THE SHARK CALLERS OF KONTU. Dennis O'Rourke, 1986. 54 min. color. 16mm/Video. Direct Cinema.
The people of Kontu in Papua New Guinea used to hunt sharks in their outrigger canoes. Now only a few sharkhunters remain who understand the ritual involved.

SONGS OF A DISTANT JUNGLE. Robert Charlton, 1985. 20 min. color. 16mm/Video. University of California Extension Media Center.
An award-winning film about a visit to the jungles of Papua New Guinea by a young musician from the Julliard School. He is shown recording and documenting the music from remote villages.

SOUTH PACIFIC. Sunset Films, 1984. 7 min. color. Video. Modern Talking Picture Service.
A trip on board the *Royal Viking* to the South Pacific.

STRANGER FROM KAHIKI. Cine-Pic Hawaii, n.d. 11 min. color. 16mm/Video. Cine-Pic Hawaii.
A Hawaiian legend about Lono, the god of agriculture, who revisits Hawaii disguised as a stranger in order to teach a young chief the many uses of the ti leaf.

STRATEGIC TRUST: THE MAKING OF NUCLEAR FREE
PALAU. Debra Dralle, CPB, 1983. 59 min. color. 16mm.
Positive Futures Center.
About the nuclear-free nation of Palau, the island republic of
America's Pacific Trust Territories. Even though the U.S. military
planned to make it a storage base for weapons, Palau managed
to circumvent the plan.

TAKEOVER. David and Judith MacDougall, 1981. 90 min. color.
16mm/Video. University of California Extension Media Center.
This is a report on a political confrontation between the
Australian government and the Aurukun Aboriginal Reserve on
one side and the state of Queensland on the other, regarding
access to bauxite deposits.

THREE HORSEMEN. David and Judith MacDougall, 1983. 55
min. color. 16mm/Video. University of California Extension
Media Center.
Examines three generations of aboriginal stockmen who are now
experiencing difficulties in their attempt to fulfill the ideals of
aboriginal stockmen earlier in this century.

TRIUMPH OF THE NOMADS: THE FIRST INVADERS.
WETA-TV, 1989. 60 min. color. Video. WETA-TV.
The first episode of a three-part series describes what Australia
was like before the Europeans came. Tells how the nomadic
aborigines survived and how, after the last of the world's Ice Ages,
the rising of the seas covered the islands that were Australia's
only link to the rest of the world.

TRIUMPH OF THE NOMADS: REIGN OF THE
WANDERERS. WETA-TV, 1989. 60 min. color. Video.
WETA-TV.
The second part of a three-part series about the aborigines of
Australia. This episode describes their arrival in Australia and
their lifestyle at that time. Explains the importance of fire in their
nomadic way of life. Shows how the aborigines mastered nature
in order to survive.

TRIUMPH OF THE NOMADS: SAILS OF DOOM. WETA-TV,

1989. 60 min. color. Video. WETA-TV.
The third and final episode of the series tells of the many things
the aborigines discovered: edible plants, mines, new medicines and
drugs, manufacturing techniques, raw materials for cosmetics, and
hidden pools of water in the deserts.

UP FOR GRABS. Curtis Levy, 1983. 55 min. color. 16mm.
   Australian Film Commission.
Tells how the Australian aborigines have gained respect and rights
from the essentially white government. In particular, studies the
struggle for land rights.

WAITING FOR HARRY. Kim McKenzie, 1981. 57 min. color.
   16mm/Video. University of California Extension Media Center.
Reports on the difficulties that Australian aborigines must face in
protecting their rituals.

WALTZING MATILDA. South Australian Film Corporation,
   1988. 8 min. color. 16mm/Video. AIMS Media.
An animated film made with clay animals representing the
Australian bush, such as kangaroos, koalas, emus, and goannas.
The clay characters sing the famous Australian song, "Waltzing
Matilda," and the full story of the song is enacted.

WESTERN SAMOA. UNICEF, 1983. 19 min. color. Video. New
   York State Education Department.
A look at the Samoan people who live in villages. Describes
traditions and culture.

THE WONDER OF WESTERN AUSTRALIA. Channel Nine
   Perth Production, 1986. 5 programs/50 min. each. color. Video.
   Wombat Film and Video.
Portrays the wild beauty of Western Australia in five parts. Part
I shows sea creatures, the golden orb weaver spider, and a big
meteorite crater. Part II, whales, sharks, quartz, the marsupial,
horses, camels, kangaroos, and the dingo. Part III, eagles, a large
bushfire, a great canyon, and an underground cave system. Part
IV, surfboarding, hang gliding, natural life on a historic beach, and
waterfalls. Part V, underwater pearl fishing, ancient shipwrecks,
Australia's gold rush, and cattle.

YESTERDAY, TODAY, AND TOMORROW: THE WOMEN
   OF PAPUA NEW GUINEA. Centre Productions, 1988. 27
   min. color. Video. Centre Productions.
Shows the women of Papua New Guinea living in a country that
has an environment very much like that of the Stone Age.
Examines ancient customs and tells about a few women who have
entered the modern world. An award-winning production.

YIRRKALA ADVENTURE. Film Australia, 1987. 50 min. color.
   Video. Films Inc.
Urban teenagers visit the Northern Territory in Australia. They
learn about aboriginal life in the bush, including dancing, playing,
and hunting for food.

NORTH AMERICA

GENERAL

BLACK AND BLUE. New Liberty Productions, 1988. 59 min. color. 16mm/Video. Third World Newsreel.
An account of two decades of mistreatment of blacks and Latinos in Philadephia.

ELECTRIC BOOGIE. Tana Ross and Freke Vuijst, 1983. 30 min. color. 16mm/Video. Filmakers Library.
Depicts the spread of break dancing to every school yard in America from its beginnings in black and Hispanic neighborhoods. Features four youths from the Bronx who are devoted fans of Electric Boogie.

LIVING IN AMERICA: ONE HUNDRED YEARS OF YBOR CITY. Gayla Jamison, 1987. 53 min. color. Video. Filmakers Library.
Ybor City is in Tampa, Florida, and is a community of Spaniards, Cubans, and Italians who settled there 100 years ago.

MISSISSIPPI TRIANGLE. Third World Newsreel, 1984. 120 min. color. 16mm/Video. Third World Newsreel.
This is a documentary about life in the Mississippi Delta that uses historical footage and interviews of longtime residents to convey the history of interethnic relations there. This is a region where

Chinese-Americans live side by side with African-Americans and whites. To give authenticity to the film, three separate film crews, each representing one of the ethnic groups, were used.

WHOSE AMERICA IS IT? Elena Mannes for CBS News, n.d. 46
    min. color. Video. Carousel Film and Video.
A discussion of immigration, legal and illegal, and how immigrants are viewed by Americans. There are concerns about the immigrants' failure to learn English and the fact that they deprive Americans of jobs. Narrated by Bill Moyers.

AFRO-AMERICANS

ABOUT TAP. George T. Nierenberg, 1984. 28 min. color.
    16mm/Video. Direct Cinema.
Features an introduction by Gregory Hines and examples by famous tap dancers to explain what jazz tap dancing is all about.

AILEY DANCES. James Lipton, 1982. 85 min. color. Video.
    Kultur.
The Alvin Ailey Dance Theater performs various ballets. Recorded live at New York City's Center Theater.

ALBERTA HUNTER: MY CASTLE'S ROCKIN'. Stuart
    Goldman, 1988. 60 min. color. 16mm/Video. The Cinema
    Guild.
Traces the long career of the legendary blues singer, jazz vocalist, and songwriter, Alberta Hunter. Tells how she returned from retirement at age 82 to perform at The Cookery in Greenwich Village.

ALICE WALKER. James Hanley, David Lee, 1988. 30 min. color.
    Video. Films Inc.
A portrait of black author Alice Walker, whose novel *The Color Purple* became a successful movie. Traces her early roots in Georgia.

AMONG BROTHERS—POLITICS IN NEW ORLEANS. Paul
   Stekler, 1986. 59 min. color. Video. Deep South Productions.
An account of the 1986 election for mayor in New Orleans in
which the voters could choose between two black candidates.

ARLINGTON ESTATE BLACKS: AND, THE FREEDMAN'S
   VILLAGE. Sylvestre C. Watkins, 1984. 29 min. color. Video.
   Sylvestre C. Watkins Co.
A TV show produced for Reston (Virginia) Community Television.
Host: Sylvestre Watkins. Guests: Agnes Mullens, Dorothy Parks
Bailey.

ATTACKING THE COLOR BARRIER. Edwin C. Wilber, 1987
   (Black American Odyssey Series, Part 2). 19 min. color.
   16mm/Video. Handel Film Corporation.
Covers the black struggle for civil rights from the turn of the
century up to the 1963 demonstration in Washington.

BENJAMIN BANNEKER AND OTHER FAMOUS BLACK
   INVENTORS. Sylvestre C. Watkins, 1984. 29 min. color.
   Video. Sylvestre C. Watkins Co.
A TV program produced for Reston (Virginia) Community
Television. Host Sylvestre Watkins discusses famous black
inventors.

BLACK AMERICANS: PART I. Dallas County Community
   College, 1980. 28 min. color. Video. Dallas County Community
   College.
Presents the history of black Americans from the Reconstruction
period through World War II.

BLACK AMERICANS: PART II. Dallas County Community
   College, 1980. 28 min. color. Video. Dallas County Community
   College.
Covers the history of black Americans from the civil rights
movement to the present time.

BLACK AND TAN/ST. LOUIS BLUES. Dudley Murphy, 1929.
   16 min. b/w. Video. Blackhawk Films.
Features Duke Ellington and his Cotton Club Orchestra, Fredi

Washington, and the Hall Johnson Choir. This also is the only surviving film of singer Bessie Smith. Other important black entertainers are presented as well.

BLACK ARTISTS OF THE U.S.A. Irene Zmurkevycg, 1981 (Art in America Series, Part 4). 25 min. color. Video. Handel Film Corporation.
Covers the artistic achievements of black artists from slave artisans to black portrait painters, and the work of the Harlem Renaissance.

BLACK BUSINESSMEN. Post Newsweek, 1980 (Go Tell It Series). 30 min. color. Video. ABC Video Enterprises.
Three successful businessmen talk about their accomplishments and share their views on black economic power.

BLACK COLLEGES: A FIGHT FOR SURVIVAL. Post Newsweek, 1980 (Go Tell It Series). 30 min. color. Video. ABC Video Enterprises.
Studies the present status of black colleges: funding, competition from white colleges, and integration.

BLACK ENTERTAINERS. Post Newsweek, 1980 (Go Tell It Series). 30 min. color. Video. ABC Video Enterprises.
Features Ossie Davis and Ruby Dee, who talk about their life in the theater and prospects for black entertainers.

BLACK MAGIC. David Hoffman, 1984. 57 min. color. 16mm/Video. Varied Directions, PBS Video.
A film about a black jump-roping team from Hartford, Connecticut, that specializes in double Dutch. The girls win a prize and get to go to England for a visit.

BLACK MEN: AN ENDANGERED SPECIES. Stan Matthews, 1988. 58 min. color. Video. KERA-TV.
Studies the influences and problems faced by black men. Covers highlights of a conference that focused on ways of improving the black man's lot.

BLACK OLYMPIANS, 1904-1984. California Afro-American

Museum, 1986. 28 min. color. 16mm/Video. Churchill Films.
Traces the history of black American athletes up to 1984. Uses archival footage and interviews with Olympic medalists.

BLACK WOMEN: LIFESTYLES. Post Newsweek, 1980 (Go Tell
It Series). 30 min. color. Video. ABC Video Enterprises.
Describes the lives of two black women, one a handicapped teenager.

THE BLOODS OF 'NAM. Wayne Ewing, 1986. 60 min. color.
Video. PBS Video.
Features black Vietnam veterans who describe the discrimination and prejudice they encountered during the war.

BOOGIE WOOGIE BLUES. Phoenix Films and Video, 1986
(Tyler, Texas, Black Film Collection). 17 min. b/w. 16mm.
Phoenix Films and Video.
A recently released film originally made in 1948. Hadda Brooks, the singer, accompanies herself on the piano in a variety of musical selections.

BOOKER. Avon Kirkland, 1983. 55 min. color. 16mm. New
Images Production.
The story of the early years of Booker T. Washington, showing his struggles against poverty and the roots of his climb to success.

BOOKER. Walt Disney Educational Media, 1984. 40 min. color.
Video. Walt Disney Educational Media.
A look at the early life of Booker T. Washington and his quest for freedom during the final days of the Civil War.

BOOKER T. WASHINGTON'S TUSKEGEE AMERICA. Comco
Prod., 1981. 25 min. color. Video. AIMS Media.
A profile of the life of Booker T. Washington.

THE BOY KING. All American Television, 1986. 48 min. color;
and 30 min. version. Video. Coronet/MTI Film and Video.
A drama about the young Martin Luther King, Jr.'s early experiences with prejudice. Shows how his family provided love and support that moved him to lead the protest against

segregation. Howard E. Rollins plays the role of Martin Luther King, Sr.

BROKEN EARTH. Robert Freulich, 1986 (The Tyler, Texas, Black Film Collection). 17 min. b/w. 16mm. Phoenix Films and Video.
A re-release of a film with an all-black cast made in 1939. Features Clarence Muse. The story concerns a farmer who prays for his sick son.

A BROTHER WITH PERFECT TIMING. Chris Austin, n.d. 90 min. color. Video. Rhapsody Films.
Stars Abdullah Ibrahim, an exile from Cape Town, South Africa, who writes music for his septet, Ekaya, that includes spirituals, slow-rolling South African *marabi* rhythms, American jazz, African traditional melodies, and samba rhythms with roots in African music. Abdullah Ibrahim performs and talks about his life and music.

THE BURNING OF OSAGE. Louis Massiah, 1986. 60 min. color. Video. WHYY-TV.
Documents the disastrous confrontation between the City of Philadelphia and MOVE, a groups of activists, which led to a widespread fire that left many people homeless and killed eleven others.

BY-LINE NEWSREEL, NO. 1. Phoenix Films and Video, 1985 (The Tyler, Texas, Black Film Collection). 17 min. b/w. 16mm. Phoenix Films and Video.
A re-release of a 1956/57 newsreel. Includes interviews with officials in the Eisenhower administration. An example of newsreels made for black audiences in segregated theaters of the South and Southwest.

BY-LINE NEWSREEL, NO. 2. Phoenix Films and Video, 1985 (The Tyler, Texas, Black Film Collection). 17 min. b/w. 16mm. Phoenix Films and Video.
A re-issue of a 1956 newsreel featuring black government officials and a scene in which a black soldier helps a crippled white

engineer. An example of newsreels made for black audiences in segregated theaters of the South and Southwest.

BY-LINE NEWSREEL, NO. 3. Phoenix Films and Video, 1985 (The Tyler, Texas, Black Film Collection). 17 min. b/w. 16mm. Phoenix Films and Video.
A re-release of a 1956 newsreel presents interviews with members of the Eisenhower administration and scenes with U.S. Air Force athletes competing in Olympic tryouts. An example of newsreels made for black audiences in segregated theaters of the South and Southwest.

BY-LINE NEWSREEL, NO. 4. Phoenix Films and Video, 1985 (The Tyler, Texas, Black Film Collection). 17 min. b/w. 16mm. Phoenix Films and Video.
A re-issue of 1956 newsreel footage showing black Republicans at the Republican National Convention in San Francisco. Also includes Morgan State football team in action and Dodger catcher Roy Campanella receiving a ball thrown by President Eisenhower to open the World Series. An example of newsreels made for black audiences in segregated theaters of the South and Southwest.

THE CALL OF THE JITTERBUG. Tana Ross, Jesper Sorensen, and Vibeke Winding, 1988. 35 min. color. Video. Filmakers Library.
Documents the dance craze called jitterbug (also knows as the lindy hop or swing dancing) in the 1930s. Its center of activity was the Savoy Ballroom in Harlem, and at the Savoy the color barrier was broken when whites and blacks danced together.

CHILDREN OF PRIDE. Carole Langer, 1983. 60 min. color. 16mm/Video. Carole Langer Productions.
About a black man who adopts 23 children who are handicapped and how he inspires them to self-improvement.

CISSY HOUSTON: SWEET INSPIRATION. Dave Davidson, 1987. 58 min. color. 16mm/Video. The Cinema Guild.
A portrait of the famous singer who has performed both gospel and popular music in her career. Covers her concerts, performances at clubs, and gospel choir rehearsals.

CLINICAL CEREBROVASCULAR DISEASE IN HYPERTENSIVE BLACKS. Emory University School of Medicine, 1986. 33 min. color. Video. Emory Medical TV Network.
Examines the problem of strokes among blacks and how it is caused by environment.

COLOR. Warington Hudlin, 1983. 25 min. color. Video. Black Filmmaker Foundation.
Tells how color and class discrimination affect the lives of blacks as exemplified by one light-skinned and one dark-skinned woman.

CROCODILE CONSPIRACY. Zeinabu Irene Davis, 1986. 13 min. color. 16mm/Video. Third World Newsreel.
A black female filmmaker made this film, a drama about a black middle-aged teacher in Watts who wants to visit her parents' homeland of Cuba. Although the crocodile is Cuba's national symbol and represents the shape of the island, it also reflects the menace that many of the teacher's friends think Cuba to be.

CRUSADE FOR CIVIL RIGHTS. Handel Film Corporation, 1987 (Black American Odyssey Series, Part 3). 21 min. color. 16mm/Video. Handel Film Corporation.
Traces the civil rights movement from 1963 to the present.

DANCE BLACK AMERICA. Suny, Bam, Pennebaker, 1984. 87 min. color. 16mm/Video. Pennebaker Associates.
Leading black American dance groups participated in the Dance Black America Festival at the Brooklyn Academy of Music in 1983. Shows various dances performed.

DEEP ELLUM BLUES. Betty Jo Taylor, 1986. 16 min. color. 16mm/Video. J. C. Penny.
Covers a performance of "Deep Ellum Blues" by the Dallas Black Dance Theater. Explains the purpose of the production.

THE DIFFERENT DRUMMER: BLACKS IN THE MILITARY—FROM GOLD BARS TO SILVER STARS. WNET-TV, 1983. 60 min. color. 16mm/Video. Films Inc.
High-ranking black officers describe how they rose in the U.S.

military.

THE DIFFERENT DRUMMER: BLACKS IN THE
MILITARY—THE TROOPS. WNET-TV, 1983. 58 min. color.
16mm/Video. Films Inc.
Traces the participation of black soldiers from World War I to
the war in Vietnam. Uses historic footage and photographs.

THE DIFFERENT DRUMMER: BLACKS IN THE
MILITARY—UNKNOWN SOLDIERS. WNET-TV, 1983. 58
min. color. 16mm/Video. Films Inc.
Explains how black soldiers' involvement in the military grew in
importance from the Civil War to World War I.

EPIDEMIOLOGY OF HYPERTENSION IN BLACKS WORLD.
Emory University School of Medicine, 1986. 30 min. color.
Video. Emory Medical TV Network.
Experts discuss the impact of modern life on the black population.

ERNIE ANDREWS: BLUES FOR CENTRAL AVENUE. Lois
Shelton, 1987. 50 min. color. 16mm/Video. Shelton
Productions.
The jazz vocalist Ernie Andrews remembers black music of the
1940s in Los Angeles and the events of his life.

ETHNIC NOTIONS. Marlow Riggs, 1987. 56 min. color. Video.
California Newsreel.
Shows how stereotypes promoted anti-black prejudice via cartoons,
movies, songs, advertisements, and household artifacts that
permeated culture from the 1820s to the civil rights era. Helps the
viewer develop a critical eye for stereotyping.

EYES ON THE PRIZE—AMERICA'S CIVIL RIGHTS YEARS:
EPISODE 1. AWAKENING (1945-56). WGBH-TV and
Blackside, Inc., 1986. 60 min. color. Video. PBS Video.
Julian Bond narrates this documentary that focuses on the 1955
lynching of Emmett Till and the 1955-56 Montgomery, Alabama,
boycott. Shows race relations in the South at mid-century.

EYES ON THE PRIZE—AMERICA'S CIVIL RIGHTS YEARS:

EPISODE 2. FIGHTING BACK (1957-62) WGBH-TV and Blackside, Inc., 1986. 60 min. color. Video. PBS Video.
Discusses the court cases of the 1940s, the 1954 Supreme Court decision *Brown v. Board of Education*, the integration of Little Rock's Central High School, and James Meredith's enrollment at the University of Mississippi.

EYES ON THE PRIZE—AMERICA'S CIVIL RIGHTS YEARS: EPISODE 3. AIN'T SCARED OF YOUR JAILS (1960-61). WGBH-TV and Blackside, Inc., 1986. 60 min. color. Video. PBS Video.
Studies the impact of the lunch counter sit-ins and the formation of SNCC on the 1960 presidential campaign and the freedom rides.

EYES ON THE PRIZE—AMERICA'S CIVIL RIGHTS YEARS: EPISODE 4. NO EASY WALK (1962-66). WGBH-TV and Blackside, Inc., 1986. 60 min. color. Video. PBS Video.
Shows the importance of marches and mass demonstrations, such as Albany, Georgia, Birmingham, Alabama, and the 1963 march on Washington, D.C., in shifting federal policy.

EYES ON THE PRIZE—AMERICA'S CIVIL RIGHTS YEARS: EPISODE 5. MISSISSIPPI: IS THIS AMERICA? (1962-64). WGBH-TV and Blackside, Inc., 1986. 60 min. color. Video. PBS Video.
Discusses the campaign for voting rights in Mississippi and the murder of three civil rights workers.

EYES ON THE PRIZE—AMERICA'S CIVIL RIGHTS YEARS: EPISODE 6. BRIDGE TO FREEDOM (1965). WGBH-TV and Blackside, Inc., 1986. 60 min. color. Video. PBS Video.
Describes the 50-mile march to Selma, Alabama, which brought thousands of blacks and whites together.

EYES ON THE PRIZE—AMERICA AT THE RACIAL CROSSROADS, 1965-1985: PROGRAM 1. THE TIME HAS COME (1964-1966). Blackside, Inc., 1990. 60 min. color. Video. PBS Video.

Presents New York's Harlem of the 1960s and the rise of Malcolm X to a position of influence. Also covers the activities of African Americans in Alabama in their drive to vote, James Meredith's "March Against Fear" from Memphis, Tennessee, to Jackson, Mississippi, John Hulett's attempt to create an independent political party in Alabama, and SNCC chairman Stokely Carmichael's call for "Black Power." Explains the symbolism of the black panther in the freedom movement.

EYES ON THE PRIZE—AMERICA AT THE RACIAL
CROSSROADS, 1965-1985: PROGRAM 2. TWO SOCIETIES
(1965-1968). Blackside, Inc., 1990. 60 min. color. Video. PBS
Video.
Studies attempts to expand civil rights in the North with particular focus on the Southern Christian Leadership Conference's efforts to achieve open housing in Chicago. Describes civil disorder in Detroit and other cities in the summer of 1967 and the findings of the Kerner Commission.

EYES ON THE PRIZE—AMERICA AT THE RACIAL
CROSSROADS, 1965-1985: PROGRAM 3. POWER! (1966-
1968). Blackside, Inc., 1990. 60 min. color. Video. PBS Video.
Discusses in detail the efforts of blacks to gain power in three communities between 1966 and 1968: in Cleveland, where Carl Stokes became the first black mayor; in Oakland, California, where Bobby Seale and Huey Newton founded the Black Panther Party for Self-Defense; and in New York City, where blacks tried to control education in the Ocean Hill-Brownsville section of Brooklyn.

EYES ON THE PRIZE—AMERICA AT THE RACIAL
CROSSROADS, 1965-1985: PROGRAM 4. THE PROMISED
LAND (1967-1968). Blackside, Inc., 1990. 60 min. color.
Video. PBS Video.
Examines Martin Luther King's concerns about the Vietnam War and the hostile response to his criticisms of U.S. policy. Reviews King's work on behalf of the poor, including his plans for the Poor People's Campaign in Washington, and the events leading to his assassination. Shows the national unrest following his death. Includes King's "mountaintop" speech in Memphis.

EYES ON THE PRIZE—AMERICA AT THE RACIAL
CROSSROADS, 1965-1985: PROGRAM 5. AIN'T GONNA
SHUFFLE NO MORE (1964-1972). Blackside, Inc., 1990. 60
min. color. Video. PBS Video.
Depicts the rise of black consciousness through three stories: 1,
the transformation of boxer Cassius Clay to Muhammad Ali; 2,
the student takeover at Howard University to move it toward a
black-oriented curriculum; and 3, the gathering of black activists
in Gary, Indiana, for the National Black Political Convention of
1972.

EYES ON THE PRIZE—AMERICA AT THE RACIAL
CROSSROADS, 1965-1985: PROGRAM 6. A NATION OF
LAW? (1968-1971). Blackside, Inc., 1990. 60 min. color. Video.
PBS Video.
Looks at the problems of the Black Panther Party with the police
and the FBI in Chicago. Discusses the FBI's plan to undermine
the efforts of black organizations and Richard Nixon's call for
"law and order" as a campaign issue in 1972. Documents the
rebellion of inmates at the Attica Correction Facility in upstate
New York.

EYES ON THE PRIZE—AMERICA AT THE RACIAL
CROSSROADS, 1965-1985: PROGRAM 7. THE KEYS TO
THE KINGDOM (1974-1980). Blackside, Inc., 1990. 60 min.
color. Video. PBS Video.
Describes the turmoil in Boston over the desegregation of the
public schools by court order. Also covers affirmative action in
Atlanta under its first black mayor and the impact of the Supreme
Court ruling in favor of Alan Bakke's admission to the University
of California-Davis Medical School.

EYES ON THE PRIZE—AMERICA AT THE RACIAL
CROSSROADS, 1965-1985: PROGRAM 8, BACK TO THE
MOVEMENT (1979-mid-1980s). Blackside, Inc., 1990. 60 min.
color. Video. PBS Video.
A visit to Overtown, a black neighborhood in Miami once known
as the Harlem of the South. Depicts the decline of Overtown and
the Miami riot of 1980. Meanwhile, in Chicago black activists
initiate a grassroots reform movement that eventually leads to the

election of Chicago's first black mayor. This program concludes with a review of the many people who contributed to the black freedom movement.

FAMOUS AMOS: BUSINESS BEHIND THE COOKIE. Coronet/MTI Film and Video, 1984. 25 min. color. 16mm/Video. Coronet/MTI Film and Video.
Shows how Wally Amos, the noted black entrepreneur, built a multi-million-dollar cookie empire with little formal business knowledge.

FIRST BLACK GRAD FROM ANNAPOLIS. Sylvestre C. Watkins, 1983. 26 min. color. Video. Sylvestre C. Watkins Co.
A cable TV production for Reston, Virginia, with Syl Watkins as host. Examines the role of blacks in the Navy. Wesley Brown, the first black graduate from Annapolis, is interviewed.

FLYERS IN SEARCH OF A DREAM. WGBH-TV, 1986. 60 min. color. Video. PBS Video.
An account of pioneering black aviators in the U.S. during the 1920s and 1930s.

FREDERICK DOUGLASS: AN AMERICAN LIFE. William Greaves, 1986. 30 min. color. Video. Your World Video.
The life story of the great black leader and abolitionist is told in dramatized form.

THE FREEDOM STATION. WETA-TV, 1989. 30 min. color. Video. WETA-TV.
This is a drama about the activities in a Maryland Underground Railroad safe house around 1850. An escaped slave girl and a farm girl from an abolitionist family meet and share their experiences. Reveals the complexities of freedom and of helping slaves escape.

FROM JUMPSTREET: BLACK INFLUENCE IN THE RECORDING INDUSTRY. WETA-TV, 1987. 30 min. color. Video. WETA-TV.
Singer, songwriter Oscar Brown, Jr., is host on this report about the impact of black musicians on the recording industry.

FROM JUMPSTREET: BLACK MUSIC IN THEATER AND FILM. WETA-TV, 1987. 30 min. color. Video. WETA-TV.
Oscar Brown, Jr., is host for this program about black performers and their contributions to stage and screen.

FROM JUMPSTREET: DANCE TO THE MUSIC. WETA-TV, 1987. 30 min. color. Video. WETA-TV.
Oscar Brown, Jr., hosts this program on the contributions of black performers to dance.

FROM JUMPSTREET: EARLY JAZZ. WETA-TV, 1987. 30 min. color. Video. WETA-TV.
Host Oscar Brown, Jr., explores the black musical experience in the early days of jazz.

FROM JUMPSTREET: GOSPEL AND SPIRITUALS. WETA-TV, 1987. 30 min. color. Video. WETA-TV.
Host Oscar Brown, Jr., describes the black musical experience in gospel and spirituals. Features performances of gospel and spirituals.

FROM JUMPSTREET: JAZZ GETS BLUE. WETA-TV, 1987. 30 min. color. Video. WETA-TV.
Oscar Brown, Jr., tells how the blues evolved as a black musical expression.

FROM JUMPSTREET: JAZZ PEOPLE. WETA-TV, 1987. 30 min. color. Video. WETA-TV.
Singer-songwriter Oscar Brown, Jr., presents performances by top black jazz musicians. Uses archival film footage and still photos of performers of the past.

FROM JUMPSTREET: JAZZ VOCALISTS. WETA-TV, 1987. 30 min. color. Video. WETA-TV.
Oscar Brown, Jr., is the host for this program that features outstanding black jazz vocalists.

FROM JUMPSTREET: SOUL. WETA-TV, 1987. 30 min. color. Video. WETA-TV.
Singer-songwriter Oscar Brown, Jr., is host for this demonstration

of soul music.

FROM JUMPSTREET: THE SOURCE OF SOUL. WETA-TV,
    1987. 30 min. color. Video. WETA-TV.
Singer-songwriter Oscar Brown, Jr., reviews the roots of soul
music.

FROM JUMPSTREET: WEST AFRICAN HERITAGE. WETA-
    TV, 1987. 30 min. color. Video. WETA-TV.
Singer-songwriter Oscar Brown, Jr., traces the black musical
heritage from its African roots.

FRONTLINE: THE   BOMBING   OF   WEST   PHILLY.
    Documentary Consortium, 1987. 60 min. color. Video. PBS
    Video.
Reviews the history of MOVE, the black revolutionary movement,
and what led to the violent destruction of a black Philadelphia
neighborhood.

GETTING TO KNOW BARBARA. CBS News, 1984. 12 min.
    color. Video. Carousel Film and Video.
About a black woman who is the head of a successful advertising
agency and how she rose from poverty.

GLORIA: A CASE OF ALLEGED POLICE BRUTALITY. O.
    Rudavsky, 1983. 27 min. color. 16mm/Video. Filmakers
    Library.
About a police shooting that involved issues of racism and power
politics.

GLORY. Edward Zwick, 1989. 122 min. color. Video.
    RCA/Columbia Pictures Home Video.
This feature film tells the story of Colonel Robert Shaw and his
54th Massachusetts regiment, one of the first black fighting units
on the Union side of the Civil War. Discusses the difficulties
experienced by the regiment in gaining acceptance and shows the
troops in action courageously fighting in the attack on Fort
Wagner. With Matthew Broderick, Denzel Washington, Morgan
Freeman, and Andre Braugher.

GO TELL IN ON THE MOUNTAIN. Films in Focus, 1984. 96 min. color. 16mm/Video. New Line Cinema.
An adaptation of James Baldwin's novel about an urban family that ponders its roots in the rural South.

GOTTA MAKE THIS JOURNEY. Eye of the Storm Productions, 1983. 58 min. color. Video. Black Filmmaker Foundation.
Each member of the vocal group Sweet Honey in the Rock discusses her background and the political and social significance of their music. Covers performances at Gallaudet College and the Sisterfire Festival.

GULLAH TALES. Gary Moss, 1986. 29 min. color. 16mm/Video. Georgia State University.
Contains dramatizations of two Gullah folktales, one from Africa and one plantation-based. Gullah is the black Creole language used on plantations of Georgia and South Carolina before the Civil War.

HALF SLAVE, HALF FREE. Janna Kroyt Brandt, 1985. 113 min. color. Video. Sony Video Software.
A dramatic realization of the story "Solomon Northrup's Odyssey" that tells the true story of a free black man who was put into slavery for 12 years. Directed by Gordon Parks.

HANDS THAT PICKED COTTON—THE STORY OF BLACK POLITICS IN TODAY'S RURAL SOUTH. Paul Stakler, Alan Bell, 1984. 60 min. color. 16mm/Video. Louisiana Committee for the Humanities.
Tells how blacks run for office and problems blacks face when they win control in a small rural community.

HOME TO BUXTON. Claire Prieto, 1988. 29 min. color. 16mm/Video. McNabb and Connolly.
In 1849 a small town in southwestern Ontario, Canada, served as home for blacks fleeing the American South. Many descendents still live here and sponsor an annual homecoming.

HOMECOMIN'. Sati Jamal and Reginald Brown, 1980. 27 min. color. 16mm/Video. BFA Educational Media.

The reenactment of a true experience of a black father separated from his family, a dilemma that affects a large number of black families in the U.S. Examines the impact of separation on the children.

A HOUSE DIVIDED. Burwell Ware, 1987. 56 min. color. Video.
    Burwell Ware.
Depicts segregation in 1962 in New Orleans via a typical event in which a black minister was refused service in a cafeteria and suffered injuries from rough handling by the police.

THE HOWARD THEATRE: A CLASS ACT. Jackson Frost, 1985. 35 min. color. Video. WETA-TV.
The Howard Theatre (c. 1910) was located in Washington, D.C., and was one of the first theaters for blacks in the U.S. Describes the artists and the neighborhood people.

I PROMISE TO REMEMBER: THE STORY OF FRANKIE LYMON AND THE TEENAGERS. Steven Fischler, Joel Sucher, and Jane Praeger, 1983. 27 min. color. 16mm/Video. The Cinema Guild.
A much-awarded film about a popular black rock-and-roll group whose music broke the color barrier. Traces their rise from Harlem street corner sessions to national success and their eventual breakup that led to a tragic end for Frankie Lymon.

IN A JAZZ WAY: A PORTRAIT OF MURA DEHN. Pam Katz, Louise Ghertier, 1986. 28 min. color. 16mm/Video. Filmakers Library.
Mura Dehn is a Russian dancer and filmmaker who, for over half a century, has documented black social dance. Gives examples of the lindy hop, bebop, and break dancing and explains what the various dances may reveal about black culture. Also features some jazz dancing by Mura Dehn herself at 82 years.

IN THE BEST OF TIMES. KCTS-TV, 1980. 29 min. color. Video. Penn State AV Services.
Tells how Seattle's blacks are not benefiting from the city's economic boom.

JAZZ IN EXILE. Chuck France, 1982. 58 min. color. 16mm/Video. Rhapsody Films.
Because of racism and lack of support, some jazz musicians moved to Europe. Includes performances and interviews that describe their experiences and why some of them are now returning to the U.S.

JAZZ IN THE MAGIC CITY. Stanley Jaffe, 1987. 30 min. color. Video. Sandy Jaffe.
How black jazz musicians in Birmingham, Alabama, learned to create jazz. Uses archival footage, interviews, and photographs.

JOE'S BED-STUY BARBERSHOP: WE CUT HEADS. Spike Lee, 1983. 60 min. b/w. 16mm. First Run/Icarus Films.
Spike Lee's master's thesis film, which was shot on a meager budget of $13,000, won the Student Academy Award. The story concerns a barber who becomes a partner to a local numbers racketeer despite his effort to lead a life outside of crime.

JOHN JACKSON: FOLK GUITARIST. Sylvestre C. Watkins, 1979. 28 min. color. Video. Sylvestre Watkins Co.
Guitarist John Jackson is guest on this TV program for which he plays a selection of folk songs.

JUST AN OVERNIGHT GUEST. Barbara Bryant, 1983. 38 min. color. 16mm/Video. BFA Educational Media.
About an abused girl who is temporarily taken in by a black family who later decide to keep her for good. Stars Richard Roundtree and Rosalind Cash. Depicts black family life in the U.S.

KICKING HIGH . . . IN THE GOLDEN YEARS. Grania Gurievitch, 1988. 58 min. color. 16mm/Video. New Day Films.
Shows the dignity of aging through this profile of black middle-class senior citizens from Queens, New York. Shows them at home and in their senior center participating in an amateur performance.

LAND WHERE THE BLUES BEGAN. Alan Lomax, Mississippi Authority for Educational Television, 1982. 58 min. color.

16mm/Video. Phoenix Films and Video.
Depicts the life of poor blacks in rural Mississippi and their style
of music—the blues. Includes interviews and performances of blues
music by local musicians sometimes using homemade instruments.
Directed and narrated by Alan Lomax.

LANGSTON HUGHES: DREAM KEEPER. St. Clair Bourne,
    1986. 60 min. color. 16mm/Video. New York Center for Visual
    History (16mm) and CPB Annenberg Project (Video).
A portrait of Langston Hughes, poet. Contains archival footage,
interviews, and poetry readings.

LOUIS ARMSTRONG, THE GENTLE GIANT OF JAZZ.
    Comco Productions, 1984. 29 min. color. Video. AIMS Media.
Uses old footage and photographs to study the life of Louis
Armstrong and his achievements in the world of music.

MAKING *DO THE RIGHT THING*. St. Clair Bourne, 1989. 58
    min. color. 16mm/Video. First Run/Icarus Films.
A behind-the-scenes look at the making of Spike Lee's successful
film *Do the Right Thing*. Shows the neighborhood where the film
was shot, Brooklyn's Bedford-Stuyvesant district, before and after
the arrival of the film crew. Some of the featured actors express
their feelings about the experience of making the film and about
incidents that influenced the script.

MARTIN   LUTHER   KING,   JR.:   LETTER   FROM
    BIRMINGHAM JAIL. Learning Corp. of America, 1988. 25
    min. color. 16mm/Video. Coronet/MTI Film and Video.
Robert Guillaume is host for this program about the segregation
and violence against blacks in Birmingham, Alabama, and the
circumstances that caused Martin Luther King, Jr., to be put in
jail. Tells how he came to write the letter that became a
fundamental document in the struggle for civil rights. Franz
Turner plays the part of King.

MARYLAND BLACKS. Sylvestre C. Watkins, 1986. 28 min. color.
    Video. Sylvestre C. Watkins Co.
A production telecast on September 18, 1986 for the Syl Watkins

show. Covers the history of blacks in Maryland up to 1985. Emphasizes black achievements.

THE MASTERS OF DISASTER. Patricia Wetmore, 1985. 29 min.
    color. 16mm/Video. Indiana University.
Some black inner-city elementary school students became champions in a national chess competition. Shows the chess team at home, at practice, on a trip to Japan, and on a visit to the White House.

MIDNIGHT SHADOW. Phoenix Films and Video, 1986 (The
    Tyler, Texas, Black Film Collection). 54 min. b/w. 16mm.
    Phoenix Films and Video.
A recent re-release of a 1939 movie about two friends who set out to find the murderer of a Texas oil entrepreneur. With an all-black cast.

MINNIE THE MOOCHER AND MANY, MANY MORE. Manny
    Pittson, 1981. 50 min. color and b/w. 16mm/Video. First
    Run/Icarus Films.
Cab Calloway takes the viewer on a tour of Harlem jazz clubs of the 1930s and 1940s. He reminisces about the star performers of the era, such as Lena Horne, Duke Ellington, Louis Armstrong, Count Basie, and Cab Calloway himself.

MIRACLE IN HARLEM. Jack Kemp, 1986 (The Tyler, Texas,
    Black Film Collection). 80 min. b/w. Phoenix Films and Video.
A re-release of a 1948 movie featuring black actors. The story concerns a swindle and two murders.

MISSISSIPPI DELTA BLUES. Anthony Herrera, 1984. 29 min.
    color. 16mm. Anthony Herrera.
A document of the land and people where the blues originated. Observes one of the last great delta blues singers performing.

MOVE: CONFRONTATION IN PHILADELPHIA. Jane Mancini,
    Karen Pomer, 1980. 60 min. b/w. Video. Temple University.
Discusses the violent removal of MOVE, a Philadelphia-based group of black political activists. Examines media bias and police harassment.

MURDER IN HARLEM. Oscar Micheaux, 1986 (The Tyler, Texas, Black Film Collection). 102 min. b/w. 16mm. Phoenix Films and Video.
This film is a re-release of a 1935 film featuring black actors. The story involves a night watchman on trial for murder. A lawyer and the night watchman's sister search for the real murderer.

THE NEGRO ENSEMBLE COMPANY. Richard Kilberg, 1987. 58 min. color. Video. Films for the Humanities.
Tells of the achievements of the famous theatrical company founded by Douglas Turner Ward and Robert Hooks. Includes scenes of the group's memorable productions.

NEVER TURN BACK: THE LIFE OF FANNIE LOU HAMER. Bill Buckley, 1983. 58 min. color. 16mm/Video. Rediscovery Productions.
Fannie Lou Hamer is a black sharecropper and activist in Mississippi who helped create the New South.

NO MAPS ON MY TAPS. George T. Nierenberg, 1979. 58 min. color. 16mm/Video. Direct Cinema Ltd.
Uses archival footage to study jazz tap dancing in the 1930s. Also provides profiles of three surviving jazz tap dancers.

ON MY OWN—THE TRADITIONS OF DAISY TURNER. University of Vermont, 1986. 28 min. color. Video. Filmakers Library.
This is about the life of a 102-year-old black woman whose ancestors were freed slaves who settled in Vermont.

OTHELLO. Liz White, 1980. 115 min. b/w. 16mm. Liz White.
The Shakespeare play is performed by an all-black cast. Has a jazz score by Jonas Gwangwa. Originally made in 1966 but released in 1980.

THE PEOPLE UNITED. Alonzo Speight, 1985. 60 min. color. 16mm/Video. Third World Newsreel.
An account of the situation in the Roxbury section of Boston. Tells of the many murders of black people, unwarranted arrests, police brutality, and the fear and anger that arose over the

incidents. With narration by Abby Lincoln.

PROPHET OF PEACE: THE STORY OF DR. MARTIN
    LUTHER KING, JR. Harold Lawrence, 1986. 23 min. color.
    Video. University of California Extension Media Center.
Based on drawings by Morrie Turner in the style of his "Wee
Pals" cartoon strip. Various characters of "Wee Pals" narrate the
story of Dr. King. Includes excerpts from two of his famous
speeches.

PSYCHOSOCIAL AND ENVIRONMENTAL FACTORS IN
    HYPERTENSION IN BLACKS. Emory University School of
    Medicine, 1986. 24 min. color. Video. Emory Medical TV
    Network.
A report on the evidence about the effect of environment on
black hypertension.

RACE AGAINST PRIME TIME. David Shulman, 1985. 58 min.
    color. Video. California Newsreel, Third World Newsreel.
Shows how present-day stereotyping is no longer a matter of
blatant distortion but of selection and omission. Looks at how
television news gets made and follows TV newsmen as they decide
what will become the news in an environment that emphasizes a
white view of black life.

RACISM 101. David Fanning, 1988 (Frontline Series). 60 min.
    color. Video. PBS Video.
Discusses controversy between black and white students at the
University of Michigan.

REFLECTIONS. Kim Watson, Caleb Oglesby, 1987. 6 min. color.
    Video. Third World Newsreel.
Uses experimental film techniques to weave images or "reflections"
on the civil rights movement. The voice of Martin Luther King,
Jr., provides the unifying thread for this program.

THE ROAD TO BROWN. William A. Elwood, 1989. 90 min.
    color; 50 min. version also available. Video. California
    Newsreel.
This is a detailed account of segregation in the southern U.S. and

the efforts of a little-known black lawyer, Charles Houston, who was a pioneer in fighting segregation on legal grounds. Shows how Houston documented the Jim Crow social structure in a movie he made in 1934. Explains the various court cases that eventually led to the landmark decision, *Brown v. Board of Education.*

ROAD TO FREEDOM. Handel Film Corporation, 1986 (Black American Odyssey, Part 1). 20 min. color. 16mm/Video. Handel Film Corporation.
A historical account of black Americans from the time of Crispus Attucks to the Spanish-American War.

SECOND AMERICAN REVOLUTION: BLACK HISTORY. Corporation for Entertainment and Learning, 1985. 58 min. color. Video. PBS Video.
Traces black history from the 19th century through the Civil War as told by Ossie Davis and Ruby Dee with Bill Moyers in his "Walk Through the Twentieth Century" TV series.

SHIRLEY VERRETT: A FILM BIOGRAPHY OF THE BLACK DIVA. RM Arts, 1985. 60 min. color. Video. Kultur.
Follows the career and private life of black diva Shirley Verrett. Film includes appearances by Claudio Abbado, Plácido Domingo, Jon Vickers, and other prominent musicians performing arias and songs.

A SINGING STREAM: A BLACK FAMILY CHRONICLE. University of North Carolina, 1987. 57 min. color. Video. Davenport Films.
Depicts the role of gospel music in maintaining family loyalty and sense of purpose for a Southern black family from the 1930s to the present.

"THERE WAS ALWAYS SUN SHINING SOMEPLACE": LIFE IN THE NEGRO BASEBALL LEAGUES. Craig Davidson, 1984. 16mm/Video. Refocus Films.
James Earl Jones serves as narrator for this history of black baseball from 1887 to 1950. Uses historical footage.

THURGOOD MARSHALL: PORTRAIT OF AN AMERICAN
    HERO. Video Productions, 1985. 28 min. color. Video.
    WETA-TV.
An account of the first black Supreme Court justice. Tells about
his efforts for the cause of civil rights.

TWO DOLLARS AND A DREAM. Stanley Nelson, 1987. 56
    min. color. 16mm/Video. Filmakers Library.
The life story of Madame C. J. Walker, a self-made black
millionairess and her daughter, the black patron of the Harlem
Renaissance. Tells how Madame Walker, the child of former
slaves, built her hair and skin products business and provides a
history of black America from 1867 to 1933.

THE VANISHING FAMILY: CRISIS IN BLACK AMERICA.
    Ruth Streeter, 1986. 64 min. color. Video. Carousel Film and
    Video.
A CBS Reports production featuring Bill Moyers who discusses
the problems of single-parent families in Newark, New Jersey.
Covers teenage pregnancy, welfare, changing values.

THE VANITIES. Phoenix Films and Video, 1986 (The Tyler,
    Texas, Black Film Collection). 17 min. b/w. 16mm. Phoenix
    Films and Video.
This film is a re-issue of a 1946 production. The film involves a
master of ceremonies of a nightclub act who presides over black
performers who sing or dance.

VIDALIA MCCLOUD: A FAMILY STORY. Theresa Mack, 1986.
    28 min. color. Video. Carousel Film and Video.
Follows three years in the life of a black family in central Florida.
Vidalia is a single parent with three boys to raise. Shows her in
various jobs—as as fruit picker and short-order cook.

VISIONS OF THE SPIRIT. Elena Featherston, 1988. 58 min.
    color. Video. Women Make Movies.
A profile of Alice Walker, noted black author, at home and on
location for the movie version of her book, *The Color Purple*.

VOICES OF THE GODS. Akuaba Productions, 1985. 60 min. color. 16mm/Video. Third World Newsreel.
Studies the practices and beliefs of African religious traditions practiced in the U.S. The African Akan and Yoruba traditions are represented.

WE SHALL OVERCOME. Jim Brown, Ginger Brown, Harold Leverthal, George Stoney, 1989. 58 min. color. Video. California Newsreel.
Chronicles the history of the song "We Shall Overcome" from its roots in South Carolina as the spiritual "I Shall Overcome" through its transformation in the civil rights movement in the 1960s to its present-day use worldwide, including South Africa where Bishop Tutu is shown singing the song. Harry Belafonte is the narrator for this documentary.

WE STILL HAVE A DREAM. Everett Marshburn and Lenora Lee, 1988. 27 min. color. Video. Maryland Public Television.
Participants in the original march on Washington for jobs and freedom remember the march and reflect on changes that have taken place in recent years.

WILD WOMEN DON'T HAVE THE BLUES. Carole van Falkenburg and Christina Dall, 1989. 58 min. color. 16mm/Video. California Newsreel.
Traces the roots of blues music in the work songs of black field hands and tells of the lives and times of Ma Rainey, Bessie Smith, Ida Cox, Alberta Hunter, Ethel Waters, and others who performed the blues in the industrial North. Includes early blues renditions that have become classics.

ZARICO. Jacques Vallée, Michel Brault, Daniel Pinard, 1986. 58 min. color. 16mm/Video. National Film Board of Canada.
A film about the folk music of the black Francophone Creole culture of Southeastern Louisiana. Various musical influences and the development of the Creole style are traced. Describes the impact of Zarico on jazz, the blues, and rock.

ASIAN-AMERICANS

ASIANS IN AMERICA: A RELIGION IN RETREAT. Centre
    Productions, 1986. 13 min. color. Video. Centre Productions.
Shows how Buddhism was decimated by Communists in most
countries of Asia and why Buddhist leaders fled to the West.
Several teachers and scholars discuss the religious persecution they
endured before their escape.

ASIANS IN AMERICA: VIETNAMESE BUDDHISM IN
    AMERICA. Centre Productions, 1986. 14 min. color. Video.
    Centre Productions.
Tells how many Buddhist leaders have fled to the U.S. where they
serve immigrant communities. Follows Dr. Thich Thien-An, who
is head of the Vietnamese Buddhist church in America, to show
the form of Buddhism practiced by this group.

ASIANS IN AMERICA: VIETNAMESE REFUGEES IN
    AMERICA. Centre Productions, 1988. 14 min. color. Video.
    Centre Productions.
Tells how most of the refugees who fled from Vietnam came to
America. Describes problems of integrating them into American
culture.

BETWEEN TWO WORLDS: THE HMONG SHAMAN IN
    AMERICA. Taggart Siegel, 1986. 28 min. b/w. Video. Film
    Ideas Inc./Third World Newsreel.
Shows how the rituals of the East Asian Hmong shaman must
compete with American customs and beliefs. Includes footage of
shamanic rituals and ceremonies, such as animal sacrifice and
trancelike healing.

BLUE COLLAR AND BUDDHA. Taggart Siegel, Kati Johnson,
    1988. 57 min. color. Video. Crosscurrent Media.
About refugees from Laos who settled in a small Midwestern
blue-collar town in the U.S. and who are experiencing some
persecution because of their attempts to preserve their traditional
culture. Winner of many awards.

CARVED IN SILENCE. Felicia Lowe, n.d. 45 min. color. Video. Crosscurrent Media.
This is the story of Angel Island in San Francisco Bay where from 1882-1943 Chinese who sought entry into the U.S. were detained for long periods of time. Covers the history of this "Ellis Island of the West" with interviews and reenactments in actual detention barracks. Winner of several awards.

CHINESE GOLD. Gold Mountain Productions, 1988. 40 min. color. Video. Chip Taylor Communications.
An account of the almost-forgotten contributions of Chinese immigrants in constructing the railroads that opened up the American West. Also discusses their other contributions to economic development.

THE COLOR OF HONOR: THE JAPANESE-AMERICAN SOLDIER IN WWII. Loni Ding, n.d. 90 min. color. Video. Crosscurrent Media.
A complete survey of Japanese-Americans in World War II. Tells about the 442nd Regimental Combat Team, the most decorated unit in U.S. history, about the linguists who helped decode top secret military plans, and about some resisters who challenged the constitutionality of the camp in which Japanese-Americans were incarcerated.

CONVERSATIONS: BEFORE THE WAR/AFTER THE WAR. Karen Ishizuka and Robert Nakamura, 1986. 29 min. color. Video. Crosscurrent Media.
Compares the lives of Japanese-Americans before World War II and after. Three fictionalized characters reveal the effects of World War II when Japanese-Americans were incarcerated.

A DOLLAR A DAY, TEN CENTS A DANCE. Geoffrey Dunn and Mark Schwartz, n.d. 29 min. color. Video. Crosscurrent Media.
This is the history of more than 100,000 Pinoys (Filipino-Americans) who immigrated to America between 1924 and 1935 to work in the farmlands. Filipino brides were not allowed into the U.S. and Filipinos could not marry white women, so they created bachelor societies where cockfights, poker games, and

dance halls served as entertainment. This video has won several prizes.

EAST OF OCCIDENTAL. Lucy Ostrander, 1986. 29 min. color. 16mm/Video. Prairie Fire Pictures.
The history of the Chinatown in Seattle, Washington. Shows how Chinese-, Japanese-, and Filipino-Americans work together to gain benefits for their people.

THE FALL OF THE I HOTEL. Curtis Choy, 1983. 57 min. color. 16mm/Video. Crosscurrent Media, Third World Newsreel.
A history of the Filipinos in San Francisco's Manilatown and the eviction of tenants from the International Hotel in 1977. The hotel has provided low-cost housing for seamen, farm and cannery workers, houseboys, and single men, but now was slated for redevelopment.

FAMILY GATHERING. Lise Yasui and Ann Tegnell, 1988. 30 min. color. 16mm/Video. New Day Films.
The filmmaker recalls her family's life in the U.S. internment camps for Japanese-Americans during World War II.

FAREWELL TO FREEDOM. WCCO-TV, 1981. 55 min. color. Video. Indiana University.
A report on the plight of the Hmong people of Laos. Many are fleeing communist persecution but remain in camps in Thailand held back by red tape in their effort to get to the U.S. Meanwhile others who have made it to the U.S. experience problems of distrust, culture shock, and unemployment.

GAMAN . . . TO ENDURE. Bob Miyamoto, 1982. 6 min. color. 16mm/Video. Third World Newsreel.
An animated film that uses the drawings of Betty Chen and the music of Nobuko Miyamoto to tell about the thousands of Japanese-Americans who were put in camps during World War II. Through the eyes of a young girl the viewer observes the internees' spirit of survival.

GREAT BRANCHES, NEW ROOTS: THE HMONG FAMILY.

Rita LaDoux, 1983. 42 min. color. 16mm. Hmong Film Project.
All about a family of refugees from Laos trying to build a life for themselves in the U.S. Takes a look at problems they face: education, job hunting, and loss of tradition.

A GREAT WALL. Peter Wang, 1986. 100 min. color. 16mm. New Yorker Films.
A comedy-drama about a Chinese businessman who returns to his homeland only to encounter surprising cultural clashes between his American family and the Beijing relatives. In English and Mandarin with English subtitles.

HITO HATA: RAISE THE BANNER. Visual Communications, 1980. 90 min. color. 16mm. Third World Newsreel.
The first feature-length drama film about the life of Japanese-Americans since the turn of the century. The story is told through a railroad laborer who lives in Los Angeles's Little Tokyo and who tries to save the homes of Little Tokyo's residents when the area is threatened by redevelopment. With Pat Morita, Sachiko, and the East West Players.

IN NO ONE'S SHADOW: FILIPINOS IN AMERICA. Naomi and Antonio De Castro, n.d. 58 min. color. Video. Crosscurrent Media.
An account of Filipino-American history from the early 1900s to the present. Reviews Filipino-American contributions to society in various fields and tells how the Filipino-Americans are working to become a significant force in the Asian-American community.

JAZZ IS MY NATIVE LANGUAGE: A PORTRAIT OF TOSHIKO AKIYOSHI. Renee Cho, n.d. 58 min. color. Video. Crosscurrent Video.
An account of an Asian-American jazz artist who achieved success despite racial and sexual prejudice.

JENNIFER'S CHINESE DIARY. Joe Conforti, n.d. 28 min. color. Video. Carousel Film and Video.
A 14-year-old schoolgirl, wondering about her identity because she is half Chinese and half American, is invited to join her father in

China. This is a report on the girl's observations and experiences in China. Includes a look at ancient and modern China. A prize-winning video.

JENNY. Ginny Hashii, n.d. 19 min. color. 16mm/Video. Carousel
	Film and Video.
A visit with a Japanese-American family who tell their eight-year-old daughter about the traditions of their ancestors. They have absorbed their ethnic heritage into their American lifestyle.

MADE IN CHINA. Lisa Hsia, 1985. 55 min. color. 16mm/Video.
	Filmakers Library.
A Chinese-American woman ponders her identity. The film uses animation, home movies, and live action footage. Also covers her visit with relatives in China where at first she encounters difficulties because she doesn't know Chinese customs.

MONTEREY'S BOAT PEOPLE. Spencer Nakasako and Vincent
	Di Girolamo, n.d. 28 min. color. Video. Crosscurrent Media.
Examines the tension between the Italian fishing community and the recently arrived Vietnamese fishermen in the Monterey Bay peninsula, California. An example of anti-Asian sentiment.

MOUNTAIN IN THE MIND. Suzanne Curran, 1986. 28 min.
	color. Video. Minneapolis Institute of the Arts.
Follows a Chinese-born artist who paints landscapes. Shows him at work in his studio in the U.S.

THE NEW AMERICANS. KCET-TV, 1981. 30 min. color. Video.
	Great Plains National.
Consists of four untitled program. Provides an account of the Indochinese who have settled in the U.S.—their culture and history.

THE NEW PURITANS: THE SIKHS OF YUBA CITY. Tenzing
	Sonam, Rita Sarim, 1985. 27 min. color. Video. Crosscurrent
	Media.
Yuba City is located in the Sacramento Valley and is the place where a large group of Sikhs has settled. Shows the conflict of lifestyles between the younger and older generations of Sikhs.

NEW SEEDS IN A NEW LAND. Chuck Kundschier, 1984. 27
   min. color. Video. University of Minnesota.
A look at two Hmong families who have settled in rural
Minnesota with the help of an agricultural project.

A NEW YEAR FOR THE MIEN. Guy Phillips, 1986. 55 min.
   color. Video. Guy Phillips.
Five people from Laos tell of their experiences in the Seattle area
of the U.S.

NISEI SOLDIER: STANDARD BEARER FOR AN EXILED
   PEOPLE. Loni Ding, 1983. 28 min. color. 16mm/Video. Vox
   Productions.
Tells how and why Japanese-American soldiers fought in World
War II. Focuses on the 442nd Regimental Combat Team. Archival
footage includes interviews with survivors, battles, and
incarceration of Japanese-Americans in camps.

OVERTURE: LINH FROM VIETNAM. Learning Corporation
   of America, 1981. 26 min. color. 16mm/Video. Coronet/MTI
   Film and Video.
An award-winning film about two Mexican-American youths who
deride the Vietnamese students in their school. As the two boys
get to know the Vietnamese better, they find that they like these
Asian-Americans after all.

THE PRICE YOU PAY. Christine Keyser, 1983. 29 min. color.
   Video. Crosscurrent Media.
Examines the problems faced by Southeast Asian refugees in their
effort to create new lives for their families in the U.S.

Q IT UP. Chinatown Youth Center, n.d. 16 min. color. Video.
   Crosscurrent Media.
A dramatic program that reveals the problem of drug abuse in the
Asian-American community. Features leading Asian-American
actors depicting the peer pressure to get high on Quaaludes and
the desire to be understood by the traditional family.

SEWING WOMAN. Deep Focus Productions, 1983. 14 min. b/w.
   Video. Third World Newsreel.
A Chinese-American woman tells about her move from the old

to the new culture and her work in a San Francisco sewing factory. An Academy Award nominee. Available with Chinese subtitles.

SLAYING THE DRAGON. Deborah Gee, 1988. 57 min. color.
    Video. Crosscurrent Media.
Portrays Hollywood's characterizations of Asian women from the Dragon Lady of the 1920s on through the years to the present with the television news anchorwoman. The impact of stereotypes on Asian-American women is described. A prize-winning film.

STARTING OVER IN AMERICA. Sylvia Komatsu, 1986. 59 min.
    b/w. Video. KERA-TV.
About Southeast Asian refugees who attempt to settle in the U.S.

TOPAZ. Ken Verdoia, 1987. 58 min. color. Video. KUED-TV.
A documentary about the plight of the Japanese-Americans who were forced to leave their West Coast homes for encampment in Utah during World War II.

UNFINISHED BUSINESS: THE JAPANESE-AMERICAN
    INTERNMENT CAMPS. Steven Okazaki, 1984. 58 min. color.
    Video. Crosscurrent Media.
Without benefit of trials or hearings over 100,000 Japanese-Americans were sent to internment camps in 1942. This is a powerful report on three Japanese-Americans who were imprisoned for taking a stand against incarceration. An Academy Award nominee.

VISIBLE TARGET. KCTS-TV, Seattle, 1985. 28 min. color.
    Video. Wombat Film and Video.
Examines the situation of the Japanese-Americans during World War II. Describes life in detention camps. Winner of many awards.

WHO KILLED VINCENT CHIN? Film News Now Foundation
    and WTBS-TV, Detroit, 1987. 60 min. color. Video. Third
    World Newsreel.
Tells the story of the first federal civil rights trial involving discrimination against Asian-Americans. A Detroit autoworker and his son beat to death a Chinese man they had misidentified as a

Japanese. When the murderers got off with a light sentence, a national movement for justice emerged.

WITH SILK WINGS—ASIAN-AMERICAN WOMEN AT WORK: FOUR WOMEN. Asian Women United, n.d. 30 min. color. Video. Crosscurrent Media.
The stories of four working women who typify the courage and idealism that inspire the invisible work done by women in the U.S. Includes study guide.

WITH SILK WINGS—ASIAN-AMERICAN WOMEN AT WORK: FRANKLY SPEAKING. Asian Women United, n.d. 30 min. color. Video. Crosscurrent Media.
Discusses the challenges faced by young Asian-American women as they try to succeed in an adult world. Uses interviews with high school students, teachers, employers, and counselors to explain the problems, Includes study guide.

WITH SILK WINGS—ASIAN-AMERICAN WOMEN AT WORK: ON NEW GROUND. Asian Women United, n.d. 30 min. color. Video. Crosscurrent Media.
Explains how ten Asian-American women managed to break the barriers of traditional male jobs, such as stockbroker, welder, and police officer. Includes study guide.

WITH SILK WINGS—ASIAN-AMERICAN WOMEN AT WORK: TALKING HISTORY. Asian Women United, n.d. 30 min. color. Video. Crosscurrent Media.
Five women—a Japanese, a Chinese, a Korean, a Filipino, and a Southeast Asian—give an account of their experiences. They discuss feminist, ethnic, and immigration issues. Includes study guide.

YUKI SHIMODA: ASIAN-AMERICAN ACTOR. Amy Emiko Kato and John Esaki, 1985. 30 min. color. 16mm. Asian American Studies Central.
Through this story of Yuki Shimoda, the Japanese-American character actor, the viewer learns about Hollywood's racial prejudice.

ZEN CENTER. Anne Cushman, 1986. 53 min. color. Video. Hartley Film Foundation.
Describes the effort of some Zen Buddhists in Los Angeles to integrate their religious practice with the American way of life.

LATINOS

¡A BAILAR! THE JOURNEY OF A LATIN DANCE COMPANY. Catherine Calderon, n.d. 30 min. color. 16mm/Video. The Cinema Guild.
Documents the Latin rhythms that continue to flourish in New York after their emergence in the post-war years of the late 1940s and early 1950s. Tells the story of Eddie Torres, who dreamed of establishing a Latin dance company. Shows recruitment of dancers, rehearsals, and preparation for opening night at the Apollo Theater in Harlem.

AÑO NUEVO. Todd Darling, n.d. 55 min. color. Video. The Cinema Guild.
Exposes the plight of Mexican workers in the U.S.—including poor working conditions and inadequate housing. Explains how the workers finally won their right to organize a union via a court case. Discusses Mexican immigration.

AQUI SE HABLA ESPAÑOL. New Jersey Network, 1983. 60 min. color. Video. New Jersey Network.
Examines the problems of the Hispanic residents of New Jersey.

ART IN THE 80'S—CHICANA ARTISTS. Sensor, 1979. 30 min. color. Video. Sensor.
Discusses and presents the work of Chicana artists Judith Hernandez, painter, and Sylvia Morales, filmmaker.

ATLANTIC CITY: ROULETTE OF POWER. New Jersey Network, 1983. 30 min. color. Video. New Jersey Network.
How Hispanics are affected in jobs and housing by casino gambling.

BALLAD OF AN UNSUNG HERO. Paul Espinosa, 1983. 28 min. color. 16mm/Video. The Cinema Guild.
A prize-winning film that describes the life of 89-year-old Pedro Gonzalez, whose action-packed life included work as a telegraph operator for Pancho Villa, a career as a radio and recording star in Los Angeles, imprisonment, deportation, and return to the U.S. 30 years later. Uses interviews with Gonzalez and his wife, archival footage, and recordings from the 1920s and 1930s.

BIRTHWRITE: GROWING UP HISPANIC. Jesus Trevino, 1989. 57 min. color. Video. The Cinema Guild.
Cheech Marin is host for this documentary about Latino writers and how their poems, short stories, and novels reflect Hispanic culture in the U.S. Presents profiles and readings of the artists represented: Edward Rivera, Alberto Rios, Rolando Hinojosa, Judith Ortiz Coler, Alijandro Morales, Lorna Dee Cervantes, and Tato Laviera.

BULLWACKIE. Wombat Film and Video, 1989. 57 min. color. Video. Wombat Film and Video.
A music film that depicts the life of Jamaicans in the Bronx through the talent of Bullwackie Lloyd Barnes, a famous musician and supporter of reggae. Shows scenes of the elements that unite the community, such as cricket matches and social clubs.

CELEBRACION DEL MATRIMONIO. Margaret Hixon, 1986. 30 min. color. 16mm/Video. University of California Extension Media Center.
Shows a Latino wedding ceremony in northern New Mexico. Focuses on the Hispanic heritage and traditions.

CELEBRATION! Karen Kramer, 1989. 29 min. color. 16mm/Video. Karen Kramer.
Shows the annual Labor Day carnival celebrated by the Caribbean community in Brooklyn. Features calypso music as well as a look at costumed participants.

CHICANOS IN TRANSITION. Centre Productions, 1986. 30 min. color. Video. Centre Productions.
Studies the lifestyle of Mexican-Americans living in a small city

in Ohio. Gives a brief history of the Chicanos from the Spanish invasion of Mexico to the present emigration to the U.S. Shows how their heritage is gradually becoming eroded.

COLOMBIANS IN NEW JERSEY. New Jersey Network, 1983. 30 min. color. Video. New Jersey Network.
Studies how Colombians are trying to adapt to their new home in New Jersey. Traces the migration of this fifth largest Hispanic group in the U.S.

DOMINICANS IN NEW JERSEY. New Jersey Network, 1983. 30 min. color. Video. New Jersey Network.
Examines the problems faced by immigrants from the Dominican Republic when they settle in New Jersey. Covers the history of this recent emigration that began in full force after the civil war in 1965.

HERO STREET, U.S.A. Mike Stroot, 1984. 28 min. color. Video. Busch Creative Services Corp.
Documents the participation of Mexican-Americans of Silvia, Illinois, in World War II and in Korea.

HISPANIC AMERICA. CBS News, n.d. 13 min. color. 16mm/Video. Carousel Film and Video.
Describes problems and solutions connected with the Hispanic population in the U.S. Looks at the growth of the Hispanics in numbers and their desire to maintain their identity. With Walter Cronkite and Ed Rabel.

HISPANIC AMERICANS. Dallas County Community College, 1980. 28 min. color. Video. Dallas County Community College.
Traces the history of Hispanic Americans and provides interviews with prominent Hispanics.

HISPANIC CULTURE: THE HISPANICS IN AMERICA. Video Knowledge, 1981. 60 min. color. Video. Video Knowledge.
Explore migration of Latinos into the U.S. Examines the impact on the communities in which they settle.

HISPANICS AND ALCOHOLISM. New Jersey Network, 1983.

30 min. color. Video. New Jersey Network.
An account of how alcoholism affects the Hispanic community in New Jersey.

HISPANICS AND HOUSING: PART I. THE PROBLEM. New Jersey Network, 1983. 30 min. color. Video. New Jersey Network.
Officials, community leaders, and residents talk about the housing problem of Hispanics in New Jersey. With English subtitles.

HISPANICS AND HOUSING: PART II. THE GOVERNMENT. New Jersey Network, 1983. 30 min. color. Video. New Jersey Network.
Discusses federal and state housing programs that affect Hispanics in New Jersey.

HISPANICS AND HOUSING: PART III. THE COMMUNITY. New Jersey Network, 1983. 30 min. color. Video. New Jersey Network.
Describes the efforts of Hispanics to improve the housing situation in Jersey City.

HISPANICS AND MENTAL HEALTH. New Jersey Network, 1983. 30 min. color. Video. New Jersey Network.
Takes a look at mental health needs of Hispanic Americans and the help given by mental health care specialists.

IN THE SHADOW OF THE LAW. Paul Espinosa, 1988. 58 min. color. Video. One West Media, Syracuse Alternate Media Project.
Portrays the daily life of Mexican families that live in the U.S. illegally, a life of fear of the Immigration Service and victimization by those who take advantage of their illegal status.

AN ISLAND IN AMERICA. Anti-Defamation League of B'nai Brith, 1983. 28 min. color. Video. Anti-Defamation League of B'nai Brith.
Examines the life of Puerto Ricans in the U.S.

JESSE TREVINO: A SPIRIT AGAINST ALL ODDS. Skip Cilley,

1984. 20 min. color. Video. Busch Creative Services Corp.
Tells how a Mexican-American artist who lost his hand during the Vietnam War becomes a success despite his handicap.

LATIN STARS IN THE 80s. New Jersey Network, n.d. 30 min.
    color. Video. New Jersey Network.
In three segments. Part 1 demonstrates how Hispanic musicians make an impact on the American music scene. Part 2 looks at Latin music stars and trends (salsa and merengue). Part 3 features jazz artist David Valentin.

THE LATINIZATION OF NEW JERSEY. New Jersey Network,
    1983. 30 min. color. Video. New Jersey Network.
This program is presented in two parts. Takes a look at the Latinos who live in New Jersey.

LATINOS IN THE MEDIA: PART I. HISTORY AND
    EVOLUTION OF LATINOS ON THE SCREEN. New Jersey
    Network, 1983. 30 min. color. Video. New Jersey Network.
Documents how Latinos have been depicted in the movies and television.

LATINOS IN THE MEDIA: PART II. A CLOSE LOOK. New
    Jersey Network, 1983. 30 min. color. Video. New Jersey
    Network.
Describes how employment, ownership, and control are depicted by the Latin media.

LATINOS IN THE MEDIA: PART III. FEEDBACK. New Jersey
    Network, 1983. 30 min. color. Video. New Jersey Network.
Representatives of Hispanic media talk with students about communications issues brought up in the first two programs of this series.

THE LEMON GROVE INCIDENT. Paul Espinosa, 1985. 58 min.
    color. 16mm/Video. The Cinema Guild.
Describes an early (1930) school desegregation case involving a Mexican-American community. The school board in Lemon Grove, California, tried to establish a separate school for Mexican-Americans. At great risk the Mexican-American community fought

the plan.

LOLA LA LOCA. Enrique Oliver, 1988. 88 min. color. 16mm.
  Lola La Loca Associates.
This is the first feature film made by the Cuban-American
filmmaker, Enrique Oliver. He also performs as an actor along
with his family and friends. The story concerns a social worker
who is looking for Lola in a setting that reveals the life and
problems of the Cuban exile.

LUISA TORRES. Centre Productions, 1981. 43 min. color.
  16mm/Video. Centre Productions.
The lifestyle of an elderly Hispanic woman who lives in northern
New Mexico documents the traditional heritage passed down
through many generations.

MACHITO: A LATIN JAZZ LEGACY. Carlos Ortiz, 1987. 58
  min. color. 16mm/Video. First Run/Icarus Films.
A portrait of Latin jazz, which is composed of Cuban rhythms and
elements of American jazz, and the performers who brought Latin
jazz to prominence. Frank "Machito" Grillo is a leading example.
Uses archival footage, recordings, street performances, and
reminiscences by key musicians.

THE MARRIAGE DINNER. Third World Newsreel Workshop,
  1986. 20 min. color. 16mm/Video. Third World Newsreel.
This is a drama that deals with the hardship faced by thousands
of Salvadorans who have come to the United States as illegal
aliens. The story concerns a Salvadoran girl who marries a middle-
class Chicano. When he is invited to a celebration dinner, he is
surprised to learn about conditions in Central America and the
problems that affect Salvadorans in the U.S.

MENTAL HEALTH UPDATE. New Jersey Network, 1983. 30
  min. color. Video. New Jersey Network.
Describes mental health care for Hispanics in New Jersey.

MEXICAN TAPES: A CHRONICLE OF LIFE OUTSIDE THE
  LAW. Louis Hock, 1985. 109 min. color. Video. Louis Hock.
Mexican aliens are shown leading a covert life in Southern

California. Shows lifestyle, employment, and fear of the U.S. immigration authorities.

MUSICA. Gustavo Paredes, 1985. 58 min. color. Video. Third
    World Newsreel.
Presents the history of Latin American music in the U.S. from the beginning of the century. Gives an overview of musical styles ("Cubop," salsa, jazz), performers, and others. Discusses stereotyped roles of Latin women as brazen sirens, and the alienation faced by Latino musicians.

LA MUSICA DE LOS VIEJOS (THE MUSIC OF THE OLD
    ONES). Jack Parsons and Jack Loeffler, 1983. 28 min. color.
    Video. Chip Taylor Communications.
Visits New Mexico's "old ones" who live in mountain villages where they perform folk music handed down through the generations. In Spanish with English subtitles.

THE NEW UNDERGROUND RAILROAD. Kathy Barber
    Hersch, 1983. 30 min. color. Video. Indiana University.
Shows how U.S. churches provide sanctuary for Central American refugees even though the U.S. government considers them illegal aliens.

ONE RIVER, ONE COUNTRY: THE U.S.—MEXICO
    BORDER. Elena Mannes for CBS News, n.d. 47 min. color.
    Video. Carousel Film and Video.
Tells about the hybrid border country that is emerging along the river that separates the U.S. from Mexico. Explains how a "good neighbor" policy in trade on the part of the U.S. might help alleviate some of Mexico's economic problems. With Bill Moyers.

PUERTO RICANS IN NEWARK. New Jersey Network, 1983. 30
    min. color. Video. New Jersey Network.
Documents the life of Puerto Ricans in New Jersey. Includes a report on the 1974 race riot there.

RACISM AMONG HISPANICS. New Jersey Network, 1983. 30
    min. color. Video. New Jersey Network.
A group of people discuss racism with regard to Hispanics in the

U.S.

SANTEROS. Teresita Productions, 1986. 29 min. color. Video.
    KCET-TV.
An account of the work of Hispanic artisans of the Southwest.

SOUTH JERSEY: A DREAM FOR HISPANICS? New Jersey
    Network, 1983. 30 min. color. 2 programs. Video. New Jersey
    Network.
A documentary in two untitled parts about the political, social,
and economic situation for Hispanics in southern New Jersey.

SPIRITUALISM AND MENTAL HEALTH. New Jersey Network,
    1983. 30 min. color. Video. New Jersey Network.
How a Caribbean spiritualist serves the psychiatric needs of the
Hispanic community.

LOS SURES. F. Moreno, 1983. 58 min. color. 16mm/Video. The
    Cinema Guild.
Men and women of the poorest Puerto Rican neighborhood in
New York discuss life on the margins of American society.

TINWORK OF NEW MEXICO. Jack Parsons and Michael
    Earney, 1980. 14 min. color. Video. Chip Taylor
    Communications.
Traces the beginnings of the Hispanic craft of tinwork handed
down from generation to generation after the opening of the
Santa Fe Trail in 1821.

VAQUERO—THE FORGOTTEN COWBOY. Hector Galan,
    1988. 28 min. color. Video. Galan Productions.
Traces the history of the Mexican-American cowboys of the
American West.

WELCOME TO MIAMI, CUBANOS. Learning Corporation of
    America, 1981. 28 min. color. 16mm/Video. Coronet/MTI Film
    and Video.
A Cuban high school student is teased by his fellow swim team
members for being different. He and his cousin, a new immigrant,
learn the importance of family and heritage.

WHAT RAMON DID. Hispanic Youth Film Project, n.d. 30 min.
color. 16mm/Video. AIMS Media.
Tells how the Latino population has been affected by AIDS to a
degree much higher than for other groups. This is the story of
Ramon, a drug user who returns to his old neighborhood only to
find that the community fears that he might be a carrier of AIDS.
This film was created by Hispanics for Hispanics. The host is Esai
Morales.

THE WRATH OF GRAPES (LA IRA DE UVAS). United Farm
Workers, 1986. 15 min. color. Video. El Taller Grafico.
The narrator is Cesar Chavez for this report on the use of
pesticides on vineyards and the health problems involved.

NATIVE AMERICANS

ABNAKI: THE NATIVE PEOPLE OF MAINE. Centre
Productions, 1984. 29 min. color. 16mm/Video. Centre
Productions.
Among four Indian tribes of Maine that have kept their identity
from ancient times, two of them successfully filed suit against the
State of Maine to regain ownership of their land. This is an
account of their efforts to obtain a legal victory and of the
cultural factors that helped with the survival of their heritage.

ALASKA: THE YUP'IK ESKIMOS. Evenari, Lansburgh, 1985. 28
min. color. Video. Chevron U.S.A.
An account of the seasonal activities of the Yup'ik people and
their attempt to maintain their culture in the presence of the new
generation who are adopting the contemporary lifestyle.

THE AMERICAN INDIAN. Dallas County Community College,
1986. 28 min. color. Video. Dallas County Community College.
The history of the American Indian up to the present day.

AMERICAN INDIAN ARTISTS—PART II. Native American
Public Broadcasting Consortium, 1982. 3 programs. 29-30 min.

each, color. Video. Native American Public Broadcasting Consortium.

A continuation of an earlier, six-part series (Part I, 1976). Three Native American artists show their work: Program 1. Larry Golsh; Program 2. Juane Quick-to-See Smith; Program 3. Dan Namingha.

AMERICAN INDIANS: A BRIEF HISTORY. Sidney Platt, 1985. 17 min. color. 16mm/Video. National Geographic.
Describes the migration of America's first Indians, who came from Asia before the white settlers arrived.

AMERICAN INDIANS: YESTERDAY AND TODAY. FilmFair Communications, 1982. 19 min. color. Video. FilmFair Communications.
Native Americans from various tribes tell how their people survived in the early days and what life for them is like today.

ANCIENT INDIAN CULTURES OF NORTHERN AMERICA. Finley-Holiday Film Corporation, 1985. 30 min. color. Video. Finley-Holiday Film Corporation.
A visit to ancient ruins with historical background provided.

ANCIENT SPIRIT, LIVING WORD: THE ORAL TRADITION. KBDI, Daniel Salazar, 1983. 58 min. color. Video. Native American Public Broadcasting Consortium.
All about the oral storytelling tradition of the Native Americans.

ANGOON ONE HUNDRED YEARS LATER. Native American Public Broadcasting Consortium, 1982. 30 min. color. Video. Native American Public Broadcasting Consortium.
A memorial commemorating the destruction of the Indian village of Angoon, Alaska, by the U.S. Navy.

ANOTHER WIND IS MOVING. Donald Stull, David Kendall, 1986. 59 min. color. Video. University of California Extension Media Center.
A history of Native American boarding schools. Explains how at first they aimed at assimilating Indian children into the American mainstream. Then later they wanted to foster a strong sense of Indian identity. Now most of the schools have been closed by the

U.S. government.

BROKEN RAINBOW. Earthworks, 1985. 70 min. color. Video.
    Direct Cinema.
Winner of many awards, including the Academy Award for best
documentary feature and the CINE Golden Eagle. Narrators
Martin Sheen, Burgess Meredith, and Buffy Sainte-Marie tell of
the U.S. government's relocation of 12,000 Navajos for the
purpose of energy development.

BY THIS SONG I WALK: NAVAJO SONG. University of
    Arizona, 1981. 25 min. color. Video. Norman Ross Publishing.
Shows how the Navajo expresses himself through song to restore
balance in his life when the harmony of his life is disturbed. In
Navajo with English subtitles.

CELEBRATION: THE PIPE IS THE ALTAR. Twin Cities Public
    TV, 1980. 26 min. color. Video. UC Video.
Takes a look at traditional Indian rituals.

CONTRARY WARRIORS: A FILM OF THE CROW TRIBE.
    Pam Roberts, 1986. 60 min. 16mm/Video. Direct Cinema.
A 97-year-old Crow leader recalls the turbulent history of the
Crow Indians.

A CONVERSATION WITH VINE DELORIA, JR. University of
    Arizona, 1981. 29 min. color. Video. Norman Ross Publishing.
Author Vine Deloria, Jr., explains the differences between Indian
and non-Indian culture, and the problems with white expectations
for Indians. Vine Deloria emphasizes the importance of keeping
the oral tradition alive.

CROW DOG'S PARADISE. James Hoagland, Mark Elliott, 1979.
    28 min. color. Video. Centre Productions.
A prize-winning film about Sioux Indians, in particular, the Crow
Dog family who try to preserve their traditional Indian culture.

DESERT REGIONS: NOMADS AND TRADERS. Wolfgang
    Bayer, 1980. 15 min. color. Video. BFA Educational Media.
Compares the Navajo Indians of Monument Valley with the

Bedouins of Jordan.

THE DRUM IS THE HEART. Randy Croce, 1982. 29 min. color.
    Video. UC Video.
A look at the present-day rituals of the Blackfoot Indians.

EYES OF THE SPIRIT. Kentucky Educational TV, 1983. 30 min.
    color. Video. Kentucky Educational Television.
Observes Yup'ik Eskimo mask carvers at work.

FOLKLORE OF THE MUSCOGEE (CREEK) PEOPLE. KOED-
    TV, 1983. 29 min. color. Video. Native American Public
    Broadcasting Consortium.
A commentary on the significance of Creek folklore by Dr. Ruth
Arrington.

FOUR CORNERS OF EARTH. WFSU-TV, 1985. 30 min. color.
    Video. Native American Public Broadcasting Consortium.
A profile of five Seminole women.

GERONIMO AND THE APACHE RESISTANCE. Neil Goodwin,
    1988. 56 min. color. Video. Peace River Films.
Documents the history of the Chiricahua Apache people from
1850 to 1913 with the help of direct descendents of warriors.

GERONIMO—THE FINAL CAMPAIGN. Centre Productions,
    1988. 30 min. color. Video. Centre Productions.
Host Will Rogers, Jr., narrates the history of the well-known
Indian warrior Geronimo's surrender to the U.S. Army in 1886,
marking the end of 350 years of war between Native Americans
and European settlers.

GREAT SPIRIT WITHIN THE HOLE. Chris Spotted Eagle,
    1983. 60 min. color. Video. UC Video.
This film tells about the restrictions sometimes placed on Indian
religious leaders when they try to give spiritual aid to Indians in
prison.

HAROLD OF ORANGE. Dianne Brennan, 1984. 32 min. color.
    16mm. Film in the Cities.

Uses trickster myths to explain the role of humor for survival among American Indians. A fictional treatment that also explores the interaction of Indians and philanthropic institutions.

HOME OF THE BRAVE. Helena S. Lad, 1983. 53 min. color. 16mm/Video. The Cinema Guild.
Shows how the Indians of North and South America are responding to efforts to take their land and to present-day influences on their traditions. Describes new organizations created to deal with their problems.

I AM DIFFERENT FROM MY BROTHER: DAKOTA NAME-GIVING. Native American Public Broadcasting Consortium, 1981. 20 min. color. Video. Native American Public Broadcasting Consortium.
Observes the name-giving ceremony for three young Sioux Indians.

IISAW: HOPIE COYOTE STORIES. University of Arizona, 1981. 18 min. color. Video. Norman Ross Publishing.
Presents Hopi singing tales that tell what happens to those who shirk work. The storyteller was born at Old Oraibi, probably the oldest continuously occupied village in North America. In Hopi with English subtitles.

IMAGES OF INDIANS. United Indians of All Tribes Foundation, 1982. 5 parts, 30 min. each, color. Video. Video Tech.
This is a five-part series on Hollywood stereotyping of Indians: 1. The Great Movie Massacre; 2. How Hollywood Won the West; 3. Warpaint and Wigs; 4. Heathen Injuns and the Hollywood Gospel; 5. The Movie Reel Indians.

INDIANS IN THE AMERICAS (REVISED). Wayne Mitchell, 1985. 22 min. color. Video. BFA Educational Media.
Covers the Indian heritage from early to modern times in North and South America.

INUIT KIDS. Paulle Clark, 1987. 15 min. color. 16mm/Video. Bullfrog Films.
Observes two 13-year-old boys, one speaks Inuktitut and English, the other only speaks Inuktitut and lives in the traditional way in

an outcamp.

ISHI: THE ENDURING PEOPLE. Centre Productions, 1983. 15
 min. color. Video. Centre Productions.
Tells about the Yehi people of northern California through the
true story of Ishi, who in 1911 came out of seclusion to relate the
history of the ancient Yehi.

JOE KILLSRIGHT: OGLALA SIOUX. Downtown Community
 TV Center, 1980. 25 min. color. Video. Downtown Community
 TV Center.
Depicts the hostile environment encountered by a Sioux seeking
work in New York City, a sharp contrast with life on the
reservation.

JOHN CAT. Beacon Films, 1985. 26 min. color. 16mm/Video.
 Beacon Films.
This film is based on a story by W. P. Kinsella and is the winner
of several prestigious awards. It tells about an older Indian named
John Cat, who, through his own disillusionment, helps two
younger Indians to become aware of racial prejudice.

JOURNEY TO THE SKY: A HISTORY OF THE ALABAMA
 COUSHATTA INDIANS. KUHT Films, 1980. 53 min. color.
 Video. Native American Public Broadcasting Consortium.
Uses a Coushatta folktale to describe the present unfortunate
situation of Indian culture.

LAKOTA QUILLWORK—ART AND LEGEND. H. Jane
 Nauman, 1983. 16mm/Video. Nauman Films.
Explains the origins of porcupine quillwork through a Lakota
(Sioux) legend.

THE LAST DAYS OF OKAK. Kent Martin, Barry Cowling, 1985.
 24 min. color. 16mm/Video. National Film Board of Canada.
Uses diaries, old photos, and interviews to tell the story of the
Inuits of northern Labrador who were wiped out by Spanish
influenza in 1919. Examines the relations between the native
residents and the missionaries who had encouraged the growth of
Inuit settlements.

LAST OF THE CADDOES. Ken Harrison, 1982. 29 min. color. Video. Phoenix Films and Video.
The setting is rural Texas of the 1930s for this program about a boy who reflects on his part-Indian heritage.

LETTER FROM AN APACHE. Barbara Wilk, 1985. 11 min. color. 16mm/Video. Centre Productions.
The story of the first Native American physician told in film animation.

LIVE AND REMEMBER. Centre Productions, 1987. 29 min. color. Video. Centre Productions.
Depicts the hardships of modern life faced by Native Americans using the Dakota Sioux Indians as example. Shows how many of the youth are experiencing acculturation with modern American values while Sioux grandparents, who would normally preserve their heritage by passing it along via the oral tradition, are out of touch with the youths. Includes interviews with Sioux people, scenes of a sweat lodge ceremony, and views of the beautiful lands and the squalid living quarters on the reservation.

THE LONGEST TRAIL. Alan Lomax, 1986. 58 min. color. 16mm/Video. University of California Extension Media Center.
Shows over 50 dances of Native Americans to explore dance traditions. Also tells how the New World was settled by people coming across the Bering Strait land bridge.

LOVING REBEL. Centre Productions, 1987. 25 min. color. Video. Centre Productions.
A profile of one of the nineteenth century's foremost advocates of Native American rights, Helen Hunt Jackson, who was also a famous writer. Features readings of her poems, novels, essays, and other writings.

MAN OF LIGHTNING. Georgia State University, 1982. 29 min. color. Video. Native American Public Broadcasting Consortium.
In dramatic form presents two Cherokee folktales that describe Indian culture before European influence.

MARICULTURE: THE PROMISE OF THE SEA. Andy Harvey, Bill Green, 1981. 21 min. color. Video. Video Out.
Shows an Indian community that is involved with mariculture (ocean farming).

MASHPEE. Maureen McNamara, 1985. 28 min. b/w. Video. Maureen McNamara.
All about Indian land claims and the issues they raise.

A MESSAGE FROM NATIVE AMERICA. David Lionel, 1982. 14 min. color. Video. Lionel Television Productions.
Presents Hopi and other Native American prophecies that indicate that peace and joy will come with a return to the way of the creator, but disaster will follow a continuation of the present course.

MINORITIES IN AGRICULTURE: THE WINNEBAGO. Briarcliffe College, 1984. 29 min. color. Video. Native American Public Broadcasting Consortium.
A review of the past and present of the Winnebago Indians of Nebraska.

MOTHER OF MANY CHILDREN. National Film Board of Canada, 1980. 58 min. color. Video. National Film Board of Canada.
An elderly woman and other members of the Hobbema Indian people talk about womanhood.

THE MYSTERY OF THE LOST RED PAINT PEOPLE. T. W. Timreck, 1987. 56 min. color. 16mm/Video. Bullfrog Films.
Describes one of the most intriguing studies made by American archaeologists and anthropologists to track down the traces left by a heretofore unknown prehistoric sea culture on the Atlantic coast.

NATIVE AMERICA SPEAKS. David Lionel, 1980. 25 min. color. Video. Lionel Television Productions.
Illustrates Native American culture. Discusses the significance of the peace pipe, the sweat lodge ceremony, and group dancing.

NATIVE AMERICAN IMAGES. Carol Patton Cornsilk, 1984. 29
  min. color. Video. Native American Public Broadcasting
  Consortium.
A look at three contemporary Native American artists.

NATIVE LAND: NOMADS OF THE DAWN. Alvin Perlmutter,
  1986. 58 min. color. Video. The Cinema Guild.
The history of civilization in the Americas and the role of myth
in Native American societies.

NATWANIWA: A HOPI PHILOSPHICAL STATEMENT.
  University of Arizona, 1981. 27 min. color. Video. Norman
  Ross Publishing.
Explains that what the Hopi does in his field of work serves as
a rehearsal for his future life. Describes how in the Hopi
philosophical system all things are related. In Hopi with English
subtitles.

THE NAVAJO. Centre Productions, 1983. 11 min. color. Video.
  Centre Productions.
Navajos talk about the problems of maintaining their culture in
the modern world.

NAVAJO CODE TALKERS. Tom McCarthy, 1986. 27 min. color.
  16mm/Video. One West Media.
During World War II the Navajos created a code that the
Japanese could not break.

NAVAJO COUNTRY. Albinson-Webb Films, 1983. 10 min. color.
  Video. International Film Bureau.
Shows that Navajos are nomads. Includes a discussion of their
creativity.

THE NAVAJO LEGEND OF THE GLITTERING WORLD.
  American Indian Cultural Foundation, 1986. 25 min. color.
  Video. Finley-Holiday Film Corporation.
Documents the cultural heritage of the Navajos in the Southwest
desert.

NORTH AMERICAN INDIANS AND EDWARD S. CURTIS.

Terry McLuhan, 1985. 20 min. color. 16mm/Video. BFA Educational Media.
Documents the history of the North American Indian with footage shot by Edward Curtis of various tribal groups at the turn of the century. Also includes Curtis's still photographs that have preserved Indian culture for modern viewers.

OLD DANCES, NEW DANCERS. KYUK, 1983. 30 min. color. Video. Kentucky Educational Television.
Observes the first annual Young People's Eskimo Dance Awareness Festival in Alaska.

ON THE PATH TO SELF-RELIANCE. The Seminole Tribe of Florida, 1982. 45 min. color. Video. Native American Public Broadcasting Consortium.
Explains how the Seminole people of Florida became successful and financially self-sufficient in recent years.

1,000 YEARS OF MUSCOGEE (CREEK) ART. Gary Robinson, The Creek Nation, 1982. 28 min. color. Video. Native American Public Broadcasting Consortium.
Various experts provide a history of Creek art.

THE ORIGIN OF THE CROWN DANCE AND BA'TS'OOSEE: AN APACHE TRICKSTER CYCLE. University of Arizona, 1981. 40 min. color. Video. Norman Ross Publishing.
An elder of the Apache people tells a story about a boy who became a supernatural being with the power to cure. In Apache with English subtitles.

OUR SACRED LAND. Spotted Eagle, 1984. 28 min. color. Video. UC Video.
Tells how the Sioux people have been restricted in their rights to worship on their unreserved land, which is sacred to them.

PEOPLE OF THE KLAMATH: OF LAND AND LIFE. James S. Culp, 1987. 28 min. color. Video. Community Media Productions.
Tells how the Native Americans of northwestern California fought and won in court over a dispute with the U.S. Forest Service.

THE PEOPLE OF UTPIAGVIK. Bob Jenkins and Carole Hodge, 1985. 46 min. color. Video. University of Alaska.
An ancient frozen family was found in 1982 in Barrow, Alaska. This is an account of the cultural and other changes that have taken place in the intervening years.

POUNDMAKER'S LODGE: A HEALING PLACE. A. Obomsawin, 1988. 30 min. color. 16mm/Video. National Film Board of Canada.
Native counselors at Poundmaker's Lodge help native people from all tribes with problems of alcoholism and drug addiction. Their work relies heavily on reconnecting the addicts with their ancient heritage.

PRIDE, PURPOSE AND PROMISE: PAIUTES OF THE SOUTHWEST. KLVX-TV, 1982. 28 min. color. Video. Native American Public Broadcasting Consortium.
Tells how the Paiute people of Arizona and Nevada live today. Also discusses their history and future.

THE PRIMAL MIND. Alvin H. Perlmutter, 1984. 58 min. color. 16mm/Video. The Cinema Guild.
Based on the book by Jamake Highwater, *The Primal Mind: Vision and Reality in Indian America*. Explores point by point the essential differences between Native American and Western cultures: dance, art, nature, and the like.

QUEEN VICTORIA AND THE INDIANS. Centre Productions, 1985. 11 min. color. 16mm/Video. Centre Productions.
A highly acclaimed animated film of a true story as told by American artist George Catlin about a group of Ojibwe Indians who made a trip to London to dance at the Indian Gallery opening. Catlin arranged for the Indians to have an audience with Queen Victoria. Raises questions about history, lifestyle, and cultural values.

RED ROAD: TOWARDS THE TECHNO-TRIBAL. KBDI-TV, 1984. 27 min. color. Video. Native American Public Broadcasting Consortium.

Tells how present-day Native Americans are responding to the technological influences on their traditional lifestyle.

RETURN TO SOVEREIGNTY. Donald Stull, David Kendall, 1987. 46 min. color. Video. University of California Extension Media Center.
Shows how the Kansas Kickapoo people have reacted to implementation of the Indian Self-Determination and Education Assistance Act of 1975, the goal of which is to promote self-sufficiency.

RUNNING ON THE EDGE OF THE RAINBOW: LAGUNA STORIES AND POEMS. University of Arizona, 1981. 28 min. color. Video. Norman Ross Publishing.
Looks at the function of Laguna storytelling. Discusses the problems involved with being an Indian poet.

SCIENCE OR SACRILEGE: THE STUDY OF AMERICAN INDIAN REMAINS. University of California-Santa Barbara, 1983. 41 min. color. Video. University of California-Santa Barbara.
Raises the question about the taking of Indian skeletal remains and artifacts for study by anthropologists in museums.

SEASONS OF A NAVAJO. Peace River Films, KAET-TV, 1984. 60 min. color. Video. Native American Public Broadcasting Consortium.
How a Navajo family deals with modern life.

SEYEWAILO: THE FLOWER WORLD. University of Arizona, 1981. 51 min. color. Video. Norman Ross Publishing.
Demonstrates the Yaqui deer songs as sung and danced at the pahko, a festival. Explains how the songs are forms of religious expression. In Yaqui with English subtitles.

SONGS IN MINTO LIFE. Curt Madison, 1985. 29 min. color. Video. River Tracks Productions.
About the oral tradition of song in the Minto Flats of interior Alaska. This is the first documentary about Athabaskan music.

SONGS OF MY HUNTER HEART: LAGUNA SONGS AND
POEMS. University of Arizona, 1981. 34 min. color. Video.
Norman Ross Publishing.
A look at what happens to Laguna Pueblo life when uranium
deposits are found nearby.

SPIRIT OF RED DOG. John Hilliard, 1983. 27 min. color. Video.
ATVN-Alaska Television Network.
The Inuplaq Eskimos who live in villages of northwest Alaska feel
they must take steps to protect their culture from outside
influences.

SPIRIT OF THE HUNT. Thomas Howe Associates, 1982. 29 min.
color. Video. Centre Productions.
Introduces the culture and religion of the Plains Indians. Focuses
on the material and spiritual significance of the buffalo for the
people of the Chippewa, Cree, and Dogrib tribes.

STRENGTH OF LIFE—KNOKAVTEE SCOTT. University of
Tulsa, 1984. 27 min. color. Video. Native American Public
Broadcasting Consortium.
Depicts the work of a Cherokee-Creek jewelry craftsman. Also
discusses the Spiro Mounds in Oklahoma.

SUMMER OF THE LOUCHEUX: PORTRAIT OF A
NORTHERN INDIAN FAMILY. Graydon McCrea, 1983. 27
min. color. 16mm. Tamarack Films.
A study of the daily life of the Loucheux, or Kutchin, Indians of
Alaska and northwest Canada. Shows a summer camp on the
Mackenzie River.

TANANA RIVER RAT. Curt Madison, 1987. 57 min. color.
Video. River Tracks Productions.
A drama with the feel of a documentary filmed in interior Alaska.
Athabaskan traditional music provides the unifying theme for a
story about brothers who, although separated by political matters
after the 1971 land claims, are forced together when a relative
drowns in the river.

THE TAOS PUEBLO. Paulle Clark, 1987. 9 min. color.

16mm/Video. Bullfrog Films.
A tour of the old pueblo in Taos, New Mexico, showing how the Indian residents try to maintain their traditions.

UKSSUM CAUYAI: THE DRUMS OF WINTER. Sarah Elder and Leonard Kamering, 1988. 90 min. color. 16mm/Video. Sarah Elder and Leonard Kamering.
An account of the traditional heritage of the Yup'ik Eskimo people of Alaska. Tells about their dance, music, and religious practices.

UMEALIT, THE WHALE HUNTER. WGBH-TV, 1979. 60 min. color. Video. PBS Video.
Shows an Eskimo whale hunter at work, and compares whaling practices of the past and present.

URBAN INDIANS. Downtown Community TV Center, 1984. 20 min. color. Video. Downtown Community TV Center.
Tells of the plight of an Oglala Sioux who became a drug addict after coming to New York in search of a job.

A WEAVE OF TIME: THE STORY OF A NAVAJO FAMILY, 1938-1986. Susan Fanshel, 1987. 60 min. color. 16mm/Video. Direct Cinema.
Covers four generations of a Navajo family from 1938 to 1986.

WHEN HOPE BECOMES DESPAIR. Tony Mussari, 1986. 56 min. color. Video. M.L.A. Productions.
Tells why some Menominee Indian teenagers tried to commit suicide and how their school helped them to have a reason to live.

WHITE JUSTICE. Morgane Laliberté and Françoise Wera, 1987. 57 min. color. Video. The Cinema Guild.
Discusses the Canadian criminal justice system with regard to the Inuit Indians in northern Quebec. Traces the history of the "white justice" imposed on the Indians, and describes the present-day circuit court system. Explains the cultural differences and difficulties.

WITH HEART AND HAND. Bill Snider, Deann Snider, 1986. 28 min. color. 16mm. Otero Savings and Loan.
A view of Southwestern Native American artists at work. Discusses the development of Native American arts and crafts.

YOU CAN'T GROW POTATOES UP THERE! Government of the Northwest Territories, 1981. 27 min. color. Video. Kinetic Film Enterprises.
A look at seal hunting of the Arctic Inuit Eskimos. Describes its role in traditional life of the Eskimos.

LATIN AMERICA

GENERAL

NEW CINEMA OF LATIN AMERICA. Michael Chanan, 1985.
    Part I: 83 min. color; Part II: 85 min. color. Video. The
    Cinema Guild.
Documents the social and artistic roots of the new national
cinemas of Latin America in a two-part report. Part I, "Cinema
of the Humble," focuses on Cuba and Nicaragua. Part II, "The
Long Road," examines repression against filmmakers, new forms
of representation in response to different circumstances in various
countries, and the development of a new women's cinema.

ONWARD CHRISTIAN SOLDIERS. Gaston Ancelovici and
    Jaime Barrios, 1989. 52 min. color. Video. First Run/Icarus
    Films.
Documents how evangelical Protestant churches are growing in
influence in Latin America. Explains how these Protestants are
often closely tied with the military.

THE TIME BOMB. United Nations, 1989. 27 min. color. Video.
    The Cinema Guild.
A report on the debt crisis in Latin America. Filmed in the
Dominican Republic, Mexico, Chile, Peru, Bolivia, Argentina, and
Venezuela. Features interviews with economists, government
officials, and striking or unemployed workers.

165

CENTRAL AMERICA

General

CENTRAL AMERICA: AN INTRODUCTION. Wayne Mitchell,
    1985. 28 min. color. 16mm/Video. BFA Educational Media.
A study of the cultural and social geography of Central America.
Makes distinctions to describe the area's seven counties.

CENTRAL AMERICA: HISTORY AND HERITAGE. Wayne
    Mitchell, 1985. 22 min. color. 16mm/Video. BFA Educational
    Media.
Covers the history of Central America from ancient times to the
present. Shows the influence of outsiders on the countries of
Central America even today.

CRISIS IN CENTRAL AMERICA: 1. THE YANKEE YEARS.
    WGBH-TV, 1985. 58 min. color. Video. Films Inc.
Covers the years from 1898 to the 1950s. Includes the Spanish-
American War, the building of the Panama Canal, the U.S.
Marine occupation of Nicaragua, and the 1945 crisis in Guatemala.

THE LACANDON MAYA BALCHE RITUAL. Jon McGee,
    1988. 40 min. color. Video. University of California Extension
    Media Center.
Depicts the ancient Mayan ritual in which an alcoholic beverage
is made, drunk, and offered to the gods. Shows some Maya
participants looking at and commenting on a tape of the
ceremony.

LAST OF THE MAYAS. Handel Film Corporation, 1981. 27 min.
    color. 16mm. Handel Film Corporation.
Documents the important features of the rich Mayan culture of
over a thousand years ago.

MAYA LORDS OF THE JUNGLE. Public Broadcasting
    Associates, 1981. 58 min. color. Video. PBS Video.
Shows archeologists at work, studying ancient Mayan civilization
for clues to the decline of the Mayas.

THE MAYANS: APOCALYPSE THEN. Centre Productions, 1988. 27 min. color. Video. Centre Productions.
Gives a close view of Mayan architectural ruins and discusses Mayan culture and history. Reveals a sophisticated civilization.

NATIONS OF THE WORLD: CENTRAL AMERICA. National Geographic, 1988. 25 min. color. 16mm/Video. National Geographic.
Explains how all seven Central American countries share an Indian and Spanish heritage and tropical climate. Also tells how these countries differ politically and economically.

SANCTUARY: A QUESTION OF CONSCIENCE. Wynn Hausser, 1986. 26 min. color. 16mm/Video. The Cinema Guild.
Documents the Sanctuary Movement, a present-day underground railroad to aid refugees who are fleeing political oppression in El Salvador and Guatemala, because the U.S. government has classified them as economic migrants, not as political refugees.

SOUTH OF THE BORDER. David Bradbury, 1987. 63 min. color. 16mm/Video. The Cinema Guild.
Explains the protest music of the people in Central America. Shot in Mexico, Guatemala, El Salvador, Honduras, and Nicaragua. Includes performances by leading Latin American musicians and scenes of the poverty and military control that the people are protesting. In Spanish with English subtitles.

STAIRWAYS TO THE MAYAN GODS. Hartley Film Foundation, n.d. 28 min. color. 16mm/Video. Hartley Film Foundation.
Studies the Mayas of Mexico and the rest of Central America. Tells how their focus on mathematics and astronomy was translated into spectacular cities of pyramids and palaces. Also suggests reasons for their ascent and decline.

Costa Rica

COSTA RICA: CHILD IN THE WIND. Jim Burroughs and Ceil Sutherland, 1987. 58 min. color. 16mm/Video. Filmakers

Library.
Documents the history of Costa Rica, the oldest democracy in Central America. Also examines Costa Rica's dependence on the U.S. and the building of a secret airstrip arranged by Oliver North. Shows how the airstrip was later dismantled by orders of the new president, Arias.

HAMBURGER: JUNGLEBURGER. Peter Heller, 1986. 58 min. color. Video. First Run/Icarus Films.
Traces the impact of fast food businesses in the Third World, with particular emphasis on Costa Rica. Production and exports of meat from Costa Rica are increasing, rain forests have been cleared for grazing at an alarming rate, some farmers have been evicted to provide room for large companies, and new markets are being developed in India and Africa.

A MAN WHEN HE'S A MAN. Valeria Sarmiento, 1982. 63 min. color. 16mm/Video. Women Make Movies.
Explains the traditions of Costa Rican culture in which the male dominates.

El Salvador

AND THAT IS WHY THE STATE IS TO BLAME. Frank Diamand and Jan van der Putten, 1984. 55 min. color. 16mm/Video. New Time Films.
A documentary about Marianella Garcia Villa, who was secretly investigating the use of chemicals and the bombing of civilians in El Salvador, and who, as a result, was killed by the Salvadoran army in 1983. Shows how during her life she publicized the horrors of the Salvadoran regime, and, as a lawyer, helped defend political prisoners.

BATTLE FOR EL SALVADOR. WGBH-TV, 1985. 58 min. color. Video. Films Inc.
See *Crisis in Central America* (below).

CRISIS IN CENTRAL AMERICA: 4. BATTLE FOR EL SALVADOR. WGBH-TV, 1985. 58 min. color. Video. Films

Inc.
Gives the background for El Salvador's civil war and explains U.S.
policy toward El Salvador.

DATELINE: SAN SALVADOR. Camino Film Projects, 1986. 28
   min. b/w. Video. Camino Film Projects.
Salvadoran citizens are shown in 1986 reacting to the repression
of the Duarte government.

EL SALVADOR: REVOLUTION OR DEATH. Frank Diamand,
   n.d. 48 min. color. 16mm/Video. New Time Films.
Describes the political and economic forces at work in El Salvador
and the role of the United States in supporting the government.
Contains an interview with Archbishop Romero, who was later
assassinated.

GUAZAPA. Don North, 1984. 45 min. color. 16mm/Video. The
   Cinema Guild.
Shows how soldiers of the Farabundo Marti National Liberation
Front and civilians support each other in Guazapa, El Salvador,
to provide the needs of daily life. Includes battle scenes.

GUERRILLA PRIEST. Yvan Patry and Françoise de la
   Cressoniere, 1982. 24 min. color. Video. The Cinema Guild.
Discusses the role of the church in El Salvador and the work of
a priest who ministers to peasants in a region controlled by the
FMLN. Includes scenes of the assassination of Archbishop Oscar
Romero and conducts an interview with the new archbishop.

IN THE NAME OF DEMOCRACY. Paul Cohen, Jose Ponce,
   1984. 31 min. color. 16mm/Video. The Cinema Guild.
Gives the details of government repression connected with the
much publicized 1982 election in El Salvador. Describes
intimidation of voters. In Spanish with English subtitles.

IN THE NAME OF THE PEOPLE. Alex Drehsler, 1984. 75 min.
   color. 16mm/Video. First Run/Icarus Films.
Martin Sheen narrates this report on El Salvador's revolution and
the guerrilla forces there. Follows the guerrillas in battle in the
city of San Salvador.

MEDIA WAR IN EL SALVADOR. Ilan Ziv, 1989. 22 min. color.
    Video. First Run/Icarus Films.
Shows how various factions in the civil war in El Salvador use the
media for their purposes.

THE POWER OF THE POOR. BBC-TV, 1987. 35 min. color.
    16mm/Video. Films Inc.
Investigates the bitter conflicts in El Salvador and the role of the
Catholic Church in the struggle.

RETURN TO AGUACAYO. Celeste Greco, 1987. 15 min. color.
    Video. Educational Film and Video Project.
Although the government of El Salvador wanted to depopulate a
farming cooperative, the peasants fought back by returning to
repopulate the area.

THE ROAD TO LIBERTY. Film Institute of El Salvador, 1983.
    65 min. color. 16mm/Video. The Cinema Guild.
A report on the new society being created in El Salvador and the
development of women's consciousness-raising groups. This film
was shot in the areas controlled by the FMLN rebels.

SEEDTIME OF HOPE. Radio Verceremos, FMLN, 1983. 27 min.
    color. Video. First Run/Icarus Films.
Discusses the role of churches in El Salvador in the fight for
justice.

STORIES FROM CUSCATLAN. Peter Chappell and Jane Ryder,
    1989. 52 min. color. Video. First Run/Icarus Films.
An in-depth look at the lives of ordinary Salvadorans as depicted
by observing three families who migrated to the capital at various
times in El Salvador's history.

Guatemala

GUATEMALA: A JOURNEY TO THE END OF MEMORIES.
    Ilan Ziv, 1986. 55 min. color. Video. First Run/Icarus Films.
Tells how a democratically elected government came into being
in Guatemala in January, 1986 and how refugees have been invited

to return to Guatemala. This film investigates what a returning refugee might see and even shows the reactions of refugees now living in Mexico to the scenes filmed.

GUATEMALA: ROADS OF SILENCE. Felix Zurita, 1988. 59 min. color. Video. The Cinema Guild.
A documentary about the terrible human rights situation in Guatemala, where in the last 30 years more than 90,000 civilians have been assassinated and 36,000 have disappeared. Shows scenes of the shantytowns where refugees live and tells about new efforts by the Indians to survive despite oppression by the military. In Spanish with English subtitles.

POPOL VUH: THE CREATION MYTH OF THE MAYA. Patricia Amlin, 1987. 29 min. color. 16mm/Video. University of California Extension Media Center.
An animated film about the creation myth of the Quiche Maya of ancient Guatemala. Uses imagery from ancient Mayan ceramics.

THE REAL THING. Peter Schnall, 1984. 36 min. color. 16mm/video. First Run/Icarus Films.
Covers a dispute over the closing of a Coca-Cola bottling plant in Guatemala City. The workers felt the reason given was not satisfactory and so they refused to leave the plant for one year. This is a success story for one small Guatemalan union that wouldn't be broken.

RIO DE LA PASION (THE PASSION RIVER). Anthony Collins, 1985. 20 min. color. 16mm/Video. IE Film Productions.
An account of the farmers who live in isolation in Pelen, a remote area of Guatemala along the banks of the Passion River.

TODOS SANTOS: THE SURVIVORS. Olivia Carrescia, 1989. 58 min. color. 16mm/Video. First Run/Icarus Films.
This is a sequel to the filmmaker's earlier film, *Todos Santos Cuchumatan*. Takes a look at Guatemala after still more years of violence. Depicts the impact of political turmoil on farming and migration patterns, and on the social and psychological aspects of the people's lives.

UNDER THE GUN: DEMOCRACY IN GUATEMALA. R. Richter and P. Goudvis, 1987. 40 min. color. 16mm/Video. First Run/Icarus Films.
Covers land reform, human rights, and military control issues in Guatemala. Tells how Guatemala changed to civilian rule after many years of military control.

WHEN THE MOUNTAINS TREMBLE. Skylight Pictures, 1984. 83 min. color. 16mm. New Yorker Films.
Describes the oppression experienced by the Indian peasantry of Guatemala and the experience of one Indian woman in particular.

Honduras

ROSALINA. Leslie Jenkins, 1987. 23 min. color. 16mm/Video. First Run/Icarus Films.
Depicts life in a Honduran refugee camp through the eyes of a Salvadoran girl who fled war-torn El Salvador with her family.

SEEING WINDOWS. Robbie Hart, 1987. 28 min. color. Video. First Run/Icarus Films.
Describes the life of a poor rural family that migrates to the Honduran capital of Tegucigalpa only to end up living in a slum outside of the city. Depicts several farming and self-help projects recently set up in Honduras to help the situation. This video was made with the assistance of the United Nations.

Mexico

ART AND REVOLUTION IN MEXICO. Films for the Humanities, 198? 60 min. color. Video. Films for the Humanities.
The work of some Mexican painters is shown to be one of the causes of the 1910 revolution.

FRIDA. Paul Leduc, 1987. 108 min. color. 16mm. New Yorker Films.
A fresh treatment of the biographical film genre, in this case, the story of Frida Kahlo, the Mexican painter who is also considered

one of the outstanding women artists of the 20th century. Covers the many facets of her life: her crippling childhood accident, her marriage to Diego Rivera, her involvement with politics, and her artistic vision.

L.E.A.R.: THE LEAGUE OF REVOLUTIONARY WRITERS AND ARTISTS. Yvette Nieves-Cruz, 1988. 31 min. color. Video. The Cinema Guild.
A look at the attempt to fuse art and politics via the League of Revolutionary Writers and Artists, which was founded in Mexico in 1931 and existed for only four years, but included some famous names, such as Diego Rivera and David Alfaro Siqueros. Presents interviews with L.E.A.R. survivors.

THE LIVING MAYA. Hubert Smith, 1985. 4 programs, 58 min. each, color. Video. University of California Extension Media Center.
A four-part series that documents how a Mayan community, and one family in particular, lives in a Yucatán village throughout one full year. Each program covers a part of the year. Program 1 examines the structure of Maya agricultural and village life. Program 2, how the family copies with illness; the village accepts a government irrigation project. Program 3, concern about the irrigation project's inequities; two sons of the family want to reject traditional life for life in the city. Program 4, the village produces a mediocre corn crop.

THE MEXICAN WAY OF LIFE. Sandler Films, 1986. 23 min. color. 16mm/Video. AIMS Media.
Depicts the contrasts of Mexico: snow-covered mountains, barren deserts, luxurious resorts, simple Indian villages. Traces Spanish and Mayan roots for modern art and architecture in Mexico. Explains the limited capacity for tilling the soil and the country's sources of capital.

MEXICO: AN INTRODUCTION. BFA Educational Media, 1984. 24 min. color. Video. BFA Educational Media.
Shows Mexico as a rapidly changing nation that is very important to the interests of the U.S.

MEXICO CITY—OLE! Around the World in Sight and Sound,
    1984. 20 min. color. Video. Around the World in Sight and
    Sound.
A travel film about Mexico with a special focus on the bullfight.

MEXICO: THE LAND AND THE PEOPLE. Roger Brown,
    Trillium Productions, n.d. 24 min. color. 16mm/Video.
    Encyclopaedia Britannica Corporation.
Covers the history of Mexico from the earliest cultures to the
Spanish conquest. Discusses the creation of the mestizos.

NATIONS OF THE WORLD: MEXICO. National Geographic,
    1988. 26 min. color. 16mm/Video. National Geographic.
Observes modern Mexico, its factories, cities, and farms. Points out
the geographical and cultural variety of the country.

NEIGHBORS: THE UNITED STATES AND MEXICO. Jesus
    Salvador Trevino and Jose Luis Ruiz, 1985. 60 min. color.
    Video. The Cinema Guild.
A study of the economic relationship between the U.S. and
Mexico. Shows the impact of factories owned by the U.S. in
Mexico and how they affect American consumers and workers.

SWIDDEN HORTICULTURE AMONG THE LACANDON
    MAYA. R. Jon McGee, 1987. 29 min. color. Video. University
    of California Extension Media Center.
A report on the four-month cycle of corn horticulture of the
Mayan people who live in the Chiapas rain forests of southeastern
Mexico. Shows the pace of life and the division of labor.

TIME OF THE ANGELS. Faith Hubley, n.d. 10 min. color.
    16mm/Video. Pyramid Film and Video.
Uses film animation to portray Mexico's history. Poems and
graphics represent the historic periods covered. The poems are
spoken in Spanish and English.

THE TRAIL NORTH. Paul Espinosa, 1983. 28 min. color.
    16mm/Video. The Cinema Guild.
Martin Sheen narrates this documentary about an anthropologist
and his ten-year-old son as they trace the journey made by their

ancestors from Mexico to the U.S.

TREMORS IN GUZMAN. John Hewitt, Sam Wonderly, 1988. 30
   min. color. Video. University of California Extension Media
   Center.
An account of what Mexicans think about the state of their
country. Some of the problems discussed—corrupt government
officials, out-of-control inflation, economic depression, and
unemployment.

WATCHER OF THE WINTER SUN. Michael Bober, 1983. 10
   min. color. 16mm/Video. Michael Bober.
Describes the winter solstice site of La Romorosa, a plateau of
northern Baja California. Includes a view of the human-figured
rock painting. Also describes the native people of the area.

WE AREN'T ASKING FOR THE MOON. Mari Carmen de Lara,
   1986. 58 min. color. Video. First Run/Icarus Films.
Reveals the impact of the September 1985 earthquake on women
garment workers in Mexico City. When factories and government
refused assistance, the women tried successfully to form a union
and sewing cooperative.

A WEEK IN THE LIFE OF A MEXICAN STUDENT. Sandler
   Films, 1986. 24 min. color. 16mm/Video. AIMS Media.
A prize-winning film about a week in the life of a 14-year-old
student in Mexico. Provides scenes of his job to pay for his
schooling, of his school classes, of his trip to Mexico City to visit
the university, and of a Mexican barbecue picnic that he attends.
Explains the chaperon system for girls.

Nicaragua

ASI FUE (SO IT WENT). Indiana University, 1984. 54 min. color.
   Video. Indiana University.
A study of Nicaragua's political situation. Discusses the civil war
and the diverse views of the people during the elections of 1984.
Samples the campaigns of seven contending parties and discusses
issues.

BALLAD OF THE LITTLE SOLDIER. Werner Herzog, 1985. 45 min. color. 16mm. New Yorker Films.
A visit to eastern Nicaragua where the long-persecuted Miskito Indians fight Sandinista troops.

BANANA COMPANY. Nicaraguan Film Institute, 1982. 15 min. color. 16mm/Video. First Run/Icarus Films.
Provides the viewer with a tour of Nicaragua's banana plantations.

BREAD AND DIGNITY. Maria Jose Alvarez, 1982. 30 min. color. 16mm/Video. Women Make Movies.
Directed by a Nicaraguan woman. A report to women of Nicaragua that explores the historical background for the recent revolution.

BREAKING THE SILENCE. Ivan Arguello, 1984. 16 min. b/w. 16mm/Video. First Run/Icarus Films.
Shows a group of volunteers from the Nicaragua telephone company as they attempt to install the first phone lines in the isolated communities inhabited by Miskito Indians, where they encounter jungles, mountains, and Contra guerrillas.

CAFE NICA: PORTRAITS FROM NICARAGUA. John Knoop, 1987. 43 min. color. 16mm/Video. Indiana University.
Focuses on the annual coffee bean harvest, which is the heart of Nicaraguan economic activity. Shows how the work is done manually with the help of volunteers from as far away as Europe. Through interviews explains the anger felt by some citizens about the encroachment of communism, about the U.S. blockade, and the attacks of the Contras.

THE CENTERFIELDER. Nicaraguan Film Institute, 1985. 18 min. b/w. 16mm/Video. First Run/Icarus Films.
Based on a story by Sergio Ramirez Mercado, vice president of Nicaragua. The setting is a prison during the Somoza regime where a man who once played center field for the National baseball team is under interrogation. In a dream sequence he attempts to escape during a game between prisoners and guards.

CHRONICLE OF HOPE: NICARAGUA. Third World Newsreel,

1985. 50 min. color. 16mm/Video. Third World Newsreel. Follows some ordinary Americans who make a trip from New York City to Nicaragua bringing medical supplies. The Americans talk to local people about life in post-Somoza Nicaragua. Discusses the Contras from the Nicaraguan perspective. In English and Spanish with English subtitles.

CRISIS IN CENTRAL AMERICA: 3. REVOLUTION IN NICARAGUA, WGBH-TV, 1985. 58 min. color. Video. Films Inc.
Covers the 1979 overthrow of the Somoza government and U.S. involvement in Nicaragua.

DREAM OF A FREE COUNTRY: A MESSAGE FROM NICARAGUAN WOMEN. Edward Le Lorrain, Kathleen Shannon, 1984. 60 min. color. 16mm. National Film Board of Canada.
Nicaraguan women talk about their participation in the overthrow of the Somoza regime and their efforts to develop a new society.

FIRE FROM THE MOUNTAIN. Adam Friedson, 1987. 58 min. color. 16mm/Video. First Run/Icarus Films.
This film, based on Omar Caberzas's autobiography, recalls his childhood years under the Somoza regime in Nicaragua. Tells how this experience caused him to become a guerrilla fighter with the Sandinistas.

INNOVATING NICARAGUA. John Mraz, 1986. 40 min. color. Video. The Cinema Guild.
Takes a look at the work of the Innovators Movement in Nicaragua. Consists of groups organized by industry that try to overcome shortages and other problems affecting production. In Spanish with English subtitles.

LIVING AT RISK. Guzzetti, Meiselas, and Rogers, 1985. 59 min. color. 16mm. New Yorker Films.
Shows how a Nicaraguan family of Sandinista supporters manage to live under the daily dangers and stresses.

MECATE: A NEW SONG. Felix Zurita de Higes, 1984. 50 min.

color. 16mm/Video. First Run/Icarus Films.
Takes a look at the cultural life of Nicaraguan peasants as
expressed in music, theater, and poetry. The Peasants Movement
for Artistic and Dramatic Expression (MECATE) has as its goal
to develop artistic potential in the countryside. Shows how people
construct masks and musical instruments from materials available
in the villages.

NICARAGUA: A DANGEROUS EXAMPLE. BBC-TV, 198? 58
   min. color. 16mm/Video. Films Inc.
A Jesuit priest who is also a revolutionary discusses the 1979
overthrow of the Somoza dictatorship and how the new
government has been criticized by a sector inside the country and
by the United States.

NICARAGUA: DEVELOPMENT UNDER FIRE. J. Jackson, R.
   Horsley, J. Reiter, and Wolf Tirado, 1986. 26 min. color.
   Video. First Run/Icarus Films.
Describes the impact of the Contras on Nicaragua's economic and
social progress. Also reports on the problems involved with
international aid.

NICARAGUA: NO PASARAN. David Bradbury, 1984. 74 min.
   color. 16mm. New Yorker Films.
Covers the Somoza regime and the coming to power of the
Sandinistas in Nicaragua. Visits with the one surviving founder of
the original Sandinistas. In English and Spanish with English
subtitles.

NICARAGUA—OUR OWN COUNTRY. Herman Engel, 1985.
   19 min. color. 16mm/Video. Churchill Films.
From the Nicaraguan perspective this production documents the
history of Nicaragua from the conquistadores to the contemporary
scene.

NICARAGUA: REPORT FROM THE FRONT. D. Shaffer, T.
   Sigel, P. Yates, 1983. 32 min. color. 16mm/Video. First
   Run/Icarus Films.
The filmmakers spent two weeks following the Contras on patrol
from their base camps in Honduras. Examines U.S. policy with

regard to Nicaragua and Honduras.

NICARAGUA: THE DIRTY WAR. Alter Cine, 1985. 58 min. color. 16mm/Video. The Cinema Guild.
Describes the efforts of the Contras against Nicaraguan civilians. Interviews Nicaraguan citizens about their experiences during the war.

NICARAGUA WAS OUR HOME. Lee Shapiro, 1985. 55 min. color. 16mm/Video. Films Inc.
Tells about the persecution of the Miskito Indians of Nicaragua and their exodus to Honduras.

NICARAGUAN WOMEN—CONTRA WAR. Centre Productions, 1988. 28 min. color. Video. Centre Productions.
Focuses on three women—a peasant, a union leader, and a Sandinista official—who work to keep the economy going. Their views of the Sandinista revolution differ, but they share a lot of fear and hatred for the Contras.

PEACE PEEPING UP: ENDING NICARAGUA'S OTHER WAR. Ana Carrigan, 1988. 57 min. color. Video. First Run/Icarus Films.
A report on the history of the relationship between the Sandinistas and the Miskito people on Nicaragua's Atlantic coast. Raises questions about the U.S. CIA's possible involvement in the war with the Indians.

THE POPE: PILGRIM OF PEACE? Jackie Reiter, Wolf Tirado, 1983. 38 min. color. Video. First Run/Icarus Films.
The pope's visit to Nicaragua is discussed and analyzed by experts.

VACATION NICARAGUA. Anita Crisfield, 1988. 58 min. color. 16mm/Video. Wombat Film and Video.
Compares the U.S. and Nicaragua through the eyes of American tourists. The contrast is even carried through to the film music, which consists of Nueva Cancion and Caribbean music, and American popular music, with songs by Little Steven, Bob Dylan, Talking Heads, and others.

VAMOS A HACER UN PAIS (WE'RE GOING TO BUILD A
    COUNTRY). Seattle to Nicaragua Construction Brigade, 1986.
    30 min. color. Video. Rain Country Video.
Tells about a group of Americans who went to rural Nicaragua
to help build a school in 1986.

THE WAR IN EL CEDRO. Don North, 1987. 50 min. color.
    Video. North Star Productions, Syracuse Alternate Media
    Project.
Ten American veterans help rebuild a health clinic in El Cedro,
Nicaragua, that was destroyed by the Contras. The situation makes
the veterans compare experiences in Vietnam with what is going
on in Nicaragua.

WITH OUR OWN TWO HANDS. National Film Board of
    Canada, 1987. 27 min. color. 16mm/Video. National Film
    Board of Canada.
A portrait of the work of Irving Boblitz, a Canadian who decided
to do something about Nicaragua's poor farming conditions and
lack of repair of farm implements. He aroused the interest of
Canadians in helping the Nicaraguan farmers and led a group of
Canadian farmers to Nicaragua.

WOMEN IN NICARAGUA: THE SECOND REVOLUTION.
    Jackie Reiter, 1982. 28 min. color. 16mm/Video. First
    Run/Icarus Films.
Examines women's efforts to gain equality and to combat
machismo in Nicaragua. Also looks at women in the army.

THE WORLD IS WATCHING. Peter Raymond, 1988. 58 min.
    color. 16mm/Video. First Run/Icarus Films.
Explains how news is reported from Central America. Emphasis
is on TV coverage of events in Managua, Nicaragua.

Panama

DIGGERS. Roman Foster, 1985. 88 min. color. 16mm/Video.
    Roman Foster.
Gives all aspects of the history of the Panama Canal and the

100,000 black laborers who built it.

A MAN, A PLAN, A CANAL, PANAMA. WGBH-TV, 1988. 58
   min. color. Video. Coronet/MTI Film and Video.
This "Nova" program won several festival awards for its coverage
of the history and operations of the Panama Canal.

SOUTH AMERICA

General

CHILDREN IN DEBT. Estela Bravo, 1987. 29 min. color.
   16mm/Video. The Cinema Guild.
Shot in Argentina, Bolivia, Colombia, Peru. Examines the impact
on children of Latin America's debt to the U.S., which brings
austerity programs to an already impoverished people. In Spanish
with English subtitles.

EQUATORIAL RIVER. Dennis Sawyer, 1988. 23 min. color.
   16mm/Video. National Film Board of Canada.
Depicts the Amazon River's tropical rain forest. Shows the variety
of plant species, fauna, and the aboriginal people who live there.

A QUIET REVOLUTION. Audrey L. Glynn, 1988. 60 min. color.
   16mm/Video. The Cinema Guild.
The work of Christian Base Communities in Brazil, Ecuador, and
Peru. These groups are organized to provide disenfranchised
citizens a way of fighting poverty, oppression, and land
distribution. Includes interviews with leaders, including Reverend
Gustavo Gutierrez, the "Father of Liberation Theology."

SOUTH AMERICA, A NEW LOOK. International Film
   Foundation, 1985. 25 min. color. 16mm/Video. International
   Film Foundation.
A revised version of an earlier film. Covers the history, geography,
religion, and problems of present-day South America.

SOUTH AMERICA SERIES: PHYSICAL GEOGRAPHY. Thomas Stanton, 1987. 20 min. color. 16mm/Video. Stanton Films.
Describes the physical features of South America: rain forests, rivers, plains, mountains, and others.

Argentina

ARGENTINA: THE BROKEN SILENCE. Victor Fridman Productions, 1987. 59 min. b/w. 16mm. Victor Fridman Productions.
An account of the history of Argentina from the time of Perón to the present. Tells about the efforts of the Alfonsin government to establish democracy.

THE COLOURS OF HOPE. David Grubin, 1985. 20 min. color. 16mm/Video. Amnesty International.
Documents the imprisonment and release of a family caught up in the political controversy in Argentina.

DON'T EAT TODAY, OR TOMORROW. Rob Hof, 1985. 43 min. color. 16mm/Video. First Run/Icarus Films.
Discusses the situation in Argentina, with a national debt of 50 billion dollars. Looks at the recent military dictatorship, the aftermath of the Falkland War, the attempt to be a democracy, and the role of multinational banks and corporations.

GRAFFITI. Matthew Patrick, 1986. 28 min. color. 16mm/Video. The Cinema Guild.
This film has been awarded many prizes and was an Academy Award nominee. Based on a story by Julio Cortazar, a leading Argentine author. A young man sneaks out at night in his curfew-controlled city to draw sketches on walls. One night he discovers the work of a mystery artist next to his own.

LAS MADRES: THE MOTHERS OF THE PLAZA DE MAYO. Susan Munoz, Lourdes Portillo, 1985. 64 min. color. 16mm/Video. Direct Cinema.
Shows how the mothers of 30,000 young people who were tortured

and killed in Argentina organized to protest.

MISSING CHILDREN. Estela Bravo, 1985. 28 min. color. 16mm/Video. The Cinema Guild.
Shows the struggle of Argentine mothers and grandmothers to locate the children who were victims of the military junta in the late 1970s and early 1980s. Uses archival footage plus interviews with all concerned, including the children, to tell how the child captives were given as "war booty" to childless military couples. In Spanish with English subtitles.

PASSING OF PERON: THE END OF AN ERA? UPI, 1984. 24 min. color. Video. Journal Films.
An account of Argentine leader Juan Perón's career. Also discusses the culture of Argentina.

THE SEARCH FOR THE DISAPPEARED. David Dugan, 1986. 60 min. color. Video. Coronet/MTI Film and Video.
Scientists in Argentina try to locate kidnapped children and identify the dead from the military reign of terror. A "Nova" program.

THE TANGO IS ALSO HISTORY. Humberto Rios, 1983. 56 min. color. 16mm/Video. First Run/Icarus Films.
A portrait of the tango's development in Argentina and how Argentina's history is reflected in the tango. Includes performances.

Bolivia

RIVER JOURNEYS: LIZZIE. Churchill Films, 1986. 57 min. color. Video. Churchill Films.
Retraces the 4,000-mile journey along the Amazon in 1896 of a woman on her way to join her husband in Bolivia.

Brazil

THE AMAZON: A VANISHING RAINFOREST. Bradford Brooks, 1988. 29 min. color. Video. The Cinema Guild.

Focuses on the work of the National Institute of Amazon Research in Brazil's Amazon River Basin. Shows the researchers studying the impact of development in the area on natural life of the river: construction of a hydroelectric dam, timber extraction, road construction, and cattle ranching.

AMAZON: THE DELICATE GIANT. Lucerne Media, n.d. 11 min. color. 16mm/Video. Lucerne Media.
Depicts the threatening conditions that will damage the ecosystem of plant and animal life of the Amazon area. Shows what steps are being taken by Brazil to cope with this problem.

BAHIA: AFRICA IN THE AMERICAS. Broadcast Video Productions, 1989. 58 min. color. Video. University of California Extension Media Center.
Brazil's cultural destiny has been influenced by Yoruba Africans in the Bahia state. Candomblé, the traditional ancestral religion, has been superimposed on Catholic saints with similar attributes. Shows life in Bahia and the importance of candomblé there.

BANKING ON DISASTER. Adrian Cowell, 1988. 78 min. color. Video. Bullfrog Films (also available in three 26-min. episodes).
This program discusses the destruction of the Amazonian rain forest. Shows the disastrous results of putting a paved road through the heart of the rain forest that was intended to help colonists from other parts of Brazil move in to farm. Follows the five years of bad times of one colonial family.

BRAZIL: 1. SKYSCRAPERS AND SLUMS. BBC-TV, 1982. 20 min. color. Video. Films Inc.
Examines economic and social developments in urban and rural areas, in this case, the life of a shoeshiner who works in a prominent business district but lives in a ghetto.

BRAZIL: 2. DROUGHT ON THE LAND. BBC-TV, 1982. 20 min. color. Video. Films Inc.
Depicts the situation in Pau Ferro, a village in central Brazil, where frequent droughts have caused the loss of income-producing crops.

BRAZIL: 3. CITY OF NEWCOMERS. BBC-TV, 1982. 20 min. color. Video. Films Inc.
Discusses the migration of rural dwellers to cities where they have found promise in factories, but also problems.

BRAZIL: 4. AMAZON FRONTIER. BBC-TV, 1982. 20 min. color. Video. Films Inc.
Shows how the Amazon River basin near the town of Santarém has become an important commercial center due to industrial and agrarian developments.

BRAZIL: 5. PROGRESS, BUT WHO IS IT FOR? BBC-TV, 1982. 20 min. color. Video. Films Inc.
Explains how coffee once dominated the Brazilian economy, but now the growing industrial sector is of equal importance.

BRAZIL, THE LAND AND ITS PEOPLE. Hugh Baddeley Productions, 1984. 18 min. color. 16mm/Video. International Film Bureau.
A view of São Paulo, Rio de Janeiro, Cuiabá, Belém, Manaus and Curitiba. Discusses exports and transportation.

THE BRAZILIAN CONNECTION. International Women's Film Project, 1982. 60 min. color. Video. The Cinema Guild.
Describes how in 1982 Brazil held democratic elections, the first in almost two decades. Studies Brazil's trade relationship with the U.S., which is so important in order for Brazil to repay its huge debt.

COMMODITIES: FREE MARKETS FOR FREE MEN. Channel Four Television/UK, 1986. 52 min. color. Video. First Run/Icarus Films.
Describes the plight of Brazil's moving ever deeper into debt despite its participation in international accords, such as the International Coffee Agreement designed to protect producer companies.

COMMODITIES: WHITE GOLD. Channel Four Television/UK, 1986. 26 min. color. Video. First Run/Icarus Films.
Depicts the beginnings of sugar production and slavery in Brazil

from the 1530s on.

HAIL UMBANDA. Jose Aruajo, 1987. 46 min. color.
16mm/Video. University of California Extension Media Center.
Reports on Umbanda in tropical Brazil, which is a blend of
Catholicism, African and American religions, and spiritualism.

MACUMBA: TRANCE AND SPIRIT HEALING. Madeline
Richeport, 1985. 43 min. color. 16mm/Video. Filmakers
Library.
A film about the African religious roots of spiritism, which
flourishes in Brazil and in the U.S. as well. Tells how spiritist
sects were once forbidden and subject to police raids. Now some
doctors are actually using spiritist techniques to help
schizophrenics, epileptics, and drug addicts.

NOMADS OF THE RAINFOREST. Grant Behrman, 1987. 59
min. color. Video. University of California Extension Media
Center.
Documents a research expedition to study the Waorani, a fierce
Indian tribe that lives in complete isolation in the Amazon rain
forest. Shows blowgun hunters and daily life and rituals.

PEOPLE OF NO INTEREST. Peter Flemington and Kristian
Paludan, 1984. 29 min. color. 16mm/Video. First Run/Icarus
Films.
Looks at major development projects at the mouth of the Amazon
River financed by multinational corporations with tax breaks and
other support from the Brazilian government: a mining project,
a smelter, and refinery on the island of São Luís.

RIVER JOURNEYS: THE SÃO FRANCISCO. Churchill Films,
1986. 57 min. color. Video. Churchill Films.
Germaine Greer travels along the São Francisco River, starting
in the Brazilian highlands and progressing to the eastern coast.

SANTA MARTA: TWO WEEKS IN THE SLUMS. Bruno
Kupperman, 1988. 54 min. color. Video. The Cinema Guild.
About daily life in a Rio de Janeiro slum. Documents the struggle
for existence along with the songs, dance, and theater of the

poverty-stricken residents.

SHARING THE LAND. Journal Films, 1988. 20 min. color.
    Video. Journal Films.
Brazil had tremendous economic growth in the 1970s. Now the
nation faces food shortages and a staggering foreign debt.
Examines the causes of these problems.

THE WAIÃPI INDIANS OF BRAZIL: CAXIRI, OR MANIOC
    BEER. Victor Fuks, 1988. 19 min. color. Video. Indiana
    University.
Studies the uses of the manioc plant, which comprises a
substantial part of the Waiãpi diet. Processing the manioc tubers
results in *kwaka* flour, which is made into *mejus*, the pancakes
eaten with meals. The *mejus* are also fermented to produce *caxiri*,
a beer that is important to festivals and musical performances.

THE WAIÃPI INDIANS OF BRAZIL: MUSIC, DANCE, AND
    FESTIVAL AMONG THE WAIÃPI INDIANS OF BRAZIL.
    Victor Fuks, 1988. 39 min. color. Video. Indiana University.
Examines five festivals celebrated by the Waiãpi people of
northern Brazil. Shows the importance of music and dance in the
culture and the importance of *caxiri*, or manioc beer, to the
festivals.

THE WAIÃPA INDIANS OF BRAZIL: WAIÃPA BODY
    PAINTING AND ORNAMENTS. Victor Fuks, 1988. 18 min.
    color. Video. Indiana University.
Discusses body ornamentation of the Waiãpi people.
Demonstrates the methods used and the types of ornamentation,
some of it for adornment and some to celebrate various aspects
of Waiãpi culture.

THE WAIÃPI INDIANS OF BRAZIL: WAIÃPI
    INSTRUMENTAL MUSIC. Victor Fuks, 1988. 58 min. color.
    Video. Indiana University.
Shows a variety of Waiãpi wind instruments. Tells how the
instruments are made and describes their special uses in music and
dance.

THE WAIÃPI INDIANS OF BRAZIL: WAIÃPI SLASH AND BURN CULTIVATION. Victor Fuks, 1988. 22 min. color. Video. Indiana University.
An account of how slash and burn cultivation is used to grow foods by the Waiãpi people, like rain forest dwellers all over the world. Gives details of the methods used and how a healthy, balanced relationship with nature is sustained.

Chile

CHELA: LOVE, DREAMS AND STRUGGLE IN CHILE. Lars Palmgren, Goran Gester, Lars Bildt, 1986. 48 min. color. Video. Filmakers Library.
Chela, a 16-year-old Chilean girl, tells about growing up under the Pinochet dictatorship. Although most of her time is spent as a typical teenager, the girl expresses her concerns by participating in street demonstrations. Shows the poor neighborhood in which she lives.

CHILE HASTA CUANDO? David Bradbury, 1986. 57 min. color. 16mm/Video. Filmakers Library.
This film was shot at great risk to report on the brutality of the Pinochet regime in Chile. Shows how the power elite lives in comfort.

DANCE OF HOPE. Lavonne Poteet and Deborah Shaffer, 1989. 75 min. color. 16mm/Video. First Run/Icarus Films.
Tells the stories of eight women in Chile using the 1988 plebescite as a backdrop. Describes their search for missing relatives. A song, "They Dance Alone," was created for them, and they have become the conscience of the nation.

DULCE PATRIA. Latin American Film Project, 1985. 59 min. color. Video. First Run/Icarus Films.
A study of the struggle in recent years against dictatorship. In Spanish with English subtitles.

HOLY FATHER AND GLORIA. Estela Bravo, 1987. 43 min. color. 16mm/Video. The Cinema Guild.

Covers Pope John Paul's visit to Chile in 1987, which evoked an outpouring of discontent with the Pinochet regime. Includes an interview with Carmen Gloria, a permanently disfigured victim of the Chilean military in 1986. Also includes interviews with people who are pro or anti Pinochet. In Spanish with English subtitles.

MEMOIRS OF AN EVERYDAY WAR. Gaston Ancelovici, 1986. 29 min. color. 16mm/Video. First Run/Icarus Films.
Interviews four people who were affected by 12 years of life under the Pinochet regime in Chile. Discusses Chile's possible future.

ONE HUNDRED CHILDREN WAITING FOR A TRAIN. Ignacio Aguero, 1988. 57 min. color. 16mm/Video. First Run/Icarus Films.
A Chilean film that tells of the experiences of a small group of children who discover a new world through the cinema. Each Saturday a professor turns a chapel in a slum neighborhood into a film projection room. Through viewing films the children learn about film history, filmmaking, and how reality can become fantasy.

RETURNING TO CHILE. Estela Bravo, 1986. 28 min. color. Video. The Cinema Guild.
Chilean young people who have been in exile with their parents discuss their memories of the 1979 coup as they return to their homeland. Shows protests in the streets, the funeral of a young man slain by the military, a speech by Pinochet, and a mother's account of the torture and killing of her son. In Spanish with English subtitles.

SWEET COUNTRY. Juan Andres Racz, 1986. 57 min. color. 16mm/Video. First Run/Icarus Films.
A comprehensive survey of Chile today. General Pinochet and others are interviewed. Activists discuss the struggle against the dictatorship.

Colombia

COLOMBIA: COFFEE MARKET. UPI, 1984. 15 min. color.

Video. Journal Films.
Explains how the international market and the weather can affect the life of the Colombians.

COMMODITIES: COFFEE IS THE GOLD OF THE FUTURE.
　　Channel Four Television/UK, 1986. 52 min. color. Video. First
　　Run/Icarus Films.
The history of the coffee industry in Colombia. Examines problems of land ownership, market control, agrarian reform, and price fluctuations.

THE EARTH IS OUR MOTHER. Peter Elsass, 1988. 50 min.
　　color. Video. Filmakers Library.
Focuses on two Indian groups of Colombia to show how they are affected by Western civilization. The Motelon people who remained in town are shown as ill, poor, and dependent. On the other hand, the Arhuaco people have retreated into the hinterland and have maintained their ancient culture.

IKA HANDS. Robert Gardner, 1988. 58 min. color. 16mm/Video.
　　MOMA Circulating Film Library.
Presents a view of the daily life of the Ika people of the Sierra Nevada of northern Colombia. A devout mystic explains the spiritual basis for the life of the Ika.

THE LEGEND OF EL DORADO. Museum of Modern Art of
　　Latin America, 1984. 25 min. color. Video. Museum of
　　Modern Art of Latin America.
Studies the myths and significance of gold in South America through a visit to the Gold Museum in Bogotá, Colombia.

TIERRA Y CULTURA. Magdalena V. and Sigi S., 1987. 38 min.
　　color. 16mm/Video. The Cinema Guild.
Indian communities of Colombia are conducting guerrilla warfare with Colombian army troops in order to protest brutal encroachments by large landowners. Discusses historical roots of the conflict back to the time of the Spanish conquistadores. Also covers Indian rituals and an interview with an Indian commander. In Spanish with English subtitles.

Ecuador

ICEMEN OF CHIMBORAZO. Gustavo Guayasamin, 1980. 21 min. color. 16mm/Video. First Run/Icarus Films.
Shows how once a week Indian peasants of Chimborazo climb above their village in rural Ecuador to cut ice from the snowcaps in order to sell it to food vendors at the market at Guaranda.

THIS IS WHAT WE THINK. Camillo Luzuriaga, 1984. 29 min. color. 16mm/Video. First Run/Icarus Films.
Tells how 100 Ecuadoran peasants struggled to combat their feudal landlord. After seven years of legal activity, they gained a portion of his estate on which they have started an agricultural cooperative.

Falkland Islands

THE FALKLANDS. UPI, 1986. 20 min. color. Video. Journal Films.
Gives the background for the Argentine effort to take over the Falkland Islands.

Paraguay

NANDUTL: A PARAGUAYAN LACE. OK Productions, 1984. 17 min. color. Video. International Film Bureau.
Demonstrates an ancient art of Paraguay—the making of *nandutl*, Paraguayan lace.

PARAGUAY: THE FORGOTTEN DICTATORSHIP. Patricio Boero, 1988. 27 min. color. Video. The Cinema Guild.
A visit to Latin America's oldest dictatorship to analyze the current power struggle. Documents human rights abuses and the development of opposition forces. In Spanish with English subtitles.

Peru

ALPACA BREEDERS OF CHIMBOYA. Kusi Films, 1984. 30

min. color. 16mm/Video. First Run/Icarus Films.
Shows how a community in the Peruvian Andes must export
alpaca fleece for economic survival.

CHOQELA: ONLY INTERPRETATION. John Cohen, 1987. 12
min. color. 16mm/Video. The Cinema Guild.
This film explains the difficulties in interpreting the Choqela
ceremony, an agricultural ritual of the Aymara Indians of Peru.

FIRE IN THE ANDES. Ilan Ziv, 1985. 35 min. color. Video.
First Run/Icarus Films.
Since 1980 there has been a guerrilla war in Peru between the
Maoist Shining Path and the Peruvian armed forces. This video
investigates the fate of eight journalists whose bodies were
discovered in a remote Andean village.

THE INCAS REMEMBERED. Lucy Jarvis, 1985. 60 min. color.
Video. Monterey Home Video.
Documents the history of the Incas of Peru from the earliest times
to the arrival of the conquering Spaniards.

MARTIN CHAMBI AND THE HEIRS OF THE INCAS. Paul
Yule and Andy Harries, 1987. 50 min. color. 16mm/Video. The
Cinema Guild.
A portrait of the Peruvian Indian photographer, Martin Chambi,
noted for his photography of wealthy families and his sensitive
photography of Peru's Indian population. In Spanish with English
subtitles. Winner of several awards.

MOUNTAIN MUSIC OF PERU. John Cohen, 1984. 58 min.
color. 16mm/Video. The Cinema Guild.
Reviews the history of music of the Andes, which today still
reflects the pre-Columbian quality of Inca culture. Shows the
importance of this music in preserving the identity of the Andean
Indians. Presents a variety of vocal and instrumental music in
performance.

OUR GOD THE CONDOR. Paul Yule and Andy Harries, 1987.
30 min. color. 16mm/Video. Filmakers Library.
Documents the "Yawar Fiesta," an annual event in Peru

celebrating the triumph of the Indians over the Spanish. Features a ritual involving a bull to symbolize Spain and a condor to represent the freedom of the Andean people.

PAUCARTAMBO—INCA RIVER. John Armstrong, 1986. 41 min. color. 16mm/Video. Wombat Film and Video.
This is an account of a kayak trip in 1985 down the Paucartambo, a river that runs from the Peruvian Andes to the Amazon basin. Has spectacular white water footage, scenes of Indian villagers, and a shaman.

PAUCARTAMBO—THE REST OF THE RIVER. John Armstrong, 1988. 58 min. color. Video. Wombat Film and Video.
Covers a daring trip down the lower Paucartambo River from the Peruvian Andes to the jungle by a seven-member expedition, which included two women. Describes the team's encounters with Quechua Indians.

PERUVIAN WEAVING: A CONTINUOUS WARP FOR 5,000 YEARS. John Cohen, 1980. 25 min. color. 16mm/Video. The Cinema Guild.
Indian weavers demonstrate the ancient Peruvian tradition of warp pattern weaving. Includes an interview with Dr. Junius Bird of the American Museum of Natural History.

VILLA EL SALVADOR: A DESERT DREAM. Robbie Hart, Luc Coté and José Bertemeu, 1989. 50 min. color. Video. The Cinema Guild.
Depicts the history of one of the best squatter settlements in Latin America, Villa El Salvador, which was established in the early 1970s on a desert prairie south of Lima, Peru. Many homes include electricity and running water; the literacy rate is 97%. Shows a people determined to improve their lot. English and Spanish versions available.

WOMEN OF PLANETA. Maria Barea, 1982. 30 min. color. 16mm/Video. Women Make Movies.
A story about women in a shantytown outside Lima, Peru. An award-winning film. In Spanish with English subtitles.

Uruguay

EDUARDO, URUGUAYO. Jan Blom, D. Sauer, F. Diamand,
    1983. 45 min. color. 16mm/Video. First Run/Icarus Films.
A clandestinely shot exposé of the oppressive military regime in
Uruguay. Follows one family in this report on torture, kidnapping,
and exile.

THE EYES OF THE BIRDS. Gabriel Auer, 1982. 82 min. color.
    Video. First Run/Icarus Films.
A dramatic theatrical feature film about a visit by the
International Committee of the Red Cross to a prison in Uruguay
called "Libertad." Reveals the awful truth about prison conditions.
Also, the committee members learn that their conversations have
been secretly recorded. Winner of first prize, Festival of New
Latin American Cinema.

URUGUAY: SHARK FISHING. UPI, 1984. 14 min. color. Video.
    Journal Films.
About a group who established a fishing community in a small
town in Uruguay.

WEST INDIES

General

AFRO-CARIBBEAN FESTIVAL. Luis Alonso, 1983. 90 min.
    color. Video. New Jersey Network.
A dance program demonstrating the performances of troupes from
Puerto Rico, Haiti, the Dominican Republic, and Africa.

CARIBBEAN MUSIC AND DANCE. Museum of Modern Art
    of Latin America, 1984. 25 min. color. Video. Museum of
    Modern Art of Latin America.
Captures the flavor of Caribbean music and dance with their
exciting rhythmic appeal.

THE CUNA INDIANS: ISLAND EXILES. Wayne Mitchell, 1983.
    22 min. color. 16mm/Video. BFA Educational Media.
Follows the daily life of one Cuna family in food preparation,
building houses, making clothing, and dancing to the music of
pipes. Explains that the Cuna Indians live in isolation on small
Caribbean islands.

LAST OF THE KARAPHUNA. Phillip Thorneycroft Teuscher,
    1983. 50 min. color. 16mm/Video. The Cinema Guild.
The Carib Indians of the West Indies are now known as the
Karaphuna. Interviews with the Karaphuna and Caribbean
ethnologists depict the history of the Caribs, who dominated the
West Indies before Columbus arrived.

ONE WORLD: 1. TRADING THE SUN. BBC-TV, 1982. 20 min.
    color. Video. Films Inc.
The first part of a series that explores perceptions about the world
by focusing on the links between Great Britain and its former
Caribbean colonies. This program about the role of tourism in the
Caribbean economy discusses the impact of much-needed foreign
money and the potentially harmful patterns of behavior brought
in.

ONE WORLD: 2. FROM THE CARIBBEAN. BBC-TV, 1982.
    20 min. color. Video. Films Inc.
Traces the economic and social problems of St. Lucia, which are
typical for small nations that are former colonies.

ONE WORLD: 3. PEOPLE ON THE MOVE. BBC-TV, 1982. 20
    min. color. Video. Films Inc.
Discusses reasons for migration and studies one Jamaican family
as an example.

ONE WORLD: 4. MADE IN BARBADOS. BBC-TV, 1982. 20
    min. color. Video. Films Inc.
Shows how developing nations often must use imported raw
materials to manufacture goods.

Cayman Islands

THE CAYMAN EXPERIENCE. H. Velle Wright, 1981. 25 min.
color. Video. Video Presentations.
A tour of the Cayman Islands in the Caribbean Sea. Covers scenic
attractions, such as beaches and gardens.

REEFS OF CAYMAN. Nancy Sefton, 1980. 25 min. color. Video.
Video Presentations.
Examines the marine life in the coral reefs of the Cayman Islands
in the West Indies.

Cuba

CRISIS IN CENTRAL AMERICA: 2. CASTRO'S CHALLENGE.
WGBH-TV, 1985. 58 min. color. Video. Films Inc.
Studies the Cuban revolution of 1959. Includes the rise of Castro,
the historic roots of the revolution, and tensions with the U.S.

CRISIS: MISSLES IN CUBA. A. Pannell, R. Wales, D. Clancy,
1987. 28 min. color. Video. Zenger Video.
In order to depict the diplomatic maneuvering of the Cuban
missile crisis, this program recreates the events of 1962. It is
designed to be stopped at important points so that the viewer can
explore policy decisions and compare them with those of the
Kennedy administration.

CUBA: IN THE SHADOW OF DOUBT. Carol Polakoff, Suzanne
Bauman, 1987. 58 min. color. 16mm/Video. Filmakers Library.
Uses interviews and archival footage to tell the history of the
Cuban revolution. Discusses its successes and failures and U.S.
policy.

CUBAN MUSIC: MARCO RIZO. New Jersey Network, 1983. 30
min. color. Video. New Jersey Network.
Marco Rizo, the Cuban musician/composer, performs traditional
and modern Cuban music.

EL DIALOGO (THE DIALOGUE). Downtown Community TV

Center, 1980. 57 min. b/w. Video. Downtown Community TV
Center.
Tells what happened after Castro and Cuban exiles met in
December 1978.

FIDEL CASTRO COMES TO NEW YORK. Downtown
Community TV Center, 1979. 35 min. color. Video. Downtown
Community TV Center.
In October 1978 Castro came to New York to address the
General Assembly of the United Nations. This program gives the
details of that visit.

HAVANA POSTMODERN: THE NEW CUBAN ART. Robert
Knafo, Coco Fusco, and Andras Mesz, 1988. 54 min. color.
Video. The Cinema Guild.
A documentary about contemporary art in Cuba. Traces influences
and provides a view of artists at work in their studios. Covers
opening night at the Havana Biennial of Third World Art. In
Spanish with English subtitles.

IMPROPER CONDUCT. Les Films du Losange, 1984. 115 min.
color. 16mm. New Yorker Films.
Compares the myth of the Cuban revolution with the realities of
Cuban life.

MODEL REVOLUTIONARIES AND WORMS. Journal Films,
1987. 42 min. color. Video. Journal Films.
Studies the "model revolutionaries" who find life easier after the
Cuban revolution, and the "worms," the defectors who no longer
believe in the revolutionary dream.

NOBODY LISTENED. Nestor Almendios, Jorge Ulla, 1988. 117
min. color. 16mm/Video. Direct Cinema.
Eyewitnesses describe human rights violations in Castro's Cuba.
Also uses archival footage.

TURNING DREAMS INTO REALITY. Monica Melamid and
Rafael Andreu, 1988. 29 min. color. Video. The Cinema
Guild.
Depicts the career of Fernando Birri, "Father of the New Latin

American Cinema." Covers his training in Rome in the 1950s, the founding of the Documentary School of Santa Fe in his native Argentina, his exile in Italy, and current work in Cuba. Includes excerpts from Birri's films. In Spanish with English subtitles.

Dominican Republic

BLACK SUGAR. Eric Michel, 1989. 58 min. color. 16mm/Video. National Film Board of Canada.
Poor Haitian farm laborers go each year to the Dominican Republic to work harvesting the sugarcane.

DOMINICAN REPUBLIC, CRADLE OF THE AMERICAS. Museum of Modern Art of Latin America, 1980. 25 min. color. Video. Museum of Modern Art of Latin America.
A report on cultural life in the Dominican Republic. Includes a discussion of pre-Columbian art.

MERENGUE: MUSIC FROM THE DOMINICAN REPUBLIC. New Jersey Network, n.d. 30 min. color. Video. New Jersey Network.
Introduces merengue music of the Dominican Republic. Features Primitivo Santos and his orchestra and Raices Latinas, a folklore dance group. In an interview Primitivo Santos talks about the history of merengue and its meaning for the Dominican people.

Grenada

GRENADA: PORTRAIT OF A REVOLUTION. Joanne Kelly, 1983. 27 min. color. Video. Video Free America.
Filmed before the U.S. invasion, this production explores the problems of Grenada.

GRENADA: THE FUTURE COMING TOWARD US. John Douglas, Carmen Ashhurst, Samori Marksman, 1984. 55 min. color. 16mm/Video. The Cinema Guild.
Discusses the U.S. military invasion in 1983 and the aims of the New Jewel Movement. Traces Grenada's history from the colonial period to the evolution of modern Grenadan society. Includes

background on the oppressive rule of Eric Gairy.

MAURICE. Estela Bravo, 1984. 27 min. color. 16mm/Video. The
    Cinema Guild.
A report on the assassination of the prime minister, Maurice
Bishop, and other members of the government in October 1983
by a counter-revolutionary group. Also discusses the subsequent
U.S. invasion.

MAURICE BISHOP SPEAKS. Larry Bullard, 1984. 40 min. color.
    Video. New Time Films.
Prime Minister Bishop was the leader of the socialist revolutionary
government that figured prominently in the 1979 revolution in
Grenada. This video documents his speech at Hunter College in
which he discussed the goals of his party and predicted the U.S.
military intervention.

OPERATION URGENT FURY. Mark Obenhaus, 1988. 58 min.
    color. Video. PBS Video.
Reporter Seymour Hersch probes the 1983 U.S. invasion of
Grenada.

Haiti

THE ART OF HAITI. Mark Mamalakis, 1982. 26 min. color.
    16mm/Video. Mark Mamalakis Productions.
In Haiti untrained painters started an art movement that has
attracted international attention. Includes interviews with painters
and features the works of more than 12 Haitian artists. Winner
of several awards.

BLACK DAWN. Robin Lloyd, Doreen Kraft, 1980. 20 min. color.
    Video. First Run/Icarus Films.
The history of the Haitian revolution and the formation of a black
republic is told as an animated folktale.

HAITI DREAMS OF DEMOCRACY. Jonathan Denime and Jo
    Menell, 1987. 52 min. color. Video. The Cinema Guild.
An unusual documentary that not only examines the concerns of

post-Duvalier Haiti but also focuses on popular music and street theater that reflect culture and political aspirations.

VOYAGE OF DREAMS. Collis Davis, Raymond Cajuste, 1983. 30 min. color. 16mm/Video. The Cinema Guild.
Describes the reasons for the exile of the Haitian boat people—injustice, oppression, economic stagnation, and the absence of free speech.

ZANTRAY '88: A PORTRAIT OF MODERN HAITI. Centre Productions, 1988. 52 min. color. Video. Centre Productions.
A report on Haiti, the poorest country in the Western Hemisphere. Tells how Haiti suffers under a repressive military dictatorship and from the Macoutes (a terrorist group), disease, poverty, and voodoo beliefs.

Jamaica

JAMAICA: SWING TO THE RIGHT. UPI, 1980, 24 min. color. Video. Journal Films.
An account of Jamaica's violent election in 1980 and the new conservative rules.

SWEET SUGAR RAGE. Sistren Theatre Collective, Jamaica, 1985. 45 min. color. Video. Third World Newsreel.
The Sistren Theatre Collective uses improvisation and theater as a means of raising consciousness among rural and urban audiences in Jamaica. The troupe represents the daily experiences of women, especially their poor working situation, with long hours, low pay, and inadequate conditions. This program tells the story of a female sugarcane worker who for 25 years has struggled for pay equity.

WOMEN'S CONSTRUCTION COLLECTIVE OF JAMAICA. Marie Kelley, 1986. 13 min. color. Video. West Glen Inc.
Shows how some black ghetto women from Kingston, Jamaica, formed their own construction business after special training in construction trade skills.

Martinique

SUGAR CANE ALLEY. Euzhan Palcy, 1983. 103 min. color. 16mm. New Yorker Films.
A shantytown black boy seeks an education in the city. Set in Martinique in 1931 when it was under French colonial rule. In French with English subtitles.

Netherlands Antilles

NETHERLANDS ANTILLES. Lucerne Media, 1981. 14 min. color. Video. Lucerne Media.
Describes Curacao and Aruba, islands in the West Indies, which serve as popular tourist attractions. Shows the recent development of the oil industry in these islands.

Puerto Rico

THE BATTLE OF VIEQUES. Zyndia Mazario, 1986. 40 min. color. 16mm/Video. The Cinema Guild.
The U.S. Navy is using the island of Vieques, a municipality of Puerto Rico, as a military base, and the residents are trying to get the Navy to leave. Shows the impact of the Navy's presence.

FRANCISCO OLLER: A 19TH-CENTURY PAINTER OF PUERTO RICO. Angel Hurtado, 1986. 25 min. color. 16mm/Video. Museum of Modern Art of Latin America.
Francisco Oller was a Puerto Rican painter who made important contributions to the development of Impressionism and introduced this style in Latin America.

MANOS A LA OBRA: THE STORY OF OPERATION BOOTSTRAP. Jaime Barrios, 1983. 59 min. color. 16mm/Video. The Cinema Guild.
In the 1950s an economic development plan for Puerto Rico called Operation Bootstrap transformed Puerto Rican life. Shows the impact of industrialization.

LA OPERACION. Ana Maria Garcia, 1982. 40 min. color.

16mm/Video. The Cinema Guild.
How Puerto Rico uses female sterilization for population control. Interviews several women who participated in the sterilization program.

PUERTO RICO: PROGRESS IN THE CARIBBEAN. Handel Film Corporation, 1988. 25 min. color. 16mm/Video. Handel Film Corporation.
Gives the history of Puerto Rico from its discovery on Columbus's second voyage to the present. Tells how Operation Bootstrap led to the successful industrialization of the island and created an area with the highest per capita income in Latin America. Spanish version available.

Saint Lucia

COME TO SAINT LUCIA. Museum of Modern Art of Latin America, 1984. 25 min. color. Video. Museum of Modern Art of Latin America.
Van Martin narrates this travelogue about the Caribbean island of Saint Lucia.

LIST OF FILM/VIDEO DISTRIBUTORS

ABC VIDEO
  ENTERPRISES
825 Seventh Ave., New York,
  NY 10019
(212) 887-1731

ADR PRODUCTIONS, INC.
P.O. Box 22581, Honolulu,
  HI 96822
(808) 524-4777

AFRICAN FAMILY FILMS
P.O. Box 1109, Venice, CA
  90291
(213) 392-1020

AIMS MEDIA
6901 Woodley Ave., Van
  Nuys, CA 91406
(818) 785-4111
(800) 367-2467

ALASKA TELEVISION
  NETWORK
2700 E. Tudor Rd.,
  Anchorage, AK 99701
(907) 561-1313

ALDEN FILMS
P.O. Box 449, Clarksburg, NJ
  08510
(201) 462-3522

AMERICAN FRIENDS
  SERVICE COMMITTEE
NARMIC
1501 Cherry St., New York, NY
  10019
(800) 223-2282 X605

AMNESTY INTERNATIONAL
322 Eighth Ave., New York,
  NY 10001
(212) 807-8400

ANTI-DEFAMATION
  LEAGUE OF B'NAI
  BRITH
Audio-Visual Department
  823 United Nations Plaza,
  New York, NY 10017
(212) 490-2525

AROUND THE WORLD IN
SIGHT AND SOUND
P.O. Box 163, Glenside, PA
19038
(215) 885-1855

ASIA SOCIETY
Education Department
725 Park Ave., New York,
NY 10021
(212) 288-6400

ASIAN AMERICAN
STUDIES CENTRAL, INC.
Visual Communications
244 S. San Pedro St., Suite
309 Los Angeles, CA 90012
(213) 680-4462

ASIAN ART MUSEUM OF
SAN FRANCISCO
Golden Gate Park, San
Francisco, CA 94118
(415) 558-2993

ATVN (ALASKA
TELEVISION NETWORK)
2700 E. Tudor Rd.,
Anchorage, AK 99701
(907) 561-1313

AUSTRALIAN FILM
COMMISSION
875 Gower St., Hollywood,
CA 90038
(213) 469-2223

BARR FILMS
12801 Schabarum Ave.,
Irwindale, CA 91706
(818) 338-7878
(800) 234-7879

BEACON FILMS
930 Pitner Ave., Evanston,
IL 60202
(312) 328-6700
(800) 323-5448

BENCHMARK FILMS, INC.
145 Scarborough, Briarcliff
Manor, NY 10510
(914) 762-3838

BFA EDUCATIONAL
MEDIA
468 Park Avenue South, New
York, NY 10016
(212) 684-5910
(800) 221-1274
and
47 Densley Ave., Toronto,
Ontario
Canada M6M 5A8
(416) 241-4483

BLACK FILMMAKER
FOUNDATION
80 Eighth Ave., Suite 1704,
New York, NY 10011
(212) 924-1198

BLACKHAWK FILMS
1235 West Fifth, Box 3990,
Davenport, IA 52808
(319) 323-9736

MICHAEL BOBER
1027 N. Ave. 49, Los
  Angeles, CA 90042
(213) 259-8145

BULLFROG FILMS, INC.
Oley, PA 19547
(215) 779-8226

BUSCH CREATIVE
  SERVICES CORP.
5240 Oakland, St. Louis, MO
  62110
(314) 289-7737

CALIFORNIA NEWSREEL
149 Ninth St. #420, San
  Francisco, CA 94103
(415) 621-6196

CAMERA 3
  PRODUCTIONS
One Madison Ave., New
  York, NY 10010
(212) 685-7880

CAMINO FILM PROJECTS
P.O. Box 291575, Los
  Angeles, CA 90029
(213) 461-7305

CAROLE LANGER
  PRODUCTIONS
28 Green St., New York, NY
  10013
(212) 925-1599

CAROUSEL FILM AND
  VIDEO
260 Fifth Ave. #705, New
  York, NY 10001
(212) 683-1660

CBC ENTERPRISES
Canadian Broadcasting Corp.
245 Park Ave., New York,
  NY 10167
(212) 949-1500

CBS FOX VIDEO
1211 Avenue of the
  Americas, New York, NY
  10036
(212) 819-3200

CENTER FOR AFRICAN
  STUDIES, UNIVERSITY
  OF FLORIDA
470 Grinter Hall, Gainesville,
  FL 32611
(401) 351-6923

CENTRE PRODUCTIONS
12801 Schabarum Ave.,
  Irwindale, CA 91706
(818) 338-7878
(800) 234-7879

CENTRON FILMS
108 Wilmot Rd., Deerfield,
  IL 60015
(312) 940-1260
(800) 621-2131

CGI
P.O. Box 604, Ontario, NY
  14519
(715) 265-1450

CHEVRON U.S.A., INC.
575 Market St., San
  Francisco, CA 94120
(415) 894-0254

CHIP TAYLOR
  COMMUNICATIONS
13 Spollett Dr., Derry, NH
  03038
(603) 434-9262
(800) 876-CHIP

CHURCH WORLD
  SERVICE
475 Riverside Dr., New York,
  NY 10015
(212) 870-2079

CHURCHILL FILMS
662 N. Robertson Blvd., Los
  Angeles, CA 90069
(213) 657-5110

CINE-PIC HAWAII
1847 Pacific Heights Rd.,
  Honolulu, HI 96813
(808) 533-2677

CINECOM
  INTERNATIONAL
1250 Broadway, New York,
  NY 10001
(212) 629-6222

THE CINEMA GUILD
1697 Broadway, New York,
  NY 10019
(212) 246-5522

COMMUNITY MEDIA
  PRODUCTIONS
P.O. Box 909, Lemont, PA
  16851

CONSTANT SPRING
  PRODUCTIONS
P.O. Box 2, Devault, PA
  19432
(215) 933-0666

CORNELL UNIVERSITY
210 Uris Hall, Ithaca, NY
  14853
(607) 255-6302

CORONET/MTI FILM AND
  VIDEO
108 Wilmot Rd., Deerfield,
  IL 60015
(312) 940-1260
(800) 621-2131

CPB ANNENBERG
  PROJECT
1111 16th St. NW,
  Washington, DC 20036

CRISFIELD FILM AND
  VIDEO
P.O. Box 788, Davis, CA
  95617
(906) 758-0900

CROSSCURRENT MEDIA
National Asian American
Telecommunications
Association
346 Ninth St., 2nd Floor, San
Francisco, CA 94103
(415) 552-9550

JAMES CULP
PRODUCTIONS
Community Media
Productions
P.O. Box 909, Lemont, PA
16851

DALLAS COUNTY
COMMUNITY COLLEGE
Center for
Telecommunications
4343 North Highway 67,
Mesquite, TX 75150
(214) 324-7988

DAVENPORT FILMS
Rt. 1, Box 527, Delaplane,
VA 22025
(703) 592-3701

CAROL KREEGER
DAVIDSON
24 Glenwood Rd., W.
Hartford, CT 06107
(203) 561-2313

DEEP SOUTH
PRODUCTIONS
825 Port St., New Orleans,
LA 70017
(504) 948-7929

THE DIASPORA FILM
PROJECT
Cultural Research and
Communication, Inc.
1700 Broadway, Room 4201,
New York, NY 10019
(212) 265-2140

DIRECT CINEMA, LTD.
(Sales) P.O. Box 69799, Los
Angeles, CA 90069
(213) 652-8000
(Rental) P.O. Box 315,
Franklin Lakes, NJ 07417
(201) 891-2840
(800) 345-6748

DOKO
COMMUNICATIONS
609 Madison Ave., Suite
1400, New York, NY 10022
(212) 570-0203

DOWNTOWN
COMMUNITY TV
CENTER
87 Lafayette St., New York,
NY 10013
(212) 966-4510

EARTHWORKS
Box 2245, Malibu, CA 90265
(213) 456-5771

EDUCATIONAL FILM
AND VIDEO PROJECT
1529 Josephine St., Berkeley,
CA 94703
(415) 849-1649

EL TALLER GRAFICO
P.O. Box 62, Keene, CA
  93531

SARAH ELDER AND
  LEONARD KAMERLING
P.O. Box 81323, Fairbanks,
  AK 99708
(907) 455-6542

EMORY MEDICAL
  TELEVISION NETWORK
Audiovisual Librarian, A. W.
  Calhoun Medical Library
Emory University, Atlanta,
  GA 30322
(404) 727-5817 (rental)
(404) 727-5678 (sales)

ENCYCLOPAEDIA
  BRITANNICA
  EDUCATIONAL CORP.
425 N. Michigan Ave.,
  Chicago, IL 60611
(800) 554-6970

EPISCOPAL RADIO-TV
  FOUNDATION
3379 Peachtree Rd. NE,
  Atlanta, GA 30326
(404) 233-5419

FELIX FILMS, INC.
530 114th St., #3R, New
  York, NY 10025
(212) 222-2879

JOHN FERRETTI
2841 Henry St., Honolulu, HI
  96817
(808) 949-6764

FILM IDEAS
3575 Commercial Ave.,
  Northbrook, IL 60062
(312) 480-5760

FILM IN THE CITIES
2388 University Ave., St.
  Paul, MN 55114
(612) 646-6104

FILMAKERS LIBRARY
124 East 40th St., Suite 901,
  New York, NY 10016
(212) 808-4980

FILMFAIR
  COMMUNICATIONS
10621 Magnolia Blvd., North
  Hollywood, CA 91601
(818) 985-0244

FILMS FOR THE
  HUMANITIES
P.O. Box 2053, Princeton, NJ
  08543
(609) 452-1128
(800) 257-5126

FILMS INC.
5547 N. Ravenswood Ave.,
  Chicago, IL 60640
(312) 878-2600 X326
(800) 323-4222 X326

FINLEY-HOLIDAY FILM
  CORP.
P.O. Box 619, Whittier, CA
  90608
(213) 945-3325

FIRST RUN/ICARUS
  FILMS, INC.
153 Waverly Place, Sixth
  Floor, New York, NY
  10014
(212) 727-1711
(800) 876-1710

FLOWER FILMS
10341 San Pablo Ave., El
  Cerrito, CA 94530
(415) 525-0942

FOGLIGHT FILMS
208 East Maynard Ave.,
  Columbus, OH 43202
(614) 268-4690

ROMAN FOSTER
108 West 15th St., #2F, New
  York, NY 10011
(212) 924-3543

GALAN PRODUCTIONS,
  INC.
400 East Anderson Lane,
  Suite 305, Austin, TX
  78752

GEORGIA STATE
  UNIVERSITY
Office of Education, Box 859
  University Plaza, Atlanta,
  GA 30303
(404) 658-3311

GREAT PLAINS
  NATIONAL
P.O. Box 80669, Lincoln, NE
  68501
(800) 228-4630

HANDEL FILM
  CORPORATION
8730 Sunset Blvd., West
  Hollywood, CA 90069
(213) 657-8990
      and
OMEGA FILMS, LTD.
70 Milner Ave., Unit 5A,
  Scarborough, Ontario
  Canada M1S 3P8

HARTLEY FILM
  FOUNDATION
Cat Rock Rd., Cos Cob, CT
  06807
(203) 869-1818

HAZARDOUS FILMS
Rd. 1, Tompkins Corners,
  Putnam Valley, NY 10579
(914) 528-6453

ANTHONY HERRERA
360 E. 50th St., #5C, New
  York, NY 10022
(212) 838-5548

HMONG FILM PROJECT
2258 Commonwealth Ave., St.
  Paul, MN 55108
(612) 871-3151

LOUIS HOCK
1215 Caminito Septimo,
  Cardiff, CA 92007
(619) 534-2915

HOME VISION
5547 N. Ravenswood Ave.,
  Chicago, IL 60640
(312) 878-3600 X325

IE FILM PRODUCTIONS
11812 Gateway Blvd., #5, Los
  Angeles, CA 90064
(213) 479-6017

IKONOGRAPHICS, INC.
P.O. Box 4454, Louisville,
  KY 40204
(502) 583-3506

INDIANA UNIVERSITY
Audio-Visual Center,
  Bloomington, IN 47405
(812) 335-8087

INTERNATIONAL FILM
  AND VIDEO
1192 Page St., San Francisco,
  CA 94117
(415) 864-2573

INTERNATIONAL FILM
  BUREAU
332 South Michigan Ave.,
  Chicago, IL 60604
(312) 427-4545

INTERNATIONAL FILM
  FOUNDATION
155 West 72nd St., Room
  306, New York, NY 10023
(212) 580-1111

INTERNATIONAL MEDIA
  ASSOCIATES
31 West 21st St., New York,
  NY 10010
(212) 645-2323

INTERNATIONAL VIDEO
  NETWORK
2242 Camino Ramon, San
  Ramon, CA 94583
(415) 866-1121

J. C. PENNEY
12700 Park Central Pl., Suite
  914, Dallas, TX 75215
(214) 387-6604

SANDY JAFFE
14 Centre St., Watertown,
  MA 02172
(617) 926-4433

JAPAN SOCIETY
333 East 47th St., New York,
  NY 10017
(212) 832-1155

JOURNAL FILMS, INC.
930 Pitner Ave., Evanston, IL
60202
(312) 328-6700
(800) 323-5448

KCTS-TV
4045 Brooklyn Ave. NE,
Seattle, WA 98105
(206) 543-2000

KENTUCKY
EDUCATIONAL
TELEVISION
600 Cooper Dr., Lexington,
KY 40502
(606) 233-3000
(800) 354-9067

KERA-Channel 13
3000 Harry Hines Blvd.,
Dallas, TX 75201
(214) 871-1390

KINETIC FILM
ENTERPRISES, LTD.
255 Delaware Ave., Suite 340,
Buffalo, NY 14202

KING FEATURES
ENTERTAINMENT
235 East 45th St., New York,
NY 10017
(212) 682-5600
(800) 223-7383

KUDLUK PRODUCTIONS
c/o Bill Steward, Dept. of
Culture and
Communications
Government of the Northwest
Territories, Yellowknife,
NWT
Canada X1A 2L9
(403) 873-7258

KUED-TV
101 Gardner Hall, University
of Utah, Salt Lake City, UT
94112
(801) 581-7777

KULTUR
121 Highway #36, West Long
Branch, NJ 07764
(201) 229-2343

LINDY WILSON
PRODUCTIONS
810 Rugby Rd.,
Charlottesville, VA 22903
(804) 293-2956

LIONEL TELEVISION
PRODUCTIONS
1551 North Western Ave.,
Hollywood, CA 90027
(213) 487-2116

LOLA LA LOCA
ASSOCIATES
835 Huntington Ave., #207,
Boston, MA 02115
(617) 739-0721

LOUISIANA COMMITTEE
FOR THE HUMANITIES
1001 Howard Ave., #4407,
New Orleans, LA 70113
(504) 523-4352

LOYOLA MARYMOUNT
UNIVERSITY
Jesuit Community
Loyola Blvd. at West 80th
St., Los Angeles, CA 90045
(213) 642-3170

LUCERNE MEDIA
37 Ground Pine Rd., Morris
Plains, NJ 07950
(201) 538-1401

MARK MAMALAKIS
PRODUCTIONS
429 West Roscoe, #403,
Chicago, IL 60657
(212) 308-2250

MARTHA STUART
COMMUNICATIONS, INC.
147 West 22nd St., New
York, NY 10011
(212) 255-2718

MARYKNOLL WORLD
FILMS
Maryknoll, NY 10545
(914) 941-7590

MARYLAND PUBLIC
TELEVISION
11787 Bonita Ave., Owings
Mills, MD 21117
(301) 356-5600

MASTERVISION, INC.
969 Park Ave., New York,
NY 10028
(212) 879-0448

MAUREEN MCNAMARA
12 Vincent St., Cambridge,
MA 02140
(617) 661-0402

MAXI COHEN FILM AND
VIDEO PRODUCTIONS
31 Greene St., New York,
NY 10013
(212) 966-6326

MCA HOME VIDEO
1755 Broadway, New York,
NY 10022
(212) 759-7500

MCNABB AND
CONNOLLY
49 Danville Dr., Willowdale,
Ontario
Canada M2P 1J2

MEADOWS MUSEUM OF
ART
Centenary College of
Louisiana
2911 Centenary Blvd.,
Shreveport, LA 71104
(318) 869-5169

METROPOLITAN MUSEUM OF ART
Fifth Ave. at 82nd St., New York, NY 10028
(212) 879-5500 X3645

MICHIGAN STATE UNIVERSITY
IMC Marketing Division, East Lansing, MI 48824
(517) 353-9229

MINNEAPOLIS INSTITUTE OF THE ARTS
2400 Third Ave. S, Minneapolis, MN 55404
(612) 870-3195

M.L.A. PRODUCTIONS
150 South Grant St., Wilkes-Barre, PA 18702
(717) 825-7031

MODERN TALKING PICTURES SERVICE
One Prudential Plaza, Suite 2020, Chicago, IL 60601
(312) 337-3252

MOMA CIRCULATING FILM LIBRARY
11 West 53rd St., New York, NY 10019
(212) 708-9530

MONTEREY HOME VIDEO
A Division of International Entertainment
21800 Burbank Blvd., #300, Woodland Hills, CA 91365
(818) 888-3040
(800) 423-5558

CHONK MOONHUNTER
2721 Bellaire Place, Oakland, CA 94601
(415) 436-6978

MOUCHETTE FILMS
548 Fifth St., San Francisco, CA 94107
(415) 495-3934

MUSEUM OF MODERN ART OF LATIN AMERICA
c/o Organization of American States-Art Museum
1889 F St., NW, Washington, DC 20006
(202) 789-6021

NATIONAL FILM BOARD OF CANADA FILM LIBRARY
c/o Karol Media
22 Riverview Dr., Wayne, NJ 07470
(201) 628-9111
and
125 rue Houde, St. Laurent, Quebec
Canada H4N 2J3

NATIONAL GEOGRAPHIC
EDUCATIONAL
SERVICES
17th and M Sts., NW, Dept.
89, Washington, DC 20036

NATIVE AMERICAN
PUBLIC BROADCASTING
CONSORTIUM
1800 North 33rd St., Lincoln,
NE 88501
(402) 472-3522

NAUMAN FILMS
P.O. Box 232, Custer, SD
57730
(605) 673-4065

NEW DAY FILMS
22 Riverview Dr., Wayne, NJ
07470
(201) 633-0212

NEW DIMENSION FILMS
85895 Lorane Hwy., Eugene,
OR 97405
(503) 484-7125

NEW IMAGES
PRODUCTIONS
919 Euclid Ave., Berkeley,
CA 94708
(415) 526-7852

NEW JERSEY NETWORK
Program Catalog Department
1018 Whitehead Rd., CN 777,
Trenton, NJ 08625
(609) 530-5180

NEW LINE CINEMA
575 Eighth Ave., New York,
NY 10018
(212) 239-8880

NEW TIME FILMS, INC.
P.O. Box 502, Village Station,
New York, NY 10014

NEW YORK CENTER FOR
VISUAL HISTORY
625 Broadway, 12th Floor,
New York, NY 10012
(212) 777-6900

NEW YORK STATE
EDUCATION
DEPARTMENT
Center for Learning
Technologies
Media Distribution Network
Room C-7, Concourse Level,
Cultural Education Center
Albany, NY 12230
(518) 474-3168

NEW YORKER FILMS
16 W. 61st St., New York,
NY 10023
(212) 247-6110

NORMAN ROSS
PUBLISHING, INC.
1995 Broadway, New York,
NY 10023
(212) 873-2100

NORTHSTAR
  PRODUCTIONS
3003 "O" St., NW,
  Washington, DC 20007

OHIO UNIVERSITY
  TELECOMMUNICATIONS
  CENTER
9 South College St., Athens,
  OH 45701
(614) 594-5244

ONE WEST MEDIA
P.O. Box 5766, Santa Fe, NM
  87502
(505) 983-8685

OTERO SAVINGS AND
  LOAN
1515 North Academy Blvd.,
  Colorado Springs, CO
  80909
(303) 597-1011

PARAMOUNT HOME
  VIDEO
5555 Melrose Ave.,
  Hollywood, CA 90038
(213) 468-5000

PBS VIDEO
1320 Braddock Pl.,
  Alexandria, VA 22314
(800) 424-7963

PEACE RIVER FILMS
12 Arrow St., Cambridge,
  MA 02138
(617) 492-7990

PENNEBAKER
  ASSOCIATES
21 W. 86th St., New York,
  NY 10024
(212) 496-9195

PENNSYLVANIA STATE
  UNIVERSITY
Audio-Visual Services
Special Services Bldg.,
  University Park, PA 16802
(814) 863-3102

GUY PHILLIPS
109 11th Ave. East, Seattle,
  WA 98102
(206) 324-8690

PHOENIX FILMS AND
  VIDEO
468 Park Ave. South, 10th
  Floor, New York, NY
  10016
(212) 684-5910
       and
c/o International Tele-Films
47 Densley Ave., Toronto,
  Ontario
Canada M6M 5A8
(416) 241-4483

POSITIVE FUTURES
  CENTER
33 Greene St., #5, New
  York, NY 10013
(212) 226-7034

PRAIRIE FIRE PICTURES
1928 Ninth Ave. West,
Seattle, WA 98119
(206) 283-3805

PYRAMID FILM AND
VIDEO
P.O. Box 1048, Santa Monica,
CA 90406
(213) 828-7577
(800) 421-2304

RAIN COUNTRY VIDEO
Log Cabin Road, Clinton,
WA 98236
(206) 321-1269

RCA/COLUMBIA
PICTURES HOME VIDEO
3500 W. Olive Avenue,
Burbank, CA 91505
(818) 953-7900
(800) 722-2748

REDISCOVERY
PRODUCTIONS
2 Half Mile Common,
Westport, CT 06880
(203) 226-4489

REFOCUS FILMS
111 Wilton Rd., Westport,
CT 06880
(203) 226-5289

RHAPSODY FILMS
30 Charlton St., New York,
NY 10014
(212) 243-0152

RIVER TRACKS
PRODUCTIONS
c/o Yvonne Yarber
P.O. Box 9, Manley Hot
Springs, AK 99756
(907) 672-3262

PERSHING SADEGH-
VAZIRI
86 Jersey St., #4, Boston,
MA 02215
(617) 262-8823

SAFI PRODUCTIONS
1401 Bentley Ave., Los
Angeles, CA 90025
(213) 479-0164

SALMON STUDIOS/FILM
AND VIDEO
2425 S.E. Salmon, Portland,
OR 97214
(503) 236-7071

SENSOR
708 Venice Blvd., Suite 2,
Venice, CA 90291
(213) 823-3428

SHELTON PRODUCTIONS
1054 Golden Gate Ave., Los
Angeles, CA 90026
(213) 660-3720

SIMARKA PRODUCTIONS,
INC.
1407 Broadway, Suite 3704,
New York, NY 10018
(212) 354-7780

SMITHSONIAN
INSTITUTION
Office of
Telecommunications,
Washington, DC 20560
(202) 357-2984

SMITHSONIAN
INSTITUTION FOLKLIFE
PROGRAMS
955 L'Enfant Plaza, SW,
#2600, Washington, DC
20560
(202) 287-3251

SONY VIDEO SOFTWARE
1700 Broadway, 16th Floor,
New York, NY 10019
(212) 757-4990

STANTON FILMS
2427 Artesia Blvd., Redondo
Beach, CA 90278
(213) 542-6573

SWANK FILMS
350 Vanderbilt Motor
Parkway, Hauppauge, NY
11787
(and other locations
throughout the U.S.A.)
(800) 876-3344

SYLVESTRE WATKINS
CO.
2234 Hunters Run Dr.,
Reston, VA 22091
(703) 648-9392

SYRACUSE ALTERNATE
MEDIA NETWORK
P.O. Box 550, Syracuse, NY
13210
(315) 425-8806

TAIPEI CHINESE
INFORMATION AND
CULTURE CENTER
900 N. Western Ave., Los
Angeles, CA 90029
(213) 461-3665

TAMARACK FILMS
P.O. Box 315, Franklin
Lakes, NJ 07414
(201) 891-8240

TELESIS PRODUCTION
INTERNATIONAL
P.O. Box 948, Mendocino,
CA 95460
(707) 877-3400

TELEVIDEOS
P.O. Box 22, Lorane, OR
97451
(800) 284-3367

TEMPLE UNIVERSITY
Department of Radio-TV-
Film, Philadelphia, PA
19122
(215) 787-8483

TERRA PRODUCTIONS
140 West End Ave., New
York, NY 10023
(212) 496-0776

THIRD WORLD
NEWSREEL
335 West 38th St., 5th Floor,
New York, NY 10018
(212) 947-9277

TRA FILM PRODUCTIONS
P.O. Box 1119, Point Reyes,
CA 94956
(415) 663-1490

TURNER PROGRAM
SERVICES
100 International Blvd.,
Atlanta, GA 30348
(404) 827-2085

TV ONTARIO
MARKETING
4825 LBJ Freeway, Suite 163,
Dallas, TX 75244
(214) 458-7447

UC VIDEO
425 Ontario St. SE,
Minneapolis, MN 55414
(612) 627-4444

UNITED NATIONS
Radio and Visual Services
Division
Department of Public
Information, New York, NY
10017
(212) 754-6953

UNIVERSITY OF ALASKA
Instructional
Telecommunications
Services
2533 Providence Dr., Bldg. K,
Room 217, Anchorage, AK
99508
(907) 786-1879

UNIVERSITY OF
ARIZONA
Microcampus
Second St. and Olive,
Building 76, Tucson, AZ
85721
(602) 621-1735

UNIVERSITY OF
CALIFORNIA
EXTENSION MEDIA
CENTER
2176 Shattuck Ave., Berkeley,
CA 94704
(415) 642-0460

UNIVERSITY OF
CALIFORNIA-SANTA
BARBARA
Instructional Development,
Santa Barbara, CA 93106
(805) 961-3518

UNIVERSITY OF
MICHIGAN
Film and Video Library
400 Fourth St., Ann Arbor,
MI 48103
(313) 764-5360
(800) 999-0424

UNIVERSITY OF
  MINNESOTA
Communications Resources
433 Coffey Hall, St. Paul,
  MN 55108
(612) 373-0710

UNIVERSITY OF
  WISCONSIN
Dept. of South Asian Studies
1244 Van Hise Hall, 1220
  Linden Dr., Madison, WI
  53706
(608) 262-3012

VARIED DIRECTIONS,
  INC.
63 Elm St., Camden, ME
  04843
(207) 236-8506

VICTOR FRIDMAN
  PRODUCTIONS
104 Chester Ave., Fairfax, CA
  94930
(415) 454-8441

VIDEO FREE AMERICA
442 Shotwell St., San
  Francisco, CA 94110
(415) 648-9040

VIDEO GEMS
731 North La Brea Ave., Los
  Angeles, CA 90038
(213) 938-2385
(800) 421-3252

VIDEO KNOWLEDGE,
  INC.
29 Brambel Lane, Melville,
  NY 11747
(516) 367-4250

VIDEO OUT
261 Powell St., Vancouver,
  BC
Canada V6A 1G3
(604) 688-4336

VIDEO PRESENTATIONS,
  INC.
Sixth and Battery Bldg.
  2326 Sixth Ave., Suite 230,
  Seattle, WA 98121
(206) 624-9241

VILLON FILMS
Brophy Rd., Hurleyville, NY
  12747
(914) 434-5579

VOX PRODUCTIONS
2335 Jones St., San Francisco,
  CA 94155
(415) 673-6428

WALT DISNEY
  EDUCATIONAL MEDIA
500 S. Buena Vista St.,
  Burbank, CA 91521
(818) 840-5290

BURWELL WARE
3 Silver Cedar Lane, Chapel
  Hill, NC 27514
(919) 942-0698

WASHINGTON MEDIA
ASSOCIATES
P.O. Box 53120, Washington,
  DC 20009
(202) 745-7600

WEST GLEN, INC.
1430 Broadway, New York,
  NY 10018
(212) 921-0966

WETA-TV
P.O. Box 2626, Washington,
  DC 20013
(703) 998-2709
(800) 445-1964

LIZ WHITE
2588 Seventh Ave., Apt. 2A,
  New York, NY 10039
(212) 283-0475

WHYY-TV12
Independence Mall West
150 North Sixth St.,
  Philadelphia, PA 19106
(213) 351-1265

WILLIAM GREAVES
PRODUCTIONS
80 Eighth Ave., New York,
  NY 10011
(212) 206-1213

WOMBAT FILM AND
VIDEO
250 W. 57th St., Suite 2421,
  New York, NY 10019
(212) 315-2502
(800) 542-5554

WOMEN FOR WOMEN IN
LEBANON
P.O. Box 9, Porter Square
  Station, Cambridge, MA
  02140
(617) 354-7001

WOMEN MAKE MOVIES
225 Lafayette St., Suite 211,
  New York, NY 10012
(212) 925-0606

YOUR WORLD VIDEO
80 Eighth Ave., Suite 1701,
  New York, NY 10011
(212) 206-1215 and 1213

ZENGER VIDEO
10200 Jefferson Blvd., Culver
  City, CA 90232
(213) 839-2436

TITLE INDEX

221

016.909 CYR
N/C C2